Regulating China's Shadow Banks

China's shadow banking has been a top issue in the past few years. Scholars, policymakers, and professionals around the world are seeking deeper insight into the subject, and the authors had unique insight into the sector through their positions high up in the regulatory apparatus. *Regulating China's Shadow Banks* focuses on the regulation of shadow banks in China and provides crucial information to demystify China's shadow banking and associated regulatory challenges.

This book defines "shadow banking" in the Chinese context, analyzes the impact of shadow banking on the Chinese economy, includes a full-scale analysis on the current status of Chinese financial regulation, and provides valuable advice on the regulation of China's shadow banks.

Qingmin Yan is a Chinese expert on financial regulation who has spent decades in positions at the China Banking Regulatory Commission and the People's Bank of China, directs much of the important policy formulation and implementation related to shadow banking.

Dr. Jianhua Li (1965–2014) was an expert on non-bank financial institutions. He pioneered much of China's regulatory approach for shadow banking and headed the CBRC's work on trust regulation before his passing.

中国金融四十人论坛书系
CHINA FINANCE 40 FORUM BOOKS

The Editorial Board

Directors

CHEN Yuan   Vice Chairman, National Committee of the Chinese People's Political Consultative Conference

XIE Ping   Executive Vice President, China Investment Corporation

QIAN Yingyi Dean, School of Economics and Management, Tsinghua University

Chief Editors (in alphabetic order)

GUAN Tao   Senior Fellow, China Finance 40 Forum

HUANG Yiping Vice Dean, National School of Development, Peking University

PAN Gongsheng Vice Governor, the People's Bank of China

YAN Qingmin   Vice Mayor, Tianjin

YUAN Li   Vice President, China Development Bank

ZHONG Wei   Director, Finance Research Center, Beijing Normal University

Executive Editor

WANG Haiming   Secretary-General, China Finance 40 Forum

Editors

Martin Chorzempa

HUANG Juan

John Lin

QUAN Shuqin

WANG Guanlong

WANG Qianzheng

XIONG Jing

The "China Finance 40 Forum Books" focuses on the macroeconomic and financial field with a special emphasis on financial policy studies to facilitate innovations in financial thinking and inspire breakthroughs, while building a high-end, authentic brand for think tank books with top academic quality and policy value.

The "China Finance 40 Forum Books" has published more than 30 monographs and article collections since 2009. Through its rigorous and cutting-edge research, this book series has a remarkable reputation in the industry and a broad influence overall.

Regulating China's Shadow Banks

Qingmin Yan
Jianhua Li

Routledge
Taylor & Francis Group

LONDON AND NEW YORK

First published 2016 by Routledge

2 Park Square, Milton Park, Abingdon, Oxfordshire OX14 4RN
52 Vanderbilt Avenue, New York, NY 10017

Routledge is an imprint of the Taylor & Francis Group, an informa business

First issued in paperback 2020

British Library Cataloguing in Publication Data
A catalogue record for this book is available from the British Library

Library of Congress Cataloging in Publication Data
Yan, Qingmin, 1961- | Li, Jianhua, 1965-2014.
Regulating China's shadow banks / Qingmin Yan, Jianhua Li.
Description: 1 Edition. | New York, NY: Routledge, 2016.
Identifiers: LCCN 2015037696| ISBN 9781138195646 (hardcover) |
ISBN 9781315637914 (ebook)
Subjects: LCSH: Nonbank financial institutions—China. | Nonbank financial institutions—Law and legislation—China. | Risk assessment—China.
Classification: LCC HG187. C6 Y3626 2016 | DDC 332.1—dc23LC record available at http://lccn.loc.gov/2015037696

ISBN: 978-1-138-19564-6 (hbk)
ISBN: 978-0-367-51649-9 (pbk)

Typeset in Bembo
by diacriTech, Chennai

Contents

List of figures

List of tables

1 A basic theory of shadow banking

This chapter primarily focuses on the following elements of shadow banking: its definition, types, relation to the traditional banking system, historical evolution and driving factors, American and European shadow banking, and why shadow banks must be regulated.

Overview of shadow banking

The term "shadow banking" is considered to have originated just as the first signs of the financial crisis were emerging in a speech by the PIMCO Managing Director Paul McCulley at the annual symposium of the Federal Reserve Bank of Kansas City in 2007 in Jackson Hole, Wyoming. McCulley used the term "shadow banking system" to describe the many institutions and services that are banks or banking in spirit rather than in name. Lying outside the regulatory system and lacking the liquidity support inherent in the traditional banking system, these "shadow banks" invest by issuing uninsured commercial paper (CP). Therefore, they are brittle and prone to liquidity crises.

Since the subprime crisis in the United States, "shadow banking" has become an important finance concept. However, it can also be viewed as the distillation of a general post-crisis rethinking of institutions and services that have long existed in the financial system. Looking at it another way, shadow banking is a way to expand credit outside the banking system. Its core is a credit relationship in which shadow banking takes credits originating in the traditional banking system and then transforms and stores them as securitized assets. These institutions perform some of banks' functions and on the surface appear to be banks, but they differ from traditional organizational structures. They exist like the banks' shadows and are thus aptly named.

Definition of shadow banking

There has long been no single precise definition for shadow banking. There are two main reasons for this lack of unanimity. The first is that the term was broadly used only after the financial crisis began, so academics and industry practitioners have not sufficiently researched the topic. The second involves significant differences in the architecture and regulatory frameworks of each country's banking system.

The evolution of shadow banks

At the aforementioned Federal Reserve Bank symposium in 2007, McCulley said, "Unregulated shadow banks fund themselves with uninsured short-term funding, which may or may not be backstopped by liquidity lines from real banks ... these levered up intermediaries operate in the shadows ...." He believed that their development was intimately related to that of money market funds (MMFs) in the 1970s. Although MMFs provide a function similar to bank deposits, they are not subjected to the same type of regulation. Like MMFs, shadow banks are outside the banking regulatory system. They are nonbank institutions that take in uninsured, short-term funds to run their operations. This definition encompasses investment banks, hedge funds, money market funds, monoline insurers, structured investment vehicles (SIVs), and others.

At the 43rd meeting of the South East Asian Central Banks (SEACEN) in March 2008, the Bank for International Settlements (BIS) Deputy General Manager Hervé Hannoun offered an in-depth explanation and analysis of shadow banking, "With the development of the originate-to-distribute model, banks and other lenders are able to extend loans to borrowers and then package these loans into asset-backed securities (ABS), collateralized debt obligations (CDO), asset-backed commercial paper (ABCP) and structured investment vehicles (SIVs)."[1] These packaged assets were, according to their credit rating, once again cut into various tranches. Higher rated tranches were sold to more risk averse investors, while lower rated tranches came into the hands of those seeking more risks. The shadow banking system brought along the entire financial system's high leverage in the form of SIVs, ABCP, CDOs, and other new services and intermediaries. For example, a 3% loss equity tranche of a CDO could reach 30× leverage. The development of this new type of product brought about shadow banking's expansion.

There are other terms beyond "shadow banking" that we can use to describe the same concept. For example, the then New York Federal Reserve Bank President Timothy Geithner pointed out fundamental changes in the financial system during the testimony to the US Senate's Committee on Banking, Housing, and Urban Affairs in June 2008. He indicated that the proportion of assets held outside the banking system was increasing, and he outlined in great length the process by which nonbanks were using short-term funds to invest in high-risk, low-liquidity, long-term assets without protection such as deposit insurance provided for banks by the Federal Deposit Insurance Corporation (FDIC). He called this process and the institutions that operated it a "parallel banking system."

Another term, "near-bank," appeared for the first time in the 2008 International Monetary Fund's (IMF) Global Financial Stability Report. These "near-banks" had long been in development and had already surpassed traditional banks in scale. Although they were similar to banks, they were not subjected to central bank regulation, nor included in the national financial safety net. Hence, they are highly levered, very risky, and played a key role in bringing about the crisis and making it as bad as it was. New York University Stern Business School Professor Nouriel Roubini proposed a broader reference to the "shadow finance system." He believes that the shadow banking system is actually the modern financial system, because it embraces almost every financial innovation in the post-war period. All these concepts ended up converging back to the original term "shadow banking system" after 2009. It is used all over the world in academic conferences and has become an official term commonly seen in reports by monetary and regulatory authorities.

At the November 2010 G20 meeting of heads of state in Seoul, the leaders agreed on new regulatory standards for bank capital. However, they had concerns about financial regulation that they believed deserved further attention, such as "strengthening regulation and supervision of shadow banking."[2] They also instructed the Financial Stability Board (FSB) to collaborate with other international standard boards in order to establish a set of policy recommendations to strengthen shadow banking regulation by 2011. In December 2010, the FSB convened a meeting of experts in London to discuss the shadow banking system. This important exchange led to the establishment of special small groups and the following starting points for further work:

1   clear up the meaning of "shadow banking system"
2   propose measures to regulate the shadow banking system
3   seek out feasible regulatory tools
4   settle the potential systemic risk and regulatory arbitrage issues.

Preliminary recommendations for regulation were ready for inclusion in the report that the FSB submitted to the G20 leaders in November 2011. The FSB used statistics until the end of 2011 as a foundation for the report, which included 11 economic areas and the Eurozone. By 2012, the report had expanded to include 25 economic areas and the Eurozone. Thus, the FSB was now responsible for monitoring an area encompassing 86% of world GDP and 90% of the world's financial assets.

Dissenting views

During the international financial crisis, shadow banks played an important role as a source of systemic risk. They were insufficiently regulated and lacked transparency. Therefore, they became a focal point for hot public discussion worldwide. However, international understanding of the subject varied widely, so this discussion often went in very different directions. We categorize the current viewpoints on shadow banking into three main types:

1   regulatory coverage theory
2   derivative risk theory
3   broad credit theory.

The regulatory coverage theory's central question is whether a certain activity or institution is part of the traditional regulatory system. It asks whether there are regulatory gaps or insufficient regulation as the main standard to judge shadow banking. This goes back to McCulley's original definition of shadow banking: as nonbank institutions that take in short-term funding outside the traditional regulatory system. The former Federal Reserve Chairman Ben Bernanke believes that they are financial intermediaries other than regulated deposit-taking institutions that transform savings into investment but are not yet regulated.

The derivative risk theory defines shadow banking as those nonbank financial intermediaries and activities that could cause systemic risk. J.P. Morgan research argues that China's wealth management products (WMPs), trusts, and other products are part of shadow banking despite the fact that they are part of the regulatory system. Their reasoning is that these products are only made up of managed assets not tied to a bank balance sheet. They could therefore easily set off a systemic crisis.

The broad credit theory defines shadow banking much more broadly as all credit activities outside savings and loans. The broad shadow banking category even includes interbank entrusted payments, bank-supported enterprise bonds, and undiscounted bank bill transfers.

The FSB's definition and analysis of shadow banking

In March 2011, the FSB's Standing Committee on Supervisory and Regulatory Cooperation announced a "two step" approach to define shadow banking. The first, broad step includes all nonbank credit intermediation, whereas the second, narrower definition for policy purposes focuses on potential sources of systemic risk and regulatory arbitrage that could reduce the effectiveness of financial regulation. Imperfect risk transfer, maturity and liquidity transformation, and leverage are especially strong markers of shadow banking under this definition. It is important to note that this definition is now both prevalent and regarded as authoritative. Of course, the FSB pointed out that there is no single international standard for what institutions and services qualify as shadow banking. Proper classification should be in reference to the economic, financial, and regulatory systems of the specific country.

According to the FSB's definition, shadow banking is essentially banking. It parallels the traditional banking system, performs credit intermediation, and has a service model similar to traditional banks. However, the regulation is either insufficient or nonexistent, making it prone to crises and regulatory arbitrage. Shadow banking is nonbank credit intermediation, meaning that the usual careful regulatory standards do not apply. They do business similar to banks, but their regulatory standards are either much lighter or simply incomparable. Shadow banks pose systemic risk through four "special characteristics":

1   liquidity transformation
2   maturity transformation
3   incomplete risk transfer
4   high leverage.

Shadow banks differ from traditional banks in another key aspect: support. They do not have government liquidity support or deposit insurance, nor are they under the banking regulatory regime. If these institutions do not pay the full costs of the risks they undertake, then they gain a competitive advantage over banks and provide an incentive for regulatory arbitrage. Banks can also use the high leverage in the shadow banking system to avoid capital controls and liquidity requirements. Some institutions only provide value through the four characteristics above. They use explicit or implicit support (including liquidity provision and guarantees) to reduce funding costs in the shadow banking system. Those exposed to this risk include banks, financial guarantee companies, real estate collateral insurers, and other buyers of default risk protection. Rating agencies, however, are not exposed. Although these various institutions acted as financial intermediaries and reduced the cost of issuing debt, debt accumulated in the shadow banking system that ultimately increased risk exposure by traditional banks. Due to inadequate transparency, these hidden risks were only discovered after the financial crisis broke out.

The functional and risk-based approaches: Two views on shadow banking analysis

Since shadow banks are part of the financial intermediary system, one must use the previous definitions as a way to consider the analysis of financial intermediaries. If we only rely on the already existing organizational forms to categorize them as shadow banking or not, we lose the ability to be forward looking. At the same time, we must realize that these institutions integrate financial markets and intermediaries. This integration is molded differently by the legal and accounting systems in different jurisdictions, so we should avoid excessive focus on concrete forms. The two main perspectives used internationally to analyze shadow banking are the functional and risk-based approaches.

The functional approach begins with the functions of financial intermediaries. Shadow banks are nonbanks that perform the functions of banks. This approach generally prescribes the use of the following three steps:

1 define shadow banking according to the traditional commercial banks' functions
2 list out related business
3 measure the extent of shadow banking.

The risk approach builds off of regulatory authorities' systemic risk-focused approach. It centers on financial activity that could cause systemic risk and the relevant regulatory needs. Shadow banking is thus defined as nonbank financial intermediation or intermediaries that could cause systemic risk. A macroprudential regulatory approach is required to research such current systemic risks. One starts from the general approach and proceeds to the particular approach, analyzing step-by-step from large to small:

1 distinguish all nonbank financial intermediation activity
2 mark all such activity that could cause systemic risk or regulatory arbitrage as potential shadow banking
3 decide on appropriate regulatory measures or risk management tools if either systemic risk or regulatory arbitrage is found.

The risk-based approach considers the four "special characteristics" of maturity/liquidity transformation, incomplete risk transfer, and high leverage to be the main causes of systemic risk, but these also constitute the core of traditional banking. Traditional banks take in short-term deposits to issue long-term loans, a textbook case of maturity transformation. These loans are relatively illiquid compared to deposits, so banks also perform liquidity transformation. If the ratio of debt to equity counts as an indicator of their leverage, banking is a highly levered, risky business.

These two approaches therefore share a relatively similar foundation. On the contrary, when measuring the size of the shadow banking system, these approaches will yield radically different results. For example, where should one start in the intermediation chain? Should one count gross or net value? If one measures according to the functional approach, one should count final assets or net debt. On the other hand, the risk-based approach would count each step in the chain, even though this would result in double counting, because they all could be proved to be sources of systemic risk.

Different organizations have their own definition and approach to define shadow banking (see Table 1.1).

Table 1.1 Main definitions of shadow banking

Organization	Perspective	Definition
Financial Stability Board (FSB)	Risk (financial stability and regulation)	Broad definition: financial intermediaries other than traditional banks Narrow definition: any institution or business that causes systemic risks including maturity transformation, liquidity transformation, high leverage and regulatory arbitrage.
European Central Bank (ECB)	Risk (financial stability and regulation)	Any financial intermediary that is not a traditional bank and is involved in liquidity transformation and maturity transformation.
United States Federal Reserve	Financial intermediation	Credit intermediary system that channels deposit funds to investors through securitization and collateral intermediation. Not directly supported by government liquidity and credit enhancement.

Organization	Perspective	Definition
International Monetary Fund (IMF)	Financial intermediation	Bank-like activities: mainly for reducing risks, especially counterparty risk. Main forms include securitization and collateral intermediation.
Deutsche Bank	Risk	Unregulated financial intermediaries.
Deloitte	Financial intermediation	Credit intermediary system that performs maturity and liquidity transformation through securitization and securities financing mechanisms.

Standards to judge shadow banking

From the previous discussion, it should be clear that different institutions and scholars do not use the same definition for shadow banking. Some use an organizational lens to define it. They believe that it is a nonbank financial intermediation system that touches upon many areas and newly distributes the three functions of banks (lending, maturity transformation, and liquidity transformation). Each intermediary has its comparative advantage. Other scholars and institutions use a combination of the organizational, instrumental, market, and structural approaches to more broadly define the shadow banking system. The FSB prefers to use an organizational and industry approach to define the shadow banking system.

According to FSB reports, the decision of whether a nonbank financial intermediary is shadow banking hinges on its ability to bring about systemic risk or regulatory arbitrage. The "four characteristics" are thus the main sources of systemic risk and become the standard markers for shadow banking. Each characteristic is defined in the following paragraph.

Maturity transformation means that the shadow bank takes short-term customer funds to make long-term investments, which creates a mismatch between the maturity of the two types of assets. Liquidity risk indicates a shadow bank that invests in insufficiently liquid products. The potential then exists that it will experience a type of bank run, meaning it is unable to sell these assets quickly enough to fulfill customer demands for redemptions in time. Imperfect risk transfer occurs when the banking and shadow banking systems transfer debt assets through derivatives and other methods, but the risk has not been completely moved from one party to another. For example, a bank may transfer assets but keep a portion of the risk through implicit guarantees or support. The risk still exists but is hidden from view. High leverage is a key characteristic of shadow banking. Although shadow banks do not take deposits, they borrow or use other tools to accumulate large amounts of debt.

They then have high leverage similar to that of banks. When judging shadow banks, we should pay attention to the following points: they exist outside of the traditional banking system, share common characteristics with banks, were insufficiently or not regulated before the crisis, and do not receive the central bank's liquidity support or public sector guarantees.

Defining characteristics of shadow banking

Shadow banking broadly defined means nonbanks engaging in credit activity and intermediation similar to those of banks. There three main characteristics are credit activity, credit intermediation, and nonbank financial institutions.

Credit activity

The so-called credit activity is a way to classify financial products by starting with a financial instrument perspective. These products can be either of two types: debt or equity. Debt products involve lending a specified sum for a specified period of time at a specified rate of interest (and compounding). At the end of this period, the borrower returns the principal and agreed interest. Loans and bonds belong to this type. On the contrary, equity gives the holder the right to a certain portion of an entity's net profits. Equity shares are the classic manifestation of this form.

Credit intermediation

Companies can obtain the aforementioned equity and debt financing directly from the markets or from financial intermediaries. This is the second characteristic of shadow banking, namely to emphasize that the issuance channels for credit products are financial intermediaries. The flow goes from lenders to intermediaries to borrowers. Categorization of these intermediaries is different depending on the standards used. The United Nations statistics for economic activity separate it into three main categories: not including insurance or pension funds, insurance and pension funds (excluding national social security funds), and auxiliary financial intermediaries. Columbia University Professor Frederic Mishkin uses different funding sources (debt) and use of funds (assets) to separate financial institutions into depository financial institutions, contractual savings institutions, and investment intermediaries.

Depository financial institutions accept personal and business deposits and make loans. These are primarily commercial banks, savings and loan associations, and mutual savings banks as well as credit unions. These institutions focus on the business of receiving deposits and making loans. They provide many types of services for their clients and create deposits while being strictly regulated. Contractual savings institutions use contracts to specify the timing and amount of payments from specific people (such as insurance premiums or pension contributions) and then pay out specified amounts of either insurance services or pension payouts. They generally invest in long-term corporate bonds, equities, or securitized loans and include insurance companies and pension funds. Investment intermediaries are generally finance companies, mutual funds, and hedge funds. They issue equities, CP, bonds, or shares to amass funds that are then used to purchase a combination of diversified equity and debt investments or market instruments as well as issue corporate loans. See Table 1.2 for an overview of the different types of financial intermediary.

Nonbank financial institutions

Shadow banking uses financial intermediaries to perform bank-like functions outside of banks. Here, "outside" means bankruptcy remote (from the bank's balance sheet) for legal and accounting purposes. This implies that banks can no longer maintain any form of support or supervision of the assets. Contractual savings institutions and investment intermediaries make up extremely important pieces of the shadow banking system's chain so that it bypasses the traditional banking system.

Therefore, shadow banking is not really an entity. It is a chain composed of many financial intermediaries related through financial markets, so it becomes the intersection between intermediary and market. Only all together can they form a network that is able to replace the economic role of banks: the shadow banking system. Traditional credit activity is either direct (over the markets) or indirect (through financial intermediaries). Shadow banking bypasses banks with markets and intermediaries together. So-called credit intermediaries can be either direct or indirect participants, with the latter participating through intermediaries that lubricate the transaction process. The shadow banking system as a whole is formed from all sorts of shadow banks connecting tougher. It takes the system, working together, to replace the functions of banks.

Table 1.2 Types of financial intermediaries

Intermediary types	Financial institutions	Main liabilities	Main assets
Depository Institutions (Banks)	Commercial banks, cooperative banks, mutual savings banks, credit associations, etc.	Deposits	Loans, bonds
Contractual Savings Institutions	Insurance companies	Insurance payments	Bonds, stocks
	Pension funds	Contributions from businesses and employees	Bonds, stocks
Investment Intermediaries	Financial companies	Commercial paper, stocks	Loans
	Mutual funds	Stocks	Bonds, stocks, etc.
	Hedge funds	Stocks	Bonds, stocks, etc.

Relationship between the shadow and traditional banking systems

Shadow and traditional banking: Associations

The existence of shadow banking has expanded the category of banking and muddied the concept of a banking system. The two systems are intimately connected. They compete and cooperate, together pushing the development and evolution of the financial system. The relationship is manifest in three main respects: similar function, close business connection, and final debt can all be seen in the end as assets of individuals.

With respect to similar function, it should now be clear that both traditional and shadow banks undertake credit intermediation. Both ensure that funds flow from savers to borrowers. As for a close business relationship, the business of each type intersects over a wide range. Traditional banks supply the basic products, such as mortgages, as well as credit and liquidity support. In actuality, there is often a bank standing behind a given shadow bank, created to reduce financing costs or perform regulatory arbitrage. One can say that each step in the shadow banking process receives support from traditional banks. As businesses of both are interwoven, so are the risks. Risks that originate in the shadow banking system can spread to banks, resulting in contagion.

Deposits are the debt of traditional banks, which are in turn a form of money. Money (assets) invested by individuals in money market funds, for example, are then the debt of each node of shadow banking. This phenomenon has been a driving factor in shadow banking's high level of development over the past years. Shadow banking relies on traditional banks, for example, as a source of loans to securitize. Both permeate each other and converge across the structure of the financial system.

Shadow and traditional banking: Differences

Traditional banks perform financial intermediary activities on one balance sheet, but shadow banks do it across many interlinked markets and institutions. From an economic perspective, intermediaries take the functional place of markets. They do so when there is information asymmetry or high transaction costs that incentivize concentration in one organization. Shadow banks are the opposite. They use market tools to replace traditional banks and perform liquidity and maturity transformation across institutions. They break down the bank's vertically integrated model with markets. Banks are pure financial intermediaries, but shadow banking is a mélange of intermediary and market. Its emergence has blurred the distinction between financial intermediaries.

Another difference is that both receive different government support. Traditional banking is a heavily regulated business. Each government has strict entry and exit rules for the industry. The Basel Agreement restricted certain bank activities from a microprudential perspective, but shadow banks to a certain extent attempt to circumvent these regulations. They bypass traditional banks with accounting and legal angles, and with it the expenses of regulatory compliance. The regulation of each is also different, which brought about the emergence of regulatory arbitrage.

The operational models of traditional and shadow banks are also different. Some of these differences are apparent from shadow banks' day-to-day operations. First, in order to have sufficient funds on hand for redemptions, traditional banks take out reserves before relending out the funds. They may also access central bank liquidity to resolve problems related to insufficient liquidity. Shadow banks, on the other hand, tend to keep a reserve in cash. Second, if a traditional bank has insufficient repayment capacity, the government will step in to grant assistance as part of the deposit insurance scheme. This is not true for shadow banks, which have no option but to put up collateral. Third, traditional banks can increase deposit rates to attract funds, but shadow banks must consult on two sides to raise repurchase rates. Fourth, deposited funds and loans granted are all on the banks' balance sheets. Since shadow banks' lending is temporary, they can use securitization to buy back the securities. In this scenario, the balance sheet does not reflect the actual debt situation of the shadow bank.

See Table 1.3 for the main differences between traditional banking and shadow banking.

The manifestation and categorization of shadow banking

Typical manifestations of shadow banking

Using the previous definitions as a starting point, shadow banking is essentially a professional division of labor based on innovative financial market instruments. They break up traditional banking's vertical integration, intermediate, and transform both liquidity and maturity. Financial products like $1 net asset value (NAV) funds lie on one end of the industry chain, and loans lie on the other. These constitute the asset and liability sides of the balance sheet.

Table 1.3 Differences between traditional banks and shadow banks

	Traditional banks	Shadow banks
Reserve position	Regulators are responsible for setting minimum liquidity	Minimum is set by mutual agreement
	May borrow from the central bank	May not borrow from the central bank
Deposit insurance/collateral	Backed by the government	Cash, asset-backed securities, loans, etc.
Interest rate	Can be raised to attract deposits	Can be increased by mutual agreement when funds are insufficient
Balance sheet	Loans are recorded on the balance sheet	Securitized assets can be recorded as collateral on the balance sheet

To sum up the research performed by the Federal Reserve, FSB, and IMF, there are two main types: securitization and collateral intermediation. We examine each in turn.

Securitization

The securitization process takes long-term, illiquid loans in special purpose vehicles and turns them into asset-backed bonds. They then turn these into relatively short-term ABCP to finish maturity transformation. This is then sold to money market funds. Since these are generally very liquid instruments, liquidity transformation is also complete, and the intermediation chain is therefore unbroken from saver to borrower. Credit enhancement from banks then enables risk transfer. Opportunities for contagion abound because the businesses of shadow banks and traditional banks are interwoven in each step of the process.[3] See Figure 1.1 for an overview of the securitization process.

Collateral intermediation

Collateral intermediation is the continued reuse of collateral created in the securitization process. Dealer banks either lend them out to increase returns or use them to either secure their own borrowing or employ them to guarantee other agreements. This in turn opens up another round of collateral reuse. Hedge funds and similar strategic investors are the beginning of this process, and money markets are the final buyers. It is now easy to see that, in developed western countries,

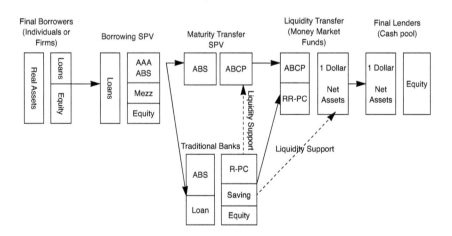

Note: PC = Private collateral.
ABS = asset-backed securities.
ABCP = asset-backed commercial paper
Mezz = Mezzanine Tranches
R = repo, RR = reverse repo

Figure 1.1 An overview of the securitization process.

money market funds complete shadow banking's debt creation. They are the perfect agents for maturity transformation due to their high liquidity and short maturity characteristics.[4]

The most common collateral originates with hedge funds and other borrowers or securities investors. Figure 1.2 uses US Treasury Bills as an example to illustrate the collateral intermediation process. Treasuries can serve as collateral, so hedge funds provide them as collateral to obtain funds from brokers (such as Goldman Sachs Investment Company). Goldman then uses the same type of collateral (treasuries) to borrow from Credit Suisse, which puts them into the money market. Money market funds can hold them either for a short time or until maturity. In this process, the same security is thus used for collateral three times.[5]

See Figure 1.3 for an illustration of these two methods integrated into the whole financial intermediation process. All in all, shadow banking touches upon all of the previously mentioned financial intermediaries. Its main products on financial markets are securitizations and collateral intermediation. In form, shadow banking encompasses each type of financial intermediary whose business centers are around these two main products.

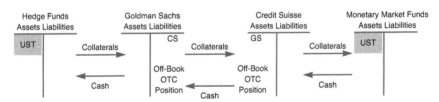

UST=U.S. Treasury bond, CS=Credit Suisse
GS=Goldman Sachs, OTC=the over-the-counter

Figure 1.2 The collateral intermediation process.

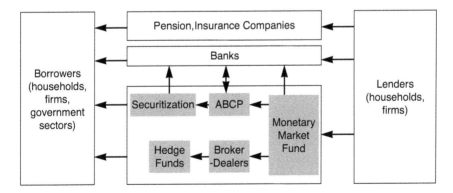

Figure 1.3 Financial intermediation process.

FSB categorization of shadow banks

Five parts that constitute shadow banks

At the 2010 G20 Global Leaders Meeting in Seoul, participants asserted that the newly agreed Basel Agreement had loopholes when it came to regulating recently emerged forms of shadow banking. They ordered the FSB and other international standards making bodies to work together to research shadow banking regulatory policy. According to this mandate, the FSB created five special working groups with the following goals:

- clarify what shadow banking is, its function, and its risks
- lay down effective regulatory measures for shadow banking
- consider special regulatory measures to counter the influence of shadow banking's systemic risk and regulatory arbitrage.

One of these groups focuses on (indirect) regulation of banks' interaction with shadow banks. The Basel Committee on Banking Supervision (BCBS) spearheads this group. The BCBS aims to improve banks' balance sheet management, especially through the regulation of risk weighting for their large exposure to shadow banks through hidden guarantees and other methods. The International Organization of Securities Commissions (IOSCO) leads the second group, which deals with regulatory research for the securities market, especially money market mutual funds. The third small group, of which the Chinese Banking Regulatory Commission is a part, is for other shadow banking entities. It researches the regulation for shadow banks that are not money market funds. The fourth working group is for the regulation of securitization. Both IOSCO and BCBS are researching the balances retained by creators of securitized securities and related disclosure. The last group is focused on research for the regulation of securities lending and repos. It includes measures to regulate margin and collateral coverage rates.

In August 2013, the FSB released a report on "Strengthening Oversight and Regulation of Shadow Banking: An Overview of Policy Recommendations,"[6] which recommended new policy in five areas to reduce the systemic risks posed by shadow banking. The first is to reduce the "spillover" effect between banks and shadow banks. Although shadow banking's intermediation supports the real economy by completing and replacing intermediation done by traditional banks, there are certain conditions (such as during the financial crisis) under which banking risks emerge from the shadow banking sector. The second is to control the spread of contagion from money market funds. Money market funds provide investors with tools such as deposits, especially when they can redeem investor funds at par in a short period of time. It is exactly under these circumstances that there is an elevated potential for contagion between investors.

The third area is to evaluate and adjust incentives related to securitization. Securitization transfers risk far from the banking sector and has even served as a source of funds, but some especially complex, securitized structured products caused pre-crisis lending standards to decline. These brought about much higher leverage than previously thought. The fourth area is to control the cyclicality of securities transactions and financial stability risks, such as repo and securities lending that come under intense pressure during market contractions. However, nonbank institutions may also use them for bank-like activities, creating a levered, maturity-mismatched link between long-term lending and short-term borrowing. The issues with this strategy were clear during the financial crisis. A decline in the value of securities that underpinned these transactions led to a violent contraction and sharp outflows in these markets. The final area for policy recommendations was to evaluate and decrease the systemic risk posed by shadow banking. The FSB's Strengthening Shadow Banking Real Regulatory Policy Framework analyzed this in more detail.

Categorizing other shadow banking according to economic function

In the course of its research, the FSB discovered wide diversity and cross-country differences in the operating model and risk structure of shadow banks. This diversity and difference was apparent both across and within specific industries. It is therefore more effective to go beyond organizational names and examine shadow banking issues according to economic function. The FSB proposes that regulatory authorities refer to the following five economic functions to evaluate shadow banks:

- management of client fund pools
- reliance on short-term funding to provide credit or make loans
- intermediary services for market activity (rely on short-term funds or client funds for securitized borrowing)
- credit auxiliaries
- securitization and financiers of financial institutions.

The first economic function mentioned in the report is management of client fund pools, which could cause a certain type of bank run. They gather investor funds and then in turn invest these funds into financial products such as publicly traded shares or private equity (PE) products. Their risk of "runs" is determined by their liquidity profile and the extent of maturity transformation, while use of leverage further elevates risk. Many firms touch on this type of activity:

- Money managers or investor funds with a low-risk propensity such as mutual funds and trusts, as well as funds with unregulated liquidity, very short-term bond funds, short-term exchange-traded funds, and bank-backed short-term investment funds are included.
- Those that rely on external financing or credit investment funds with a high level of trading concentration (mutual funds or trusts) are another category. The capital they provide directly to investment funds (such as primary broker dealers) or indirectly through derivatives leave them exposed to risk of a run, especially when the funds are invested in long-term or more complicated

financial instruments. Examples include credit hedge funds levering up through short-term bank investments, securities lending, or repurchase agreements.

- Holders of large bond positions in the credit market or part of it (mutual funds or trusts) engage in immediate or very short-term repurchase agreements that put them in danger of runs.

The second economic function is the use of short-term funds to provide credit or loans. This credit is provided outside the banking system and includes both secured and unsecured loans to corporate or retail clients (such as car loans, mortgages, or commercial property loans). All these types can lead to liquidity and maturity transformation, and they have the following possible organizational forms:

- Institutions that are not carefully regulated like banks.
- Financing companies that raise funds from ABCP, CP, or repurchase agreements (repos).
- Institutions that heavily rely on a parent company for financing, and the parent's industry are highly cyclical.
- Institutions that finance banks but get around banking regulatory measures.

The third economic function includes financial services intermediaries that rely on short-term financing or client-provided collateral for financing. These intermediaries could be brokers (assist the sale and purchase of derivatives and on/off market securities, including market makers) or providers of hedge funds' primary dealer services. They take the following forms:

- Securities brokers who finance themselves with large amounts of short-term bank credit or wholesale market financing (main funding sources are ABCP, CP, repos, and short-term bank credit).
- Securities and primary dealers that rely on client assets to obtain finance for their own business or others.

The fourth economic function is facilitation of credit creation, such as balance sheet support or credit insurance/enhancement. These help banks and nonbanks grant loans. These are also financial intermediaries and can bring about the danger of imperfect risk transfer or excessive leverage. Organizational structures are the following:

- Financial guarantee companies that guarantee structured products and pose a potential risk to the system through inappropriate risk pricing (excessively reducing financing costs so that they no longer reflect the real risk levels).
- Financial guarantee companies that finance themselves over the wholesale funding markets or short-term bank credit and perform credit enhancement for banks and nonbanks in areas such as credit card loans or corporate loans.
- Mortgage insurance companies that perform credit enhancement to the extent that borrowing conditions do not reflect the borrower's true situation (risk is not properly disclosed and interest rates are not reasonable, raising risks throughout the financial system).

The final economic function is securitization-based credit intermediation and funding of financial entities. This can be done with or without assistance from banks/risk transfer and is part of both the financial intermediation machine and banking system. Excessive liquidity/maturity transformation, leverage, and regulatory arbitrage can all emerge from this process under certain conditions. For example, securitizers may buy up or provide credit enhancement for asset pools that consist of bank- or nonbank-held loans. They then use these as collateral to issue their own ABCP or other securities.

Historical evolution and driving forces

Financial intermediaries other than banks have existed on the sidelines throughout the history of banking. These are the embryonic forms of today's shadow banks, which have taken different shapes in various historical periods. One of these periods was in America after the adoption of Regulation Q in 1933. Regulation Q capped deposit rates to protect the newly formed deposit insurance system from ruinous interest rate competition for now government-insured deposits. Sure enough, nonbank financial intermediaries sprung up to meet the demand for higher investor returns, such as the Eurodollar market and money market mutual funds. Another example came after the Second World War, as many countries tried to control their money supply by restricting loan growth. The result was a migration of loans off of balance sheets. Once again, after the first set of Basel Accords were published, many structured financial products emerged to avoid regulatory supervision. It is these very products that evolved into today's shadow banking. From the previous examples, it should be clear that shadow banking is essentially markets' avoidance of regulation. We can concretely analyze the reasons for its existence by looking at it through a lens of supply and demand.

From the demand side, shadow banking tries to fulfill investor demand for low-risk, high-return investment channels. Since 2000, institutional demand for safe, highly liquid financial instruments has sharply increased. These institutions include large corporations and financial intermediaries like PE firms and pension funds. Figure 1.4 shows American companies' possession of cash and cash equivalents, which clearly took off after 1980. In addition, firms like PE funds needed more safe assets as reserves to manage liquidity for their immense assets. These were to guard against unexpected cash outflows.

Existing bank deposits were insufficient to fulfill this new demand for liquid assets. One reason lies in the design of deposit insurance schemes. American and European deposit insurances are mainly designed to protect small depositors, so the compensation per depositor is limited. Large deposits would therefore be mostly uninsured (high-risk), so institutional investors needed new, short-term, highly liquid financial instruments. Securitization, collateral intermediation, and other forms of shadow banking jumped in to satisfy this demand. High-quality collateral implied low risk, so institutional investors flocked to these securities.

Second, we look at the supply angle. Shadow banking has a certain cost advantage compared to traditional banks. One of the primary ways shadow banks reduce operational costs is through avoidance of traditional banking regulation, which allows

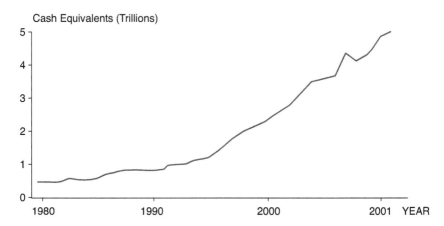

Figure 1.4 Company holdings of cash equivalents in the United States (1980–2010).

them to skirt capital requirements and leverage restrictions. Another factor is financial innovation. In the recent years, new forms of and structures for financial products have increased efficiency and reduced financing costs. For example, shadow banks use structured debt instruments to spread risk more broadly and efficiently than banks.

Comparison of shadow banks in major economies

Overview

The FSB defines shadow banking as the financial intermediation system outside of banks. Using this definition means shadow banking rapidly increased in scale before the financial crisis broke out. In 2002, shadow banking activity in 20 countries/areas and the Eurozone was estimated at $26 trillion, and it reached $62 trillion in 2007 before declining in 2008. However, it passed its previous peak with $67 trillion in 2011.[7] Figure 1.5 shows different financial institutions' scale and growth rate from 2002 to 2011. In this figure, "Other Financial Intermediaries" refers to broadly defined shadow banking. Figure 1.6 shows different types of financial institutions' holdings as a percentage of all financial assets. Here we also see a peak for shadow banking in 2007, holding 27% of all assets. Despite this, shadow banking is still dwarfed by traditional banking, coming in at only half the size of their traditional counterparts.

Figures 1.7 and 1.8 show the share of shadow banks in 20 countries/areas and Europe in 2005 and 2011, respectively. According to the data, America, the Eurozone, England, and Japan have the highest shares of worldwide shadow banks. Together they made up 91% of shadow banking in 2005 and witnessed a slight decrease to 87% in 2011. America had the largest individual share, at 44% in 2005 and 35% in 2011. Eurozone and English shadow banking saw increases in their respective shares from 2005 to 2011. America and the Eurozone have the largest share of shadow banking (68% together in 2011), and the following section analyzes their shadow banking sectors in more detail.

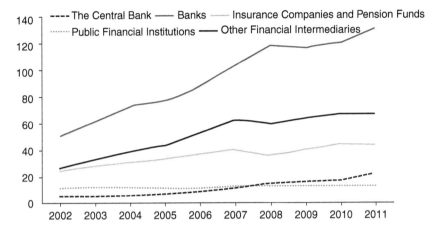

Figure 1.5 Assets of financial institutions (in trillions).

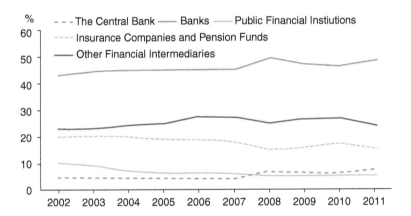

Figure 1.6 Share of aggregate financial assets by type of institution.

Concrete examples

America: The subprime disaster

Securitization was the main pre-crisis model for American shadow banks. Since different researchers have defined shadow banking in different ways, they have provided varied estimates of the sector's size (see Figure 1.9).

To gain a clearer view of American shadow banking's structure, we examine the flow of funds data. This gives us a breakdown of different types of debt products as a percentage of the total (see Figure 1.10). Traditional bank loans generally decline as a proportion of the total from 1945 onwards, while money market mutual funds, repos, and securitization continually gain ground. Of course, securitization started to decline after the financial crisis, but repos stayed constant.

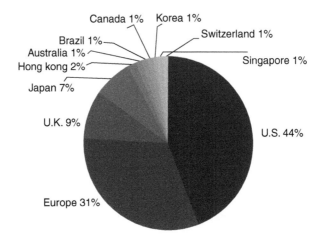

Figure 1.7 Share of shadow banking in 20 countries and regions in 2005.

Source: National flow of funds data. See *Global Shadow Banking Monitoring Report 2012*, www.financialstabilityboard.org/search/?q=shadow+bank+20&dr=-1&mp= any&_st=false&c=10&sb=0

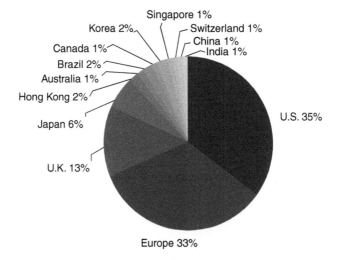

Figure 1.8 Share of shadow banking in 20 countries and regions in 2011.

Source: National flow of funds data. See *Global Shadow Banking Monitoring Report 2012*, www.financialstabilityboard.org/search/?q=shadow+bank+20&dr=-1&mp= any&_st=false&c=10&sb=0

Eurozone: The subprime disaster

The Eurozone's main securitization products are asset-backed bonds and relatively short-term ABCP. Asset-backed bonds are also most commonly used for collateral

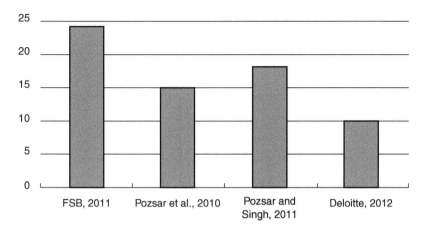

Figure 1.9 Estimates on the size of US shadow banking (in trillion dollars).

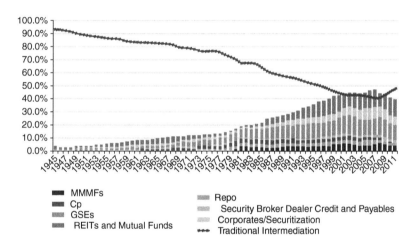

Figure 1.10 Structure of US shadow banking.

intermediation and securitized lending. Figure 1.11 shows that asset-backed bonds were the most common collateralized securities in the Eurozone before the crisis, but since then have almost completely disappeared. Figure 1.12 sheds further light on the matter. Loans are the most common form of backing for ABS, of which 72% was issued to households. This leaves corporates to be responsible for only the remaining 24%.

Money market mutual fund is another primary channel for shadow banks in the Eurozone. Figure 1.13 shows that although Eurozone MMFs are large, they are pale in comparison with the size of American MMFs. Since institutional investors are the primary purchasers of MMFs, this trend is consistent with the aforementioned explosion in global demand for certain assets.

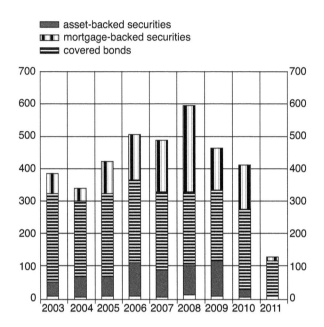

Figure 1.11 Asset-backed securities in the Eurozone (in trillion euros).
Source: The European Central Bank.

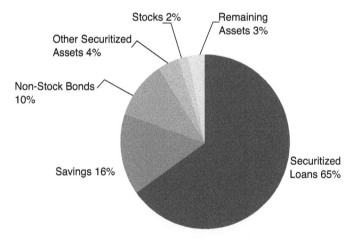

Figure 1.12 Asset shares of financial vehicle corporations (FVC) in 2010.

To conclude, pre-crisis shadow banking mainly occupied itself with securitization. But risks that emerged during the crisis period resulted in a sharp contraction in these markets. At present, recurring utilization of collateral, collateral intermediation loans, and repos are making up an increasing proportion of shadow banking.

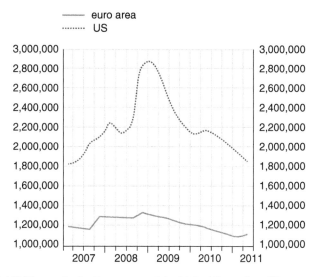

Figure 1.13 MMF assets in the Eurozone and the United States (in million euros).

Why shadow banking requires additional regulation

Credit intermediation outside the traditional banking system can exert a certain accumulated effect. For example, it can increase the available funding sources and strengthen liquidity. However, the financial crisis originating in America demonstrated the capacity of a daily growing shadow banking system to cause systemic crises. Causality could be direct or work through their relationships with the traditional banking system. They can also raise systemic risk throughout the financial system through regulatory arbitrage, a break out from the strict banking regulatory systems. It is therefore imperative to regulate these areas.[8]

Systemic financial risk

Shadow banking is recognized as the main source of systemic risk in the latest financial crisis. The FSB attributes this to the "four characteristics": maturity transformation, liquidity transformation, credit risk transfer, and high leverage. Shadow banks use short-term debt to fund medium- to long-term operations, which creates a maturity mismatch. They invest liquid funds in financial products that have a risk of being too illiquid to be redeemed for cash in time to satisfy investor redemptions. Banks often keep a portion of assets sold to shadow banks or provide hidden guarantees that cause incomplete risk transfer. Many high-leverage financial products have emerged in recent years, especially structured products whose operational leverage is boosted to raise returns. The risks are both great and easily transmitted to the traditional banking system.

The outbreak of risks for banks in a traditional financial system is the "bank run," but shadow banks have their own type of this phenomenon. During the financial crisis, for example, the breakdown of the repo chain, in which shadow banks were the main players, is widely considered to be a type of "bank run." They therefore received a great deal of attention due to the systemic risks they pose. Risks spread all around the world with shadow banking's cross-border allocation of capital. As financial globalization deepens, the interconnectedness of worldwide shadow banks increases with it. Systemic risk in the financial system of one country could easily evolve into a worldwide crisis that gravely threatens the world economy.

Regulatory arbitrage

Regulatory arbitrage arises when the standards used to regulate banks and shadow banks are not the same. It allows shadow banking to launch an accumulation of systemic risk. We have seen that shadow banking's existence itself is to a certain extent due to avoidance of regulation. It uses accounting and legal methods to carve assets out of highly regulated banks and puts them into lightly regulated financial markets and intermediaries. Clearly, strict microprudential regulation focused on banks is woefully inadequate to prevent the buildup of excessive risk.

Market self-regulation cannot deal with shadow banking's regulatory arbitrage on its own. In game theory, this is a classic prisoners' dilemma. If one bank does not use shadow banking to sell its loans, it will use up more of its core capital and have higher costs. Thus, shadow banking has become a "strictly dominant strategy." No matter what their competitors do, banks reach their individually optimal outcomes when they participate in the shadow banking system. Shadow banks thus easily lead to market failure and non-Pareto optimal outcomes. Regulatory organs must therefore intervene to alter the use of shadow banking channels for financial returns. They must help change financial institutions' choices and bring the assets onto the balance sheet under the existing framework to encourage stability and restraint.

Notes

1 www.bis.org/speeches/sp080403.pdf, p. 8.
2 http://online.wsj.com/public/resources/documents/G20COMMUN1110.pdf
3 See Claessens, Stijn, Pozsar, Zoltan, Ratnovski, Lev, and Singh, Manmohan. "Shadow Banking: Economics and Policy," *International Monetary Fund*, December 4, 2012, p. 8.
4 See Claessens, Stijn, Pozsar, Zoltan, Ratnovski, Lev, and Singh, Manmohan. "Shadow Banking: Economics and Policy," *International Monetary Fund*, December 4, 2012, pp. 14–15.
5 See Claessens, Stijn, Pozsar, Zoltan, Ratnovski, Lev, and Singh, Manmohan. "Shadow Banking: Economics and Policy," *International Monetary Fund*, December 4, 2012, pp. 14–15.
6 www.financialstabilityboard.org/publications/r_130829a.pdf
7 See "Global Shadow Banking Monitoring Report 2012." FSB. http://www.financialstabilityboard.org/publications/r_121118c.pdf
8 See FSB, "Recommendations to Strengthen Oversight and Regulation of Shadow Banking," October 27, 2011; and FSB, "Shadow Banking: Scoping the Issues," April 12, 2011. http://www.financialstabilityboard.org/publications/r_110412a.pdf

2 The emergence of Chinese shadow banking and where it stands today

After an overview of the fundamental theories of shadow banking internationally, this chapter focuses on shadow banking in China. Since the Chinese financial market is still in a relatively early stage of development, shadow banks in China are different from those that triggered the recent financial crisis abroad. Thus, we first define Chinese shadow banking in both a broad and narrow sense. Then we explore the past and present of broad shadow banking, including an analysis of its composition and overall size. Finally, we study the driving factors of Chinese shadow banking, its positive effects, and potential risks. Then, we the foundation for a definition of narrow shadow banking and an understanding of the Chinese regulatory framework.

Definition of Chinese shadow banking

Introduction

There is no widely accepted definition of "shadow banking" among Chinese scholars. On October 10, 2012, the IMF noted in its Global Financial Stability Report that China should pay attention to its shadow banking problem, which could generate risks for traditional banking. People's Bank of China (PBOC) Governor Zhou Xiaochuan pointed out during an interview on November 11, 2012, that like many other countries China has "shadow banks," but the size and associated problems are much smaller than those of developed countries before the financial crisis. Shang Fulin, Chairman of the China Banking Regulatory Commission (CBRC), stated: "Trust and financial products are currently regulated by the CBRC. As a next step, the CBRC will research the content, function, size, structure, and risk of shadow banking under present conditions. It will improve industry standards, crack down on illegal behavior, and strengthen regulation of certain aspects of shadow banking, such as leverage ratios and consolidated credit risk. At the same time, the CBRC will promote bank reform and innovation to provide better and safer financial services." Afterwards, other experts came up with their own interpretations. Overall, their opinions were divided. Some regarded shadow banking negatively, others dismissively, but most saw it as a strong driving force. It thus remains a hotly discussed concept in China.

In September 2011, Yi Xianrong, Director of the Chinese Academy of Social Sciences' (CASS) Institute of Finance and Banking (IFB), argued that only business related to debtor–creditor relationships and activities outside bank balance sheets should be considered "shadow banking." Yuan Zengting, Deputy Director of the Center for Financial Products of IFB of CASS, recommends a focus on bank products and business lines. In China, "shadow banking" mainly refers to typical business lines and products in banks' wealth management departments, especially loan pools, entrusted loans, and loan products that originated from cooperation between banks and trusts. Liu Yuhui, Director of the CASS Financial Lab, separates shadow banking into two categories: unregulated securitization activities in banks and unregulated private finance. The former is mainly embodied in bank-trust cooperation, but also includes entrusted loans and intermediation from saving to investment performed by micro-loan firms, guarantee companies, trusts, finance companies, and financial leasing firms. The latter includes underground banks, private lending firms, and pawnshops.[1]

Some Chinese experts believe that shadow banking includes both organizations that practically function as banks and their activities.[2] Others emphasize regulation and treat shadow banks as financial institutions outside the supervisory and regulatory system. Most scholars insist that shadow banking includes all financial institutions other than commercial banks. For example, Li Jianjun, Professor of Finance at the Central University of Finance and Economics, defines shadow banking as the totality of all non-bank financial institutions, informal financial organizations, and their product systems.[3] Yuan Zengting, another CASS researcher, pointed out that shadow banking is more than financial institutions with independent legal personalities. It also covers business departments and financial tools, which are similar to or can be substitutes for traditional banking activities. In other words, it includes not only non-bank institutions and their businesses but also shadow banking departments and their businesses inside banking system.[4]

Some experts believe that any credit creation that does not submit deposit reserves to the central bank should be considered shadow banking. According to this standard, commercial banks' wealth management products (WMPs) and entrusted lending are both shadow banking. They do not pay deposit reserves to central bank, are capable of creating almost limitless amount of credit, and will not be able to receive any bailout from the central bank in the event of a default.[5]

There are other experts who stress the distinction between the broad and narrow sense of shadow banking. The broad sense of shadow banking refers to all credit intermediary systems other than banks. Since every component is divided by its related organizations and businesses, some of them reflect debt (e.g., financial products) and some reflect assets (e.g., trust loans and entrusted loans) of the financial institution. In this way, the estimated size of shadow banking does not reflect its actual credit support to real economy or its net risk exposure (excluding possible overlap).

In the narrow sense, shadow banking includes credit intermediary institutions and businesses that are outside traditional banks and may lead to systematic risk.[6] Some scholars define the broad and narrow standards by regulation. From the broad perspective, all non-bank loan channels providing credit activities belong to shadow banking. Only those outside the view of regulators are narrow shadow banking.

In a financial summit that took place on January 11, 2013, Yang Zaiping, the Executive Vice President of the China Banking Association (CBA), argued that it would not be proper to count formal financial products of Chinese banks as shadow banking, nor should these formal financial products and trusts be considered comparable to pawnshops or underground banks.[7]

Shadow banking was discussed as an independent issue during the 2013 China Development Forum. Ba Shusong, the Deputy Director-General of the Financial Research Institute at the Development Research Center of the State Council (DRC), indicated that Chinese shadow banking products are quite different from that of the United States and European countries, in both their nature and constitution. Currently, shadow banking generally is strictly regulated. For example, financial products of banks, trusts, and enterprise finance companies must be reported to regulators and fulfill net capital requirements. Although the concept of "shadow banking" is still unclear, it will remain useful due to banks' leading role in the financial system.

Dispute over shadow banking in China

Currently, the meaning of "shadow banking" in China varies greatly depending on who is using it and in what context. Despite the discrepancies, most use it in a disparaging manner. These varied opinions appear to fit into three categories, which define shadow banking in a progressively narrower sense.

The first level covers the widest range. It states that Chinese shadow banking consists mainly of institutions that fulfill banks' roles without inclusion on the bank's balance sheet, non-bank financial institutions, as well as private lending firms that resemble commercial banks. Either directly or indirectly, they replicate the core business and functions of commercial banks. This basically covers every subject of public financing. They range from legal activities such as trust loans, entrusted loans, and micro-loans all the way to financial innovations that either have bypassed existing laws, such as bank-trust cooperation, or have clearly unlawful activities such as guarantee companies that take deposits or issue loans, or usurious private lending.

The second refers to only those non-bank financial institutions and businesses that have copied commercial banks' core business without permission or supervision. Some call these "gray" or "black market" financing. They include loan sharks, guarantee companies that take deposits and issue loans, and innovations used by non-bank financial institutions to avoid regulation. This definition excludes non-bank organizations that are certified for credit business, such as trusts and micro-credit companies that can legally issue loans. On the other hand, it includes illegal financing, illegal lending, hidden financing, and hidden lending activities.

The third level of shadow banking excludes illegal private credit. It categorizes non-bank legal lending and disguised off-balance sheet bank lending as shadow banking.

In fact, current financing activities can be separated into the following types: qualified legal institutions and businesses for bank lending; illegal activities such as illegal financing and usury; and financial innovations that aim to circumvent the present legal restrictions, for example, non-bank institutions and businesses that attract deposits and issue hidden loans. Other versions are often just different combinations of the aforementioned types. Institutions and businesses that have bank loan qualifications are under financial supervision, but they do not receive the same level of direct restrictions inherent to banking regulation or monetary policy, thus attracting public attention.

If private credit activities are currently against the law or unregulated, then they should be controlled in the short term. At the same time, if they seem lawful and reasonable, then there should be remedies to legalize them in the long term. For example, regulators must consider how to ensure private lending firms meet legal standards. Businesses that are not restrained by traditional regulations may be innovations that could benefit the development of financial institutions and the financial system. Through innovation, they have discovered new ways to perform legal banking activities, such as bank-trust cooperation. These activities are market oriented and certainly capable of increasing financial efficiency. Their existence could also benefit economic development. While there should be regulations and standards, these innovations should be allowed to grow.

Implications of Chinese shadow banking

Shadow banking has a positive value despite serving as a scapegoat for the financial crisis. For example, it can provide new funding and liquidity source to market participants and enterprises. It thus pushes for an efficient allocation of credit in the economy. This book maintains that shadow banking itself is a neutral concept and should be considered without preconceived notions. On the one hand, it can play a positive role in deepening financial market reform and improving financial system. On the other hand, it may lead to systemic risks and regulatory arbitrage.

It is clear that there is no unanimous definition of shadow banking in China. These definitions often lack clarification and practical standards. This book seeks to define shadow banking based on several key words of previous studies, such as credit intermediaries, level of supervision, systemic risk, and regulatory arbitrage.

Essential factors

NON-BANK CREDIT INTERMEDIARY

Credit intermediary is a broad concept that refers to entities that can link both sides of credit as well as fulfill the role of credit financing and transfer, either entirely or in part. Credit intermediaries generally have five functions: credit creation, maturity transformation, risk diversification, settlement, and transaction cost management. It is the most fundamental function of traditional banks, including commercial banks, thrift institutions, and credit unions. Banks gather idle funds as liabilities and invest in economic sectors that become assets.

Apart from the traditional banking system, there are many other credit intermediaries that can realize credit creation and funds allocation. They are called non-bank credit intermediaries and play roles similar to those of banks. Overall, financing is the ultimate goal and credit is the medium. Indirect financing used to constitute the majority of financing. Direct financing was a much smaller market of secondary importance. Now, both begin to converge and work together.

LEVEL OF SUPERVISION

Many descriptions of shadow banking simply focus on aspects such as being outside of regulatory system, lightly or unregulated or enjoying a lower level of regulation than banks. However, our definition of shadow banking is mainly to help financial markets and regulators adopt proper measures and rules to identify shadow banking.

The aim of financial supervision is to protect the public interest, enhance market confidence, promote financial knowledge, and maintain financial market stability through prudential regulation. Shadow banking supervision is based on the idea that it can lead to systemic risk and market turmoil. A lack of proper regulation is generally the cause of systemic risk. An organization or business which is identified as a shadow bank should depend on its current level of supervision.

SYSTEMIC RISK

Systemic risk is the possibility that one event can trigger a series of losses within a financial system or market. In finance, systemic risk refers to instability caused by some special events that lead to deterioration of the financial system, which often has catastrophic result.[8] Non-bank financial institutions have maturity mismatch and high leverage. They can play the role of traditional banks, but their competitive advantage and profit margins are the results of higher risks, the kind of risks that traditional banks actively avoid. When they lack adequate supervision, they are more dangerous than traditional banks.

REGULATORY ARBITRAGE

Regulatory arbitrage refers to the cost advantage and profit gained by non-bank financial institutions due to less regulatory restrictions compared with banks. Their businesses are often off-balance sheet, they receive inadequate supervision, and they are free from compliance with capital adequacy or reserve requirements. This gives them an advantage over traditional banks. It also pushes more and more institutions to reduce their regulatory compliance costs and increase profit margins. Regulatory arbitrage is an essential part of shadow banking.

It is necessary to note that many non-bank financial institutions and businesses have regulatory arbitrage as their goal, but some of their aims are based on solid legal basis and satisfy market demand. These should be viewed as both positive and valuable. In this way, regulatory arbitrage is a necessary prerequisite for shadow banking, but an institution cannot be defined as a shadow bank just because of regulatory arbitrage. To make consistent judgments, we must examine an institution's regulatory arbitrage, systemic risk, and level of regulation together.

Broad and narrow shadow banking

On a broad scale, shadow banking is a credit intermediary system consisting of financial entities and businesses that do not belong to traditional banking. It can be either an independent credit activity or a part of the credit activity chain. Again, shadow banking is itself a neutral concept. Of course, shadow banking usually uses maturity transformation and high leverage to create credit and raise money. Without efficient supervision, it has higher systemic risk than traditional banks. Yet, this is only a small fraction of the shadow banking system.

Thereby the authors consider it necessary to distinguish between broad and narrow shadow banking. Broad shadow banking is defined as credit intermediaries that are not traditional banks. Not all of them cause systemic risk. Regulation should focus on non-bank credit intermediaries characterized by limited supervision, high systemic risk, regulatory arbitrage, maturity mismatch, liquidity transformation, high leverage, and risk transfer. In order to make things clear, we call the latter "narrow shadow banking." This must be carefully regulated to enhance risk management.

In particular, shadow banking includes both institutions and certain lines of business that fit our definition. "Shadow banking system" thus may be a better way to capture the essence of the concept. Because of this, some definitions focus on institutions, while others focus on their functions (lines of business). In fact, more often than not, the shadow banking system lies within traditional banks. They are often bank departments or agents of financial institutions. Most shadow banks do not operate independently. Rather, they are embedded in more financial activities. This book examines Chinese shadow banking by analyzing both institutions and businesses that may be associated with shadow banking. Afterwards, we will be able to decide if they are shadow banking.

Criteria of Chinese shadow banking

In this book, shadow banking is defined as a non-bank credit intermediary or a business that has at least one of the following: maturity transformation, liquidity transformation, high leverage, and risk transfer. Moreover, it is under either limited or non-existent regulation and has the potential to cause systemic risk as well as regulatory arbitrage. Based on this, there are three steps to identify a shadow bank (Figure 2.1).

Is it a credit intermediary or does it function as a credit intermediary?

Broad shadow banking consists of credit intermediaries that are not traditional banks, including independent institutions and businesses. Therefore, the first step is to check whether the institution is in the credit intermediary business, including whether it creates credit and raises funds. For those that meet this standard, the following two steps should be used to determine if they are truly shadow banks.

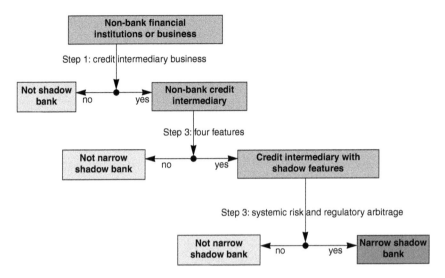

Figure 2.1 Identification of Chinese shadow banking.

Does it involve the following: Maturity transformation, liquidity transformation, high leverage, and risk transfer

Maturity transformation, liquidity transformation, high leverage, and risk transfer are four major risk factors of shadow banking as defined by the Financial Stability Board (FSB). Credit intermediaries or businesses that cause no systemic risk are not shadow banking.

MATURITY TRANSFORMATION

Maturity transformation is the first core function of commercial banks. It turns short-term debt into long-term assets and balances deposit and loan maturities. Some non-bank credit intermediaries can perform the same function. Early law allowed commercial banks to monopolize short-term debt (deposits). However, with the development of modern money market, the disadvantage of passive liabilities like deposits became clear. Commercial banks gradually started to actively seek liabilities and use a variety of money market tools. Traditional commercial banks usually use the "current debt & long-term creditor" model, including "taking short-term deposits & issuing long-term loans," "short-term liabilities in the money market & issuance of long-term loans." Short-term liabilities include commercial paper or asset-backed commercial paper (ABCP), whose maturities run under a year. The most fundamental function of maturity transformation is to create money and credit. Through maturity transformation, commercial banks create two-sided claims for both depositors and banks, which then can solve information asymmetry problems and decrease transaction costs.

Maturity mismatch is a related concept, which is also called imperfect maturity transformation. This can happen to commercial banks and pose both liquidity and interest rate risk. However, risks in the banking system have explicit guarantees from the lender of last resort. In comparison, non-bank financial institutions have higher maturity mismatch risk as their investments are usually unregulated, non-standard credit assets. They consequently receive no protection from central banks. Regardless of its nature, the safety of maturity transformation depends on the participants' creditworthiness, which is influenced by its coverage, value of long-term investment assets, and redemption value of its collateral.

The maturity transformation of American shadow banking happens in the money market, and it is typical in money creation. By using asset-backed securities (ABS), ABCP and repos, shadow banks obtain short-term and extremely short-term commercial financing from institutions such as the money market fund (MMF). After a long chain of derivatives, shadow banks finally invest in liabilities that have longer maturity than that of the liability. The maturity transformation function of shadow banks gave rise to multiple claims on the same asset base. Some examples include ABCP, MMF, and money market tools that are typically considered quasi-money.

Maturity transformation is a key characteristic for the definition of shadow banks. Many Chinese non-bank financial institutions finance themselves through methods that are a mix of direct and indirect financing. They often sell a type of monetary liability and make loans, which combines short-term liabilities with medium- and long-term assets. It is often not bond indenture. Rather, it is a kind of financial market tool or security that includes a monetary claim. The asset is an indirect financial market asset. As for its term and business model, long-term loans on the asset side requires the shadow banks to have a maturity transformation function. Non-bank financial institutions with "short-term liabilities + mid-and-long term assets" therefore have the potential to be shadow banks.

LIQUIDITY TRANSFORMATION

Liquidity transformation is the second core function of commercial banks. Like maturity transformation, it emphasizes commercial banks' transfer of non-liquid deposits into current deposits. At the same time, it turns short-term liabilities into long-term assets. The liquidity is changed twice in the process. The history of developed countries proves that a growing number of commercial banks no longer depend on saving deposits. They are turning to the money market for funding even at the start of disintermediation. Commercial banks' new mediums for liquidity transformation are becoming substitutes for deposits, such as financial products and MMFs, but the nature of the transformation processes remain the same. In China, many non-bank financial institutions also use the same models for liquidity transformation.

In the process of liquidity transformation, we must also consider liquidity risk and liquidity premiums.[9] Since depositors may withdraw their money at any time, commercial banks are now susceptible to liquidity squeezes. Liquidity premium is one of the basic reasons for the existence of financial intermediaries and the earliest income source of commercial banks. Maturity and liquidity transformations are the primary processes of credit creation and a major standard in classifying credit intermediaries.

HIGH LEVERAGE

High leverage implies both high debt and credit creation. Leverage comes from net liabilities and is driven by maturity and liquidity transformations. In practice, provided that equity capital is constant, any increase in debt (e.g., implicit liabilities, contingent liabilities, credit enhancement, and overestimation of collateral values) and liability innovation (e.g., repos, rehypothecation, and extensions of the asset/liability transformation chain) can produce high leverage. In the US shadow banking system, high leverage includes on-balance sheet leverage, such as financing from primary dealers or through repos, and off-balance sheet leverage embedded in derivatives. In both commercial banks and shadow banks, high leverage increases the probability of eventual insolvency.

Leverage is also a procyclical phenomenon. It allows a small amount of capital to punch above its weight, boosts asset prices, and can turn a minor external shock into a serious financial crisis. When high leverage pushes up asset prices, debtors can make enough profits to compensate for the interest expense. On the contrary, when asset prices fall, debtors can easily see their equity wiped out and be forced into bankruptcy.

RISK TRANSFER

Risk transfer is used in risk management. In developed countries, it mostly refers to the tools commercial banks use to transfer credit risk. These tools include collateralized debt obligations (CDOs) and credit-default swaps (CDSs). Risk transfer does not equal risk elimination. There are two ways to eliminate credit risk: first, debtors pay off their debt at maturity and, second, the last counterparty that takes credit risks can absorb potential default losses in their entirety. In other words, none of the risk transfer process can eliminate risk. According to the FSB, credit risk transfers by commercial banks or shadow banks are often accompanied by the rise of other risks. For example, when a commercial bank buys CDS for credit enhancement, it will face new counterparty risk in addition to that it already faced. The FSB regards this imperfect credit risk transfer process as another source of systemic risk.

In China, the majority of credit risk transfer performed by commercial banks and near-banks are credit asset transfers and informal ABS. Enterprises use financing guarantees and loan exchange for risk transfer. All of these methods and their regulation are in the process of development. While their market demand is great, credit asset counterparties may not have the capacity to bear potential default risk.

Maturity and liquidity transformations, high leverage, and imperfect credit risk transfer are the main reasons of systemic risk, but they do not trigger systemic risk every time. In most cases, reasonable supervision and risk prevention can help ensure systemic risk does not break into systemic crisis. This implies that credit intermediaries with the aforementioned four features are not necessarily shadow banks. The determining factors are whether it is under supervision and whether it can trigger systemic risk, as well as regulatory arbitrage. Moreover, to cause systemic risk, the four features do not have to exist at the same time. In fact, as long as one of the features exists, the intermediary may be a shadow bank. Therefore, it is necessary to analyze it further through the third step.

WILL IT CAUSE SYSTEMIC RISK?

Maturity and liquidity transformations, high leverage, and imperfect credit risk transfer may lead to systemic risk. Maturity and liquidity transformations are core functions as well as qualifying standards for credit intermediaries. Non-bank credit intermediaries with high leverage and imperfect credit risk transfer are more likely to produce risk. Thus, the focus of regulation should be on non-bank credit inter-mediaries. The lack of regulation is a major cause for systemic risk.

All in all, only through the aforementioned three steps can we determine whether or not an institution belongs to shadow banking. In Chapters 3–5, this book examines the broad shadow banking system using the previously outlined steps. The outcome should also reveal the current scope of narrow shadow banking in China.

Broad Chinese shadow banking system

From the history of shadow banking systems outside China, we know that shadow banking is tied to developments in financial markets and financial products. The Chinese financial market had a late start, especially in financial derivatives. Likewise, shadow banking also started late in China. The bulk of Chinese shadow banking is scattered among different institutions and lines of businesses.

Main forms of Chinese shadow banking

Discussions in Chapter 1 showed that shadow banking is not just an individual subject, but a chain of businesses linked by a number of financial intermediar-ies through various financial markets. It is a crossover of financial markets and financial intermediaries with credit products as its core business. Correspondingly, broad shadow banking in China predominately engages in credit activities. The typical operating process is the following: social capital – general assets management products – private use. Credit creation, conversion, and financial intermediation are achieved through this chain. Credit institutions engaged in such activities include trust companies, securities companies, insurance companies, small loan companies, consumer finance companies, financial leasing companies, auto finance compa-nies, finance companies, money brokers, and pawnshops. Types of financial services involved include banking, trust banking, securities financing, financial services for funds, insurance, financial services, asset securitization, MMFs, and repos. All of these agencies and businesses are part of broad shadow banking, but not all non-bank credit intermediation leads to systemic risks. In fact, some of them are under the supervision of the CBRC and consequently operate strictly in accordance with the law. In addition, non-bank credit intermediaries include many different types of business. There is a chance that some of them may cause systemic risk.

To identify shadow banking is a large task. We discuss Chinese narrow shadow banking in Chapters 3–5. Chapter 6 talks about shadow banks' influence on China's macroeconomy, monetary policy, and the entire financial system. It adopts the definition of broad shadow banking and risk perspective analysis for the sake of data convenience, accuracy, maximum risk control, and financial market stability.

Scale analysis of broad Chinese shadow banking

Estimation issues in the shadow banking system

As seen earlier, shadow banking is not composed of just one kind of institution (Table 2.1). Rather, it includes businesses or even some activities typical to credit intermediaries. Therefore, analyses of the shadow banking system can make large errors. Balance sheets sometimes can show the assets and liabilities of shadow banks, but they cannot accurately display the scale of credit creation activities. It is necessary to have detailed research, statistical analysis, and core structural data to estimate shadow banking system stocks at the end of the year. In comparison, incremental analysis is better in describing the scale of activity. The increments can display how much new long-term credit (legal and illegal) comes from shadow banking system within a certain time period. It more accurately reflects the true activities of shadow banking and the structure of activity within the financial system.

There is another method to calculate both the stock and flow of money. On the one hand, we can directly measure the liabilities of financial intermediations. For example, we can look at short-term financial tools and their activity level, which can replace commercial banks through absorption of deposits and subsequent investment. On the other hand, we can measure the assets of financial

Table 2.1 Chinese shadow banking system in a broad sense

Organizations that are regulated by China Securities Regulatory Commission (CSRC), CBRC, and China Insurance Regulatory Commission (CIRC)	*Financial institutions that are regulated by ministries and local governments*	*Organizations that are currently not being regulated*	*Latest shadow banking activities in the financial market*
Banks	Pawnshops	Internet finance	ABS
Trusts	Guarantee	companies	Securities lending
Securities	companies	Private lending	Repurchasing
Funds	Financial leasing	third-party financial	MMF
Insurance companies	companies	agencies	
Financial companies	Private equity firms		
Factoring services	Micro-lenders		
Third party payment	Financial asset		
companies	exchanges		

intermediations indirectly. We measure the entire long-term credit investments in the country and deduct foreign currency loans, long-term RMB loans in commercial banks, entrusted loans, corporate compliance bonds, notes, and a few others. The remaining will be the total for long-term credit assets.

A direct estimation for scope is difficult for a few reasons: First, information about deposits taken by many non-bank financial institutions is not shown on the balance sheet, so it is hard to obtain reliable statistics. Second, some businesses and institutions have received more stringent regulation from CBRC, which has changed their nature. Features like maturity transformation are becoming sporadic phenomena instead of the norm. It is difficult to give them an accurate qualitative description. The financial products of commercial banks are good examples. Establishing accounts one-on-one directly eliminates maturity and liquidity transformations. The financial products that roll investments over into long-term liabilities are under control.

Indirect statistics can roughly state the overall size. Funds from banks are ultimately devoted to mid- and long-term credit by the shadow banking system. The scale of social financing includes the total amount of credit assets of all legal credit intermediaries, but it does not contain private loans and specific structural data. We can monitor China's shadow banking activities by using data for the scale of social financing and private loans.

Currently, many domestic scholars and organizations include institutions or activities in their estimations of the total size of the shadow banking system from an institutional perspective. Their inflated results exaggerate the total size of the shadow banking system beyond the actual level. In fact, they are using a broad shadow banking estimation that is unable to differentiate narrow shadow banking and its lurking systemic risk.

Relation and trend analysis for the shadow banking system

ANALYSIS OF AGGREGATE FINANCING FOR THE REAL ECONOMY

This indicator, aggregate financing to the real economy, fully reflects the relation between the financial and economic systems as well as the total financial support for the real economy. It refers to the scale of total social financing that the real economy receives from the whole financial system during a certain period of time, including RMB loans, foreign currency loans, entrusted loans, trust loans, undiscounted bank acceptance bills, corporate bonds, equity financing of non-financial enterprises, investment real estate, and 10 other types of financial instrument. As for the financial system, there are banks, securities, insurance, and other financial institutions from an institutional perspective. From a market perspective, we have credit markets, bond markets, stock markets, insurance markets, and intermediary markets.[10]

The amount of aggregate financing to the real economy for first half of 2013 was RMB 10.15 trillion, RMB 2.38 trillion more than the same period in 2012 (Table 2.2). Among them, RMB loans increased to RMB 5.08 trillion, an increase of RMB 221.7 billion; foreign currency loans increased to RMB 579.1 billion, an increase of RMB 302.6 billion; entrusted loans increased to RMB 1.11 trillion, adding RMB 629.1 billion; trust loans reached to RMB 1.23 trillion, an increase of RMB 895 billion; undiscounted bank acceptances rose to RMB 516.4 billion, an decrease of RMB 93.2 billion; net financing from corporate bonds was RMB 1.22 trillion, up by more than RMB 396.5 billion; and domestic non-financial corporate equity financing totaled RMB 124.8 billion, a decline of RMB 24.7 billion. Aggregate financing to the real economy in June was RMB 1.04 trillion, RMB 742.7 billion less than the same period in 2012.

Structurally, for the first half of 2013, RMB loans accounted for just over 50% of total social financing, a decline of 12.4 percentage points from the previous period in 2012; foreign currency loans accounted for 5.7%, an increase of 2.1 percentage points; entrusted loans accounted for 10.95%, an increase of 4.8 percentage points; trust loans accounted for 12.14%, an increase of 7.8 percentage points; undiscounted

Table 2.2 Aggregate financing to the real economy for first half of 2013

Time / Project	2013.01	2013.02	2013.03	2013.4	2013.05	2013.06	Total	Ratio
	Units(RMB 100 million)							%
Aggregate financing to real economy	25,446	10,704	25,502	17,624	11,860	10,375	101,511	100
RMB loans	10,721	6,200	10,625	7,923	6,694	8,605	50,768	50.01
Foreign currency loans	1,795	1,149	1,509	847	357	133	5,791	5.70
Entrusted loans	2,061	1,426	1,748	1,926	1,967	1,990	11,118	10.95
Trust loans	2,108	1,825	4,312	1,942	971	1,162	12,319	12.14
Undiscounted bankers' acceptances	5,798	-1,823	2,731	2,218	-1,141	-2,620	5,164	5.09
Corporate bond	2,248	1,453	3,869	2,033	2,219	410	12,234	12.05
Domestic non-financial corporate equity financing	244	165	208	274	231	126	1,248	1.23

Source: Statistics and Analysis Department of the People's Bank of China.

Notes: There are 10 indicators for aggregate financing to the real economy, of which the table lists seven. Thus, the total amount of our seven indicators is smaller than the aggregate financing amount, as shown in Table 2.3.

bankers' acceptances accounted for 5.09%, a decrease of 2.7 percentage points; corporate bonds accounted for 12.05%, an increase of 1.5 percentage points; domestic non-financial corporation financing accounted for 1.23%, down by 0.7 percentage points.

As can be seen from Table 2.3 and Figure 2.2, in addition to RMB loans, other financing accounted for a small fraction in 2002 when RMB loans accounted for 91.9% of total social financing, leaving other financing at only a relatively insignificant 8.1%. However, by 2010, the situation was entirely different. RMB loans proportion fell below 60% of the total. Besides, with the rapid development of financial innovation, RMB loan as a proportion of social financing declined to 52.0% by 2012. Therefore, in order to improve the effectiveness of financial regulation, it is necessary to take both RMB loans and other financing methods into consideration.

DATA ANALYSIS

For a more intuitive understanding of the supply and demand issues of social capital, this part analyzes the scale of local government financing platforms, bank financing, trusts, aggregate financing to the real economy, and RMB loan balances since 2010 (Table 2.4).

Figure 2.3 shows that from 2010 to 2012, the scale of aggregate financing to the real economy and local government financing platform debts rose continuously. The bank financing and trusts were expanding rapidly, but RMB loan balances grew slowly. This implies that bank financing and trust loans are beginning to occupy greater proportions of total social financing, but RMB loans are losing ground.

BROAD SHADOW BANKING SCALE AND GDP

As mentioned earlier, broad shadow banking includes financial intermediaries involved in facilitating the creation of credit across the global financial system, but whose members are not subject to regulatory oversight. The broad shadow banking system also refers to unregulated activities by regulated institutions. Strictly speaking, the size of broad shadow banking should also be based on all these institutions and lines of business. Given that some institutions or businesses do not publish accurate data and most businesses are rather small, we use bank financing, trust assets, securities asset management, fund, and insurance assets to represent the size of broad shadow banking since 2010 (Table 2.5).

Figure 2.4 shows that broad shadow banking has expanded from RMB 12.31 trillion in 2010 to RMB 27.45 trillion by 2012, an increase of 59%. Broad shadow banking also occupies an increasing percentage of GDP, reaching 30.6% in 2010, 37.9% in 2011, and 52.9% in 2012. By June 2013, the total scale of shadow banking reached RMB 33 trillion. However, the scale of broad shadow banking has little to do with that of narrow shadow banking. Not all broad shadow banking engenders systemic risk and regulatory arbitrage. In addition, some are subject to CBRC regulation, for example, bank and trust financial products.

Table 2.3 Aggregate financing to the real economy since 2002 (RMB 100m)

Time	Total amount	RMB loans	Foreign currency loans	Entrusted loans	Trust loans	Undiscounted bankers' acceptances	Corporate bond	Domestic non-financial corporate equity financing
				Breakdown aggregate financing to the real economy				
2002	20,112	18,475	731	175	–	-695	367	628
2003	34,113	27,652	2,285	601	–	2010	499	559
2004	28,629	22,673	1,381	3,118	–	-290	467	673
2005	30,008	23,544	1,415	1,961	–	24	2,010	339
2006	42,696	31,523	1,459	2,695	825	1500	2,310	1,536
2007	59,663	36,323	3,864	3,371	1,702	6,701	2,284	4,333
2008	69,802	49,041	1,947	4,262	3,144	1,064	5,523	3,324
2009	139,104	95,942	9,265	6,780	4,364	4,606	12,367	3,350
2010	140,191	79,451	4,855	8,748	3,865	23,346	11,063	5,786
2011	128,286	74,715	5,712	12,962	2,034	10,271	13,658	4,377
2012	157,631	82,038	9,163	12,838	12,845	10,498	22,551	2,508

(continued)

Table 2.3 Aggregate financing to the real economy since 2002 (RMB 100m) (continued)

Time	Total amount	RMB loans	Foreign currency loans	Entrusted loans	Trust loans	Undiscounted bank-ers' acceptances	Corporate bond	Domestic non-financial corpo-rate equity financing
				Proportion (%)				
2002	100	91.9	3.6	0.9	–	-3.5	1.8	3.1
2003	100	81.1	6.7	1.8	–	5.9	1.5	1.6
2004	100	79.2	4.8	10.9	–	-1.0	1.6	2.4
2005	100	78.5	4.7	6.5	–	0.1	6.7	1.1
2006	100	73.8	3.4	6.3	1.9	3.5	5.4	3.6
2007	100	60.9	6.5	5.7	2.9	11.2	3.8	7.3
2008	100	70.3	2.8	6.1	4.5	1.5	7.9	4.8
2009	100	69.0	6.7	4.9	3.1	3.3	8.9	2.4
2010	100	56.7	3.5	6.2	2.8	16.7	7.9	4.1
2011	100	58.2	4.5	10.1	1.6	8.0	10.6	3.4
2012	100	52.1	5.81	8.14	8.15	6.66	14.31	1.59

Source: Statistics and Analysis Department of the People's Bank of China.

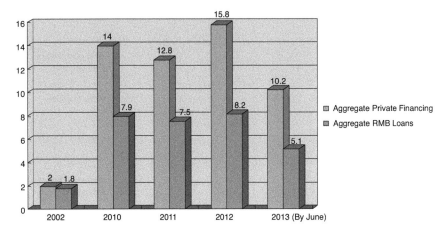

Figure 2.2 Comparison of aggregate financing to real economy and RMB loans.

Table 2.4 Comparison of local government financing platforms, bank financing, trusts, aggregate financing to the real economy, and RMB loans balance

Year Project	2010	2011	2012	2013 (by June)
Local government finance platform	7.77	10.3	11.4	9.2
Bank financing	1.7	4.58	7.12	9.08
Trust size	3.04	4.81	7.47	9.45
Aggregate financing to the real economy	14.02	12.83	15.76	10.15
RMB loans balance	7.9	7.5	8.2	5.1

Therefore, the sustainable growth of broad shadow banking may not have a great impact on Chinese macroeconomic and financial market stability.[11]

Notably, the proportion of broad shadow banking in GDP we measure statistically is significantly larger than reality due to cross-holding problems in its classification. For example, bank financial products contain elements of trust and securities assets (Figure 2.5).

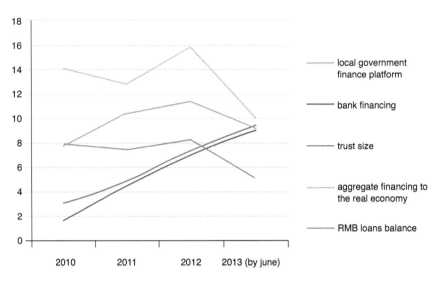

Figure 2.3 Local government financing platforms, bank financing, trust, aggregate financing to the real economy, and RMB loan balances.

Table 2.5 Broad shadow banking from 2010 to 2013 (unit: RMB trillion)

Item \ Year	2010	2011	2012	2013 to June
Bank financing	1.7	4.58	7.12	9.08
Trust assets	3.04	4.81	7.47	9.45
Securities asset management	–	0.28	1.89	3.42
Funds	2.52	2.19	3.62	3.48
Insurance assets	5.05	6.01	7.35	7.88
Shadow banking scale	12.31	17.87	27.45	33.31
GDP	40.2	47.2	51.9	24.8
Broad shadow banking as a percentage of GDP	30.6%	37.8%	52.9%	

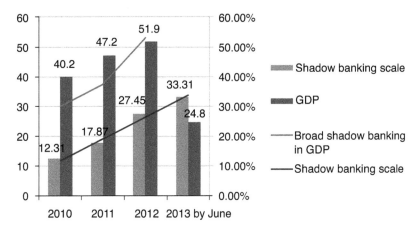

Figure 2.4 Broad shadow banking and GDP.

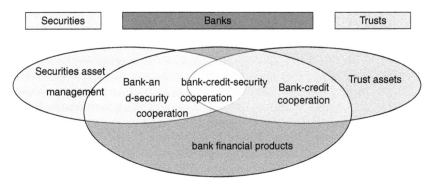

Figure 2.5 Cross-holding.

China's broad shadow banking system and traditional commercial banks

Overall, the relationship between China's shadow banking system and commercial banks is both competitive and complementary. As an alternative credit channel for banks, the shadow banking system competes for high-quality customers. As complements, shadow banking deals with enterprises that banks can or will not service. This relationship and the unique role of shadow banks then ultimately increase the efficiency of the entire financial system.

The third prominent relationship between shadow banking and commercial banks in China is cooperation and reciprocity, mainly in reference to bank collaborations with non-bank financial institutions and use them to make off-balance sheet loans. Many industry insiders call this cooperation channel a "channel business" or "bridge model." Banks make out the majority of finance and investment, while other institutions work as toll bridges, for example, bank-trust cooperation, bank-securities cooperation, or cooperation between the three institutions. Commercial banks' active disintermediation implies that commercial banks are not satisfied with their on-balance sheet business. They have a desire for expansion beyond what regulations allow, so they engage in regulatory arbitrage. The disintermediation also implies that commercial banks are an important source of shadow banking system funding channels, which some scholars call "shadow of banking." Finally, it implies that part of the credit risk and liquidity risk of the entire financial system are concealed and could eventually reach bank balance sheets once a crisis breaks out, which would put the central bank in a difficult position.

Forces behind, influence, and development of broad shadow banking in China

Factors driving broad shadow banking's development in China

Shadow banking in China is inevitable regardless of inherent drawbacks or external development demand of the financial system

First, non-bank financial institutions provide supplements for commercial banks when continuous rapid growth demands multi-level financial services and innovative tools. In any case, China's market-oriented financial system is making immense progress. In order to ensure monetary and financial stability, regulatory policies should be based on real-time conditions to control credit aggregates, money supply, and the price of money within the system instead of a one-off liberalization. Thus, it is necessary for financial regulation to both encourage a variety of shadow banking businesses and strictly control the formal credit system to maintain financial stability. Constrained commercial banking systems will inevitably breed shadow banking systems. In this view, there is no "original sin." Shadow banking is thus an integral part of Chinese financial reform.

Second, with respect to financial development, Chinese commercial banks still enjoy high franchise value and low costs. At the same time, due to institutional constraints, the main business of non-bank financial institutions has developed relatively slowly. In other words, some could have done better. The industry has great profit margins as China's financial system has begun to disintermediate and step into the era of asset management. When the legal framework for separate operations is unclear, non-bank financial institutions have acquiesced to improve their ability to innovate and enter the asset management industry. There, asset homogenization occurs in the absence of main business heterogeneity. Without well-developed securities markets, most funds escaping from banks come, directly or indirectly, into the debt markets to gain their piece of economic growth.

Shadow banking to meet supply and demand

First, from the demand side, shadow banking thrives on current conditions. Commercial bank deposit rates are capped, and investors are seeking higher yielding investment products. Table 2.6 lists the current progress of China's deposit interest rate marketization, which has gradually liberalized the range of fluctuation. The upper deposit rate cannot exceed 1.1 times the benchmark deposit rate. However, since China's benchmark deposit rate is far below the market equilibrium interest rate, increasing the floating range cannot meet investors' needs (Table 2.7).

Banks have developed many high-yield WMPs without interest rate ceilings to meet customers' needs, which make commercial banks' financial products one option for shadow bank financing. This also applies to MMFs, another significant financing source for shadow banking.

Second, from the supply perspective, PBOC and CBRC regulations on loan size, loan-to-deposit ratio, and capital adequacy ratio have aided the development

Table 2.6 Deposit interest rate marketization progress

Time	Progress
October 2004	Lift control over the lower bound, upper bound is benchmark deposit rate
June 2012	Upper bound is 1.1 times benchmark deposit rate

Table 2.7 Benchmark deposit rates

Type	Maturity	Benchmark rate	Five main state banks	China Merchants Bank	China Everbright Bank	Bank of Nanjing	
						Under 10,000	More than 10,000
Demand deposit		0.35	1	1.1	1.1	1	1
Fixed deposit	3 mo.	2.60	1.1	1.1	1.1	1	1.1
	6 mo.	2.80	1.09	1.1	1.1	1	1.1
	12 mo.	3.00	1.08	1.1	1.1	1	1.1
	24 mo.	3.75	1	1	1	1	1.1
	36 mo.	4.25	1	1	1	1 (<200,000)	1.1 (≥200,000)
	60 mo.	4.75	1	1	1	1 (<300,000)	1.1 (≥300,000)

Source: Banks' official websites.

of shadow banking. China's commercial banks' loan pricing has been more diverse since 2003, and lending rates have fallen to a small degree. Only 11.4% of loans saw their interest rates float downward in the first quarter of 2013. If the regulations really worked, most loan interest rates would have floated downward (Table 2.8). In this sense, China's lending rate controls are not effective.

For current commercial banks' lending, the most influential regulations are quantity orientated, such as aggregate lending limits, loan-to-deposit tests, and capital adequacy requirements, so that banks transfer normal loans into unregulated types. For example, short-term financial products issued by commercial banks are invested in non-financial institutions' financial products, such as long-term capital trust schemes or brokered channels to support infrastructure, real estate construction, and consumer credit. This also creates a maturity mismatch due to different durations of financial products and transfers credit risk through implicit guarantees. This chain, a mainstay of the broad shadow banking system, is updated continuously to avoid regulatory changes. For example, financial products can purchase asset management businesses directly from brokerages, and then buy trust plans indirectly.

Positive effects of China's broad shadow banking

As a new operation that combines direct and indirect financing, the shadow banking system is neutral and plays multiple roles in real economic development, financial system improvement, and risk creation.

One of the most important positive aspects is that it opens up a wide range of new investment channels for residents and businesses. Most liabilities of shadow

Table 2.8 Loan interest rate marketization progress

Time	Measure
January 2004	Upper bound: 1.7 times benchmark loan rates Lower bound: 0.9 times benchmark loan rates
October 2004	Upper bound: no limitations Lower bound: 0.9 times benchmark loan rates
October 2008	Lower bound of personal housing mortgage loans interest rage: rise from 0.85 to 0.7 times benchmark loan rates
June 2012	Lower bound: 0.8 times benchmark loan rates
July 2012	Lower bound: 0.7 times benchmark loan rates
July 2013	Lower bound cancelled

banking institutions are financial products that have higher yield and risk than deposits and money. These wealth management tools adapt to the rise of financial management, enrich investment channels, and meet investor demands for both products and services. Trends in global finance prove that this is a lasting change. We will never return to the simple deposit management era.

Broad shadow banking also improves the efficiency of the financial system such that small- and medium-sized enterprises (SMEs) benefit. Although SMEs are not favored by commercial banks, they can fill their financing gaps through small loan companies, pawnshops, and private lending. However, due to regulation, small loan companies and pawnshops cannot take deposits to expand their business. High market demand and financing costs pushed some SMEs to turn to shadow banking for survival and development.

Competition between shadow banks and commercial banks is also pushing commercial banks to restructure in innovative ways. Although China's commercial banks dominate the financial system, they cannot escape the constraints of low deposit rates and the challenge of disintermediation. With the monopoly advantage of taking deposits, domestic commercial banks take initiative against disintermediation by innovating in products, channels, and mechanisms.

Shadow banks also reveal the inherent weaknesses and future direction of China's financial system. Some passive effects make shadow banking system lack sustainability (e.g., frantically pushing up the price of money). SMEs cannot afford such high prices, and shadow banking could very well prove to be a Ponzi scheme. The nature of Chinese shadow banking is still indirect financing because participants are mainly financial intermediaries rather than investors. Enterprise loans have not been fully explored by financial markets, and investors cannot always use direct financial tools. This situation indicates that the corporate bond market remains underdeveloped and must be a priority for the future.

Passive influence of China's broad shadow banking

The liability side of Chinese shadow banking system has grown out of commercial banks and other areas of the formal financial system. It obtains finance in innovative ways, but its asset side has not achieved equal marketization. The asset side still relies on crude methods of credit provision. The consequences of this long-term game are highly competitive credit markets and sprawl. Highly competitive prices bring cheap loans and increase social welfare. However, sprawl promotes asset price bubbles, snowballing debts, and high risk down the road.

As for the macroeconomy, the Chinese shadow banking system evades macro-control and indirectly invests in areas normally spurned by big banks. They may have high pollution, high energy consumption, and excess capacity. Bubbles then get bigger and zombie companies continue to limp on, further bloated with bad debt. This passive support causes systemic risk and structural problems for the economy.

As for risks, China's shadow banks and commercial banks have many of the same risk factors because they have similar business. However, lack of regulation makes the shadow banking system's risk more dangerous. In addition, there are legal and systemic risks. Specifically, current shadow banking largely depends on short-term credit, which inevitably causes a maturity mismatch. This also describes the entire indirect financing system. The financing channels and rapid operations of shadow banking may lead to Ponzi schemes and liquidity risk. Some contracts are signed through commercial banks and sold over bank counters. Investors cannot gain recourse from banks, which take on no legal responsibilities (legal risk). China's shadow banking is more secretive than western countries. Systemic risk arises because central banks cannot monitor them, and the lender of last resort cannot provide aid on time.

According to our previous definition, non-bank credit intermediaries are part of broad shadow banking. They are similar institutions and engage in business similar to banks. However, more specific criteria are necessary to decide whether they are part of narrow shadow banking. This book classifies these institutions and business according to the state of their regulation. The next three chapters discuss each aforementioned question separately.

Notes

1 Fang, Yingding, and Wang, Lijuan. "Shadow Banking," Pedigree. http://finance.people. com.cn/h/2011/0913/c227865-478718279.html
2 Wen, Weihu, and Chen, Rong. "Pay Attention to Shadow Banking Activities to Prevent Risks from Materialize," *Southwest Finance*, 2010(2).
3 Li, Jianjun, and Chen, Rong. "Top Design of Shadow Banking Regulatory System," *Macroeconomics*, 2011(8).
4 Yuan, Tingzhen. "On Nature and Regulation of Chinese and Foreign Shadow Banks," *Chinese Finance*, 2011(1).
5 Zhang, Xiaojun and Qian, Yao. "China's Shadow Banks: the Current Situation and Regulatory Responses," *Journal of Hubei Institute for Nationalities (Philosophy and Social Sciences)*, 2013(4).
6 China's Broad and Narrow Shadow Banking. http://bank.cngold.org/c/2013-05-20/ c1833295.html
7 Yang, Zaiping. "Understanding 'Shadow Banks'." http://news.xinhuanet.come/ fortune/2013-01/14/c_124227247.htm
8 Daula, Tom. "Systemic Risk: Relevance, Risk Management Challenges and Open Questions." PowerPoint Presentation.
9 Zhou, Liping. "Non-Bankization of Core Functions of Commercial Banks and Its Effects." *The Banker*, 2012(10).
10 "An Illustration of the Size and Composition of Social Financing." Statistics and Analysis Department of the People's Bank of China. www.pbc.gov.cn/pblish/diaochatong-jisi/3172/2011/20110520190935664550535/20110520190935664550535_.html
11 This issue is deeply studied in Chapter 6.

3 Financial institutions supervised by the "three commissions" and their businesses

China has implements a financial system with "separate operation and separate regulation" for businesses and institutions in different financial sectors. Non-bank financial institutions and businesses regulated by the China Securities Regulatory Commission (CSRC), China Banking Regulatory Commission (CBRC), and China Insurance Regulatory Commission (CIRC) include wealth management (hereafter may be referred to as WM) through the following entities: banks, trust companies, securities firms, fund management companies, insurance companies, and businesses of financial institutions (finance companies, financial leasing companies, auto finance companies, and consumer finance companies).

Bank wealth management businesses

Historical development

Wealth management refers to business activities in which banks, as financial advisors entrusted and authorized by clients, manage investment and asset management activities in accordance with the investment guidelines and venues agreed by clients. Such business is referred to as "asset management" or "wealth management" internationally and dates back to the eighteenth century. However, it did not grow to be a major bank business until the 1990s.

In China, some preliminary forms of bank WM business appeared in 2002. Foreign banks such as Standard Chartered Bank (SCB), ABN, and Citibank successively released structured WM products (WMPs). Since the rate of return of such products was higher than the deposit interest rate of the same maturity, and risks were controllable, they were able to attract numerous high-quality clients, putting pressure on Chinese banks. In order to compete, domestic banks started to release WMPs and strengthen their marketing efforts, following foreign banks. Such efforts stimulated the development of the Chinese banks' WM business.

As WMP of domestic banks began to take shape, the CBRC began to research and formulate relevant laws and regulations in early 2004. It then promulgated the *Interim Measures Concerning Managing Personal Financial Management Services of Commercial Banks* (No. [2005]2 of the CBRC, hereinafter referred to as the *Interim Measures*) and the *Guidelines for Risk Management of Commercial Banks' Wealth*

Management Business for Individuals (No. [2005]63 of the CBRC) in November 2005. The promulgation of both the regulations symbolized the beginning of real development of domestic banks' WM business.

Development incentives

Bank WM businesses developed from scratch and grew quickly, becoming one of the business sectors with the largest assets under management (AUM) in China's asset management.

First, it satisfies the growing demands of people for the preservation and appreciation of asset value. At present, the interest rate in China is not completely market-driven. After accounting for inflation, the real interest rate of bank deposits was relatively low and was below zero in some years. With people's rapid accumulation of wealth, demands for the preservation and appreciation of asset value grew. Meanwhile, WMPs of banks are more market-oriented on returns, which meets market demands as well. In 2011, 160 banking financial institutions in China made a profit of over RMB 175 billion for WMP investors. In 2012, 18 major banks that conducted WM businesses in China created investment returns of RMB 246.4 billion for their clients.[1]

Second, it satisfies diverse financing demands of the manufacturing economy in China. The Chinese economy recovered in 2010 and 2011, which was partially driven by the government's stimulus measures in 2008. However, due to the lack of new economic development incentives, economic growth has significantly slowed down in the recent years. Some manufacturing enterprises experienced difficulties in operation, and those qualified bank loans had insufficient demands for financing. At the same time, industries with great demands for capital were restricted by limits in bank credit. Bank's WMPs, in compliance with the national macroeconomic policies and regulatory rules, are more flexible than bank loans in terms of funding size, venues, use of funds, and funding cost, satisfying the diverse financing demands of the manufacturing economy and relieving enterprises' excessive dependence on indirect financing from banks. Statistics indicate that from January to March 2013, newly issued bank loans made up 54.1% of the total social financing, a decrease of 12.6% by year-on-year (yoy) basis.

Third, it satisfies the demands for innovative development in China's financial market. The multi-level financial market is still under-developed. Meanwhile, there is an enormous demand for social financing, but financing channels are far from diverse. Bank's WMPs connect investor capital with social financing demands, which improves the price discovery mechanism of financial markets, enhances financing efficiency, cultivates new direct financing methods, and thereby stimulates the innovative development of the financial market.

Fourth and finally, it satisfies banks' needs for strategic transformation. In response to the demands of capital management requirements such as *Basel III*, the interest rate liberalization and financial disintermediation, banks have taken initiatives to adjust their development strategies and make substantial efforts to develop WM businesses. In this way, capital is better utilized, profitability is improved and competitiveness is enhanced. Over the years, the continuous and sound development of the WM business promoted the operational transformation and strengthened bank competitiveness.

Market scale

By the end of June 2013, there were over 300 banking financial institutions with WM businesses. These had released a total of nearly 40,000 WMPs and had an AUM of RMB 9.08 trillion.[2] These products can be categorized into WMPs for individuals, institutional clients, and private bank clients. These can further be classified by type of return, such as return guaranteed, principal guaranteed, and those with no guarantee. We can also separate them by operational pattern: principal guaranteed, with projected interest, and those based on net asset value (NAV). We can also categorize them according to investment targets into products that invest mainly in bonds, money market instruments, debt products, deposits, funds and stocks, derivatives, qualified domestic institutional investor (QDII), and alternative investments.

Risk characteristics

First, products with maturity mismatch also imply liquidity risk. It is problematic that many banks invest short-term WM funds in long-term assets. Among all WMPs, those with maturities within 6 months make up 65% and those within 1 year make up 90%, but investments in long-term assets make up over one-third of all WMPs. Additionally, approximately RMB 3.33 trillion worth of WMPs invest in non-standard assets. The maturity mismatch between the capital source and invested assets is thus quite large. In order to make payments to clients on time, some banks seek to ensure liquidity by creating new WMPs, selling of other products or deploying their own capital. They have limited solutions to the maturity mismatch issue, which paves the way for a series of hidden problems such as insufficient liquidity or banks being forced to make advance payments to clients with their own capital.

Second, mismatches of cost and proceeds result in collateral repayment risk. Currently, WMPs issued by banks generally have high expected returns. The average expected return of WMPs from major banks is about 4%–5%, far higher than the average deposit interest rate. But investment strategies are restricted for such high-cost capital, and high yields are thus difficult to obtain. Besides, from the macro perspective, as economic growth in China has slowed down and corporate profits have slumped, WM faces great risks by investing in non-standard debt assets. However, in practice, returns on investment paid by banks to investors need to be almost equivalent to expected earnings. Moreover, in the context of financial disintermediation and escalating competition in WM, the expected interest rate set by banks is actually rising. Under the expectation of "rigid payoff" (implicit guarantee from banks), if banks fail to pay the expected earnings, clients may complain, appeal to higher authorities, or even disturb normal business on purpose.

Therefore, some banks have to pay the return on the WMP, resulting in collateral repayment risks.

Third, regulatory circumvention results in compliance risks. Some banks' intention to circumvent regulation is obvious from the way they design and operate their WMPs, which leads to an increase in compliance risks. For example, some banks issued WMPs that intentionally circumvent national macro industrial policies, while some products are substitutes for on-balance sheet loans, thus bypassing regulations on capital usage and loan-to-deposit ratios. Some banks use WMPs to purchase on-balance sheet low-quality or even non-performing assets, which conceals the actual asset status and risk. Meanwhile, many WMPs are involved in inter-industry cross-funding, making up as much as 37.5% of the total amount. This also conceals risks and makes them both more complicated and contagious.

Fourth, incompetent management results in reputational risk. Public opinion suggests that the WM business has always been the focus of reputational risk in the banking industry. Among all banking products, WMPs received the most complaints from clients. Some banks frequently have serious management deficiencies in both the business process and the sales management. Moreover, problems such as failure to discover potential risks due to inadequate due diligence, insufficient information disclosure, illegitimate prioritization in payment of earnings, and misrepresentation in product selling appear often. Some bank branches even sell third party WMP without proper authorization, a practice that sometimes leads to social unrest. All of the above aggravate reputational risks.

Operational principles

The operational principles of bank WM are quite different from those of the traditional banking business. The following WMPs are taken as examples.

T + 0 open-ended WMPs

This kind of product has no fixed term or definite maturity date. It meets investor demand for cash management, enhances utilization efficiency, and improves the productivity of previously idle money. Such products can be subscribed and redeemed on a daily basis, and the money can be credited to client's account immediately. The detailed operational principle is as follows: clients subscribe the product, and then the product invests in bonds, money market instruments, money market funds, and other assets in line with the regulation to gain interest. If the principal and interest of the investment can be paid on time, then banks pay the expected returns when the clients redeem the product. Such an operational pattern is different from that of traditional bank deposits, where all deposits are included in a pooled fund, and banks themselves manage the collected money. Banks assume the credit risks, and there is no correspondent relationship between the assets in the pooled fund and liabilities from deposits. Banks can lend or invest in bonds and other assets after surrendering deposit reserves to the central bank and are 100% responsible for the risks and earnings. With T + 0 open-ended WMP, however, clients entrust funds as a portfolio, and clients should assume the risk of loss. Banks manage each investment in accordance with the investment guidelines and scope agreed in the product manual and set up separate management, accounting and bookkeeping for each product.

T + N open-ended WMP based on NAV

This kind of product is open for subscription regularly on prescheduled dates and is subscribed and redeemed at a price in accordance with the NAV released on the day of subscription or redemption. The detailed operational principle is as follows: banks release the NAV of a WMP, and clients subscribe and redeem such product based on NAV. Generally, these products reserve some cash for liquidity and the investor redemption, and the remaining funds are invested in various assets. The operational pattern of such WMP is different from those of traditional bank deposits. Such products are open regularly and are subscribed and redeemed according to NAV. Once again, the banks set up separate management, accounting, and bookkeeping for each product.

WMP with fixed terms

This kind of product has fixed terms, definite interest-incurring date, and maturity date as well as provides an expected interest rate. When a product matures, if the assets invested are able to pay the principal and earnings as agreed, the banks pay the return on investment to clients as agreed in the product manual. Like the other types of WMP, administration for each product is separate, and clients entrust funds as a portfolio.

Shadow banking determination

After comparing relevant regulatory requirements on bank's WM business with the principle of identification for shadow banking, we may conclude that from the policy perspective, Chinese banks' WM business is not shadow banking.

Strict and independent regulatory framework

Since 2005, the CBRC has been promulgating the *Interim Measures, Administrative Measures on Sales of Wealth Management Products by Commercial Banks* (Order No. [2011]5 of China Banking Regulatory Commission) and over 20 other regulatory rules and systems. They cover business management, risk management, financing services for clients, investment management, cooperation between banks and trust companies, transfer of credit assets, and sales management to provide systematic guidelines for the sound development of bank's WM business. Meanwhile, a product-reporting mechanism is adopted: all WMPs must be reported to the regulatory authority before issuance, and the regulatory authority will both continuously monitor their business and conduct on-site inspections when necessary. With changes in regulatory policies and market development, banks have also updated and adjusted internal policies, systems, and processes to meet compliance requirements and risk controls.

Definite and clear legal relationships

WM is built on a motto of "acting as a trustee while managing wealth on behalf of customer." Banks accept a client's entrustment and invest in accordance with the client's guidelines in order to preserve and appreciate the client's wealth. Clients assume risks arising from the investment and reap its return. Banks charge relevant fees as agreed by clients and assume no investment risks. In accordance with *Notice of the China Banking Regulatory Commission on Relevant Issues Concerning Regulating the Investment Operation of Wealth Management Business of Commercial Banks* (No. [2013]8 of the China Banking Regulatory Commission, hereinafter referred to as "Document No.8"), banks shall have one-to-one correspondence between WMP and invested assets and maintain a separate management, accounting, and booking for each product. The balance sheet, income statement, and cash flow statement shall be set up for each product, presumably applying the principle of "buyer's responsibility" on the premise of fully realizing the principal of "seller's accountability." Credit conversion may exist in bank's WM, depending on the product's characteristics.

In WMP with principal guaranteed, banks guarantee the principal or earnings of a product. In this case, credit conversion exists. However, the raised capital and the invested assets are incorporated in the on-balance sheet accounting management with corresponding reserves and risk-weighted assets calculated. In this manner, risks of such products are well controlled.

For WMP with principal not guaranteed, banks guarantee neither the principal nor the returns. Clients assume credit risks arising from the investment, and banks should perform their fiduciary responsibility with adequate due diligence. Banks should strictly abide by regulatory requirements. They should ensure that all financial statements are in place and establish clear ownership for each product. Meanwhile, banks should reinforce information disclosure, particularly with regard to non-standardized debt assets, to adequately inform investors of risks and ensure that buyers (clients) are responsible and the sellers (banks) are accountable.

Second, banks should match the risk preference between WMP and invested assets through risk management and limits on risk exposure. They should also ensure to sell appropriate WMP to suitable clients during the process of product design and implementation. In the end, risks of standardized assets and non-standardized assets should be controlled through different approaches. For standard assets, the risks can be managed and transferred to investors through market pricing in an openly traded market. However, non-standardized credit assets require strict entry requirements, credit risk approval, risk exposure limit, investment approval, and post-investment managerial measures, management measures that are in reference to those of banks' on-balance sheet loans. They must strictly control and calculate the credit risks arising from such assets. Meanwhile, for both classes of assets, banks should establish comprehensive evaluation methods and appraisal systems. To conclude, after adequate due diligence, banks may apply the principle of "buyer's responsibility," and there is no credit conversion.

Maturity mismatch does exist in some products, but overall liquidity risks are under control

Although some banks have maturity mismatch in their WM business, the liquidity risks are generally under control. Our preliminary investigation suggests that most banks and their branches have one-to-one correspondence between their WMPs and assets, but maturity mismatch does exist in some products. Banks have strict management for the liquidity risks of such products. First, banks set liquidity risk management or quota targets for investment portfolio. For example, they have set standards regarding the percentage of high-liquidity assets, the percentage of maturity mismatch, leverage ratio, and ratio of product with different terms to control liquidity risks.

Second, banks conduct liquidity stress tests and contingency exercises regularly and formulate specific contingency plans to deal with liquidity risks in relevant products. Then, according to regulatory requirements, liquidity risks of WMP are incorporated into the bank's unified risk control system for comprehensive control. Last, regulatory authorities have quotas regarding the amount of products that can be invested in non-standardized debt assets and have disallowed pooled funds for non-standardized products, which limits the scale of non-standardized assets with low liquidity and generally reduces liquidity risks. To conclude, banks have set up a multi-layer liquidity risk management system in the WM business to ensure that overall liquidity risks are under control.

Bank WMP shall not invest in high-risk financial products

It is important to note that no highly levered operations are involved. The CBRC limits the investment range of capital from WMP in various regulations. For example, it is explicitly specified in *Circular on Revising the Scope of Overseas Investment for Overseas WM Services on Behalf of Customers of Commercial Banks* (No. [2007]114 of the CBRC) that "(banks) may use swaps, forwards, and other derivative financial tools circulating in the financial market only for risk hedging purposes, and are prohibited from using them for speculation or leverage purposes"; and it is also explicitly specified in *Circular on Further Standardizing Issues Related to Individual WM Business and Investment Management of Commercial Banks* (No. [2009]65 of the CBRC) that "(bank WMP) shall not invest in high-risk financial products that may lead to material losses of principal or financial products that are too complicatedly structured."

The correspondence between WMP and the invested assets is explicitly specified in the Document No.8 (of the CBRC), which stipulates that banks shall have separate management and accounts for each product. As a result, the source and use of invested capital do not involve leverage. In practice, the underlying assets of WMP are mainly fixed-income assets such as bonds, deposits, and money market instruments, making up over 80%. In other words, there are no leveraged investments through other source of financing.

Adequate information disclosure

The CBRC has specific and strict requirements regarding the information disclosure of WMPs. Relevant regulations are demonstrated as follows: (a) *Administrative Measures on Sales of WMP by Commercial Banks* has various provisions on the information disclosure in sales documents of WMP and requires that banks shall sell appropriate products to suitable clients; (b) *Circular on Further Reinforcing Issues Related to Risk Management of WM Business of Commercial Banks* (No. [2011]91 of the CBRC) stipulates that banks shall fully disclose product-related information, state-specific types and proportions of various underlying assets, and keep improving transparency by continuous disclosure before, during, and after investment; (c) Document No.8 expressly specifies that banks shall fully disclose investment in non-standardized debt assets to investors, including the name and project of the financing party, remaining term, the distribution of yields to maturity, and transaction structures; and (d) any changes in the risk condition of invested non-standardized debt assets shall be disclosed to investors within 5 days.

At present, banks with competent management capacity and complete IT systems have already launched online information disclosure systems. Investors of WMP can obtain online information regarding product establishment, operation, and payment upon maturity. Such information may also include the information on capital users, name of the invested project, terms, and the rate of return for each product. In this way, clients are able to have adequate knowledge of the risk and return of their investment and realize the right-to-know regarding their investment in WMP.

Together with the Central Settlement Company, the CBRC has set up operation of the "National WMP Information Registration System for the Banking Industry." It completes the whole process: registration, electronic report, online review, and statistical analysis for all WMP. Any information related to each product will be incorporated in the system for management and monitoring. The real-time, dynamic monitoring of WMP will significantly enhance information transparency.

The earlier analysis suggests that banks have strict, independent regulatory frameworks and systems for the WM business, along with no high-leverage operations in their management. Parties involved assume clear responsibilities of credit risks. Liquidity risks arising from maturity mismatch are well contained, and the information is fully disclosed. All of these indicate that systematic risks are unlikely to be induced by these WMP.

Further issues of concern

From the regulatory perspective, bank's WM business does not constitute shadow banking. However, some of the businesses in practice do have features of regulation circumvention and regulatory arbitrage. Certain products fail to have one-to-one correspondence between capital source and investment assets and thus qualify as shadow banking products. Meanwhile, since the infrastructure construction for bank WM is not yet complete and the Chinese capital management market is still in a preliminary development stage, there is room for banks to circumvent regulation. As a result, there are some criticisms of bank's WM. Some of these critics argue that such business should be characterized as shadow banking.

Risks due to nonconforming operations

Banks whose WMP and underlying assets fail to establish one-to-one correspondence shall bear credit risks. At present, a few banks failed to realize such correspondence as prescribed by Document No.8, and for these banks, no separate accounting and management is available for each product. The non-correspondence between WMP and underlying assets will result in unclear ownership as well as an ambiguous relationship between credit risks arising from underlying assets. Accordingly, neither "buyer's responsibility" nor "seller's accountability" can be achieved. If credit risks arose in the investments, investors could be identified due to such non-correspondence. According to the Document No.8, however, banks need to incorporate the assets on their balance sheets for accounting, calculation of risk-weighted assets, and maintain capital, so that the banks should bear the credit risks in such cases.

Incomplete infrastructure

1   The management systems for WM need to be further improved. First, with the expansion of bank WM business, it is necessary to incorporate sales management, investment operation, information disclosure, evaluation, liquidation, and other aspects of each product into the bank's management system not only for enhancing business management efficiency but also for managing business risks and improving the overall management quality. Second, according to Document No.8, for each product, banks should have separate management, keep separate accounts, and prepare separate balance sheets, income statements, and cash flow statements, which require support from competent IT systems. However, some banks with limited IT system construction and weak business management system are unable to provide effective support for investment portfolio management, asset configuration, real-time evaluation, dynamic risk monitoring, and accounting. Additionally, compared to the statistical information system of traditional on-balance sheet deposit and loan businesses, WM, as a hybrid industry and cross-market financial product, is not completely accounted for by regulatory authorities. It is necessary to set up statistical channels and systems that are in line with the nature of WM business.

2   The management framework must be further improved. To safeguard investor's interests and prevent problems of potential bribery and conflict of interests, banks should adopt a system that separates its own financial business from that for clients and separate front, middle, and back offices. However, some

banks failed to meet this requirement. For example, a few banks have no independent management departments or teams for WM businesses, and such business is managed by a variety of departments in the banks. Some banks fail to separate their front, middle, and back offices and have not set up sound managerial systems for checks and balances. Others fail to segregate on-balance sheet financing and that for clients, and the independence of investment decision-making is challenged by third parties and clients. Banks with such circumstances are not only unable to make concerted efforts to stimulate the sound development of WM businesses but also unable to completely separate interests of investors from that of the banks. It therefore leaves the bank open to potential cases of bribery.

3   The incentive that stimulates the continuous, sound development of WM business needs to be optimized. The sound, compliant development of WM business depends on self-discipline of banks. Therefore, there should be a reasonable risk-control culture and an effective incentive mechanism within each bank. For the time being, some banks still have serious loopholes in their WM business and sales management. They have no complete managerial systems regarding the qualification, training, and evaluation for relevant employees. They also focus too much on sales performance or profits while neglecting compliance and risk-reporting procedures. Such a problematic practice likely results in inadequate due diligence, incomplete information disclosure, and misleading sales to clients. It may thus bring reputational risks.

The competition mechanism must be further standardized

In China's asset management market, banks, as asset management institutions, have complete regulatory frameworks and strong risk management, yet are in a disadvantageous competitive position. First, online financial companies and the third-party WM institutions, with little or inadequate regulations, have rapidly expanded, which has had a significant impact on the WM market and incurred potential risks. Second, WM schemes from securities firms, asset management companies, insurance companies, trust companies, and other institutions have more advantageous positions than the WMPs of banks. Those asset management schemes are able to open transaction accounts in the open market for investment, while banks are limited in this respect and can only make external investments through asset management schemes of other institutions. This adversely affects investment efficiency and increases financial and operational risks.

In addition, the transformation from non-standardized debt assets to "standardized" assets needs to be normalized. After the quota control was established for investment in non-standard debt assets with WMP, a few banks have been trying to "standardize" the non-standard debt assets by transferring the product quota of other asset management institutions in the open market and breaking the quota control. Unlike asset-backed securitization (ABS), which goes through the processes of public rating, market bidding, bankruptcy remoteness, and other systemic arrangements and technical means, such "standardization" simply transfers the quota among investors through agreements. The quotas transferred are not the standardized assets in essence and lack an active trading market.

Clarification of bank's legal position as the fiduciary of WM

Bank's WM business has an independent legal and regulatory framework that covers a variety of activities such as operations management, risk management, overseas WM for clients, investment management, cooperation between banks and trust companies, loan assets transfer, and sales management. According to the prevailing legal systems, WM ensures that the buyers assume the responsibility and that the seller is accountable. However, in terms of the legal relationships of bank's WM, there are still abundant disputes and difference of understanding, for example, as the fiduciary of a WM scheme, whether a bank can be the holder of a mortgage or other collateral. It is also unclear with regard to a bank's liquidation order as the fiduciary when an invested enterprise goes bankrupt. The legal status of the bank as a fiduciary when opening transaction accounts in the open market is also far from clear.

Development trends

WM will be a major business of banks

The rapid growth of wealth has laid a solid foundation for the development of the bank's WM business. According to statistics from Boston Consulting Group, the total investable assets of individuals in China exceeded RMB 73 trillion in 2012, the number of families with high net worth reached 1.74 million, and the compound growth rate over the past 3 years topped 38%. The rapid growth of wealth thus laid a foundation for the development of the WM business.

Compared with Western developed countries, the WM market in China is still at a preliminary stage of development. For example, in the United Kingdom, by the end of 2011, the scale of the WM industry exceeded 5 trillion pounds, with over 0.55 trillion pounds managed by BlackRock, the largest investment management company. Moreover, WM has already been a major business for foreign banks, contributing significant incomes and revenues. For example, JP Morgan divides its business into four sections including corporate and investment banking, asset management, commercial banking, and private banking.

As banks transform from the asset holders to the asset manager, WM will be a major business parallel to their traditional business lines. Over the recent years, as the People's Bank of China has loosened its regulation of loan interest rates, the interest rate liberalization reform will have an increasing influence on the structure of assets, liabilities, and operating models of banks. Engaging in this transformation is inevitable for banks. It is widely accepted by the market that the WM business uses little capital and is effective in helping bank's transformation. All major banks are reevaluating the positioning and development of the WM business, making great efforts to promote this capital-saving business to be bank's major business in the near future.

Direct investment will be the development trend of bank's WM business

For a long time, bank's WM business has not enjoyed the legal status of being an investor, and the investment made was usually completed through the asset management schemes of other financial institutions. In other words, they invested in the target assets indirectly through "channels." This model increases financing costs, prolongs the operation process, and aggravates operational risks. Meanwhile, if losses occur in the invested assets, they will be transferred and expanded in different financial industries and markets, thus increasing the possibility of cross-industry risks. Therefore, it is necessary to complete the regulatory framework to gradually clarify the primary operator of banks' WM business and to make a strict distinction between business for clients and that for the bank's own assets. This will prevent financial risks from spreading across markets.

Standardized assets will be the major underlying assets of WMP

It is one of the goals of bank's WM to increase the percentage of "standard, public, transparent, and rated" investment tools. According to a preliminary survey, investment in non-standardized debt assets reached as much as 30.62% of the total.[3] One of the major reasons is that the securities market in China is far from being developed and that the direct financing market needs to be further improved. For example, in the United Kingdom, the underlying assets of asset management by British banks can be divided as follows: stocks 42%, bonds 38%, cash 8%, and property 3%, which is to say, the standardized assets in the open investment market make up over 90%. In accordance with the relevant instructions of the central government to vitalize credit and to support manufacturing economies, ABS in China will be the next major focus of development. This indicates that WMP will be able to invest in more "standardized, open, transparent, and rated" investment instruments.

Competitive advantages of banks will safeguard the continuous, sound development of WM business

Compared with other types of institutions, banks have the following advantages in the WM business: product distribution, risk management, and advanced management techniques.

First, banks have extensive sales channels and numerous distribution networks for their products. For investors who want to purchase WMP, those issued by banks are the most convenient. Second, they have a strict risk management system. Risk management is the core competence of the banking industry. Through many years of development, banks have formulated and implemented comprehensive risk precaution and mitigation measures to "improve the system, standardize management, mitigate risks, and safeguard operation" and still keep improving. Risk management has become an important part of banks' corporate culture. Third, banks have developed advanced management techniques. The new *Basel Accord* put forward higher requirements for the risk management of banks and also provided banks a unified standard and method for risk control and management. Banks also have accumulated abundant managerial experiences and techniques, bringing more standardized systems in the WM business. More advanced risk management techniques and stricter post-investment management will safeguard the continuous and sound development of WM business.

International comparison

In developed countries and regions like Europe, the United States, and Japan, WMPs are regarded as a financial product provided by banks for the purpose of asset management. Types of WMP provided by banks in developed countries include unit trust/common funds, structured investment products, exchange-traded funds (ETF), pension funds, hedge funds, and private equity (PE) funds. In China, in accordance with *Interim Measures*, WM schemes (WMP) are capital investment and management plans developed for, designed for, and sold to specifically targeted investors by banks based on the analysis and research on specifically targeted investors. WMPs are still at a preliminary stage of development in China. While the levels of developments vary significantly among China's banks, Chinese WMPs are quite different from their Western counterparts with respect to product types, product forms, investment directions, fee structures, investor profiles, and source of funds. The main attributes of foreign banks in this market that differentiate them from their Chinese counterparts are clear legal status of being the fiduciary of WMP, can open transaction accounts in various open markets for WMP, and get involved in the trading and investment in the open market, and WM has already become a major business of foreign banks as a major contributor of incomes and revenues. Such situation is shown in Table 3.1.

Table 3.1 WMP at Chinese and major western banks

	Western banks	*Banks in China*
Type of product	Mainly unit trust, structured investment products, ETF, pension funds	Mainly bank's WMP
Form of product	Mainly products with a range of rates of return, NAV, and closed-form products	Mainly fixed-term products and open-ended products (without fixed term)
Investment direction	Mainly stocks, bonds, and funds traded in open market	Mainly bonds, money funds, and assets of project financing
Fee structure	Charged according to a fixed percentage or commission depending on performance	No fixed forms and in a way similar to a fixed percentage and commission on performance

(continued)

Table 3.1 WMP at Chinese and major western banks *(continued)*

	Western banks	*Banks in China*
Investor profiles	Mainly institutional investors	Mainly individual investors
Source of funds	From both international and domestic investors, each making up around 50%	Mainly from the domestic investors
Contributions to the incomes of intermediary businesses	Making up around 38% on average and 68% at the most	Making up around 10% on average

Source: Synthesis of financial statements from 2002 to 2012 of 20 banks including Deutsche Bank, JP Morgan, and State Street.

Trust wealth management business

Historical development

As an ancient asset management mechanism, trusts date back to the Roman law, but the modern trust system originated in the United Kingdom. For China, however, it was exotic. In October 1979, the first professional trust investment company in China, China International Trust & Investment Corporation, was established. In 1980, the State Council required that "banks should try out trust business as pilot programs," and the People's Bank of China promulgated the *Circular on Vigorously Developing Trust Business* in September of the same year. Later, trust companies started to develop and explore asset management businesses that were adapted to China's local conditions. The development process of the Chinese trust WM business since Reform and Opening Up is shown in Table 3.2.

Having gone through the five stages, Chinese trust industry got rid of the mixed operation system highly similar to the banking industry and confirmed the new separate operation system with trust as the main business. This eventually developed into one of the four major financial industries. Since the third quarter of 2012, the CSRC and CIRC have enacted new policies concerning asset management, loosening the restraints on asset management of other financial institutions, and the "pan-asset management era" arrived. Trust companies are facing new challenges. They will have to make efforts to improve their active management ability and initiate business transformation and innovation for further development.

Development incentives

There are a number of major reasons for the rapid development of Chinese trust WM business:

1 Institutional advantages: Trust provides a favorable external WM system for society. It strictly separates rights, obligations, responsibilities and risks of clients, trustees, and beneficiaries. It also safeguards trust assets and guarantees the

continuous, stable operation of trust assets for specific purposes. Such a unique asset isolation mechanism appeals to many investors, laying a foundation for its continuing development.

2 Trusts satisfy strong demands for investment and WM: For over 30 years since Reform and Opening Up, the Chinese economy has grown steadily and continuously. As people's wealth rapidly accumulates, they have growing demands for investment and management of their assets. Trust, as a unique WM method, meets people's demands for investment by virtue of its unique institutional advantages.

Table 3.2 Development process of trust WM business since reform and opening up

Development stages	Start and end	Important events	Major business models
Pilot	1979–1999	Five major upheavals, then explored its way forward	Debt business: to absorb deposits with high interest rates (in disguised form) and vigorously develop debt business like deposits and loans Securities business: including stock brokerage, self-operated securities investment, and Initial public offering (IPO)
Stagnation	1999–2002	Promulgated *Trust Law* and *Measures on the Management of Trust Investment Companies*	Redefined the trust investment scope according to the principle of "trust as foundation, separate regulation, scale management and strict regulation" Separated trust industry from the banking industry and securities industry Up to 2002, only about 50 trust companies survived
Development with guidelines	2002–2006	In 2002, China implemented *Interim Measures Concerning Capital Trust Management of Trust Investment Companies* together with the *Trust Law* and the *Measures on the Management of Trust Investment Companies* is called "one law, two regulations"	Collective trust schemes were the most important and mature business in Chinese trust industry at that time Investment mainly focused on traditional industries like infrastructure, real estate, industrial commercial enterprises, and bank loan assets

(continued)

Table 3.2 Development process of trust WM business since reform and opening up *(continued)*

Development stages	Start and end	Important events	Major business models
Rapid expansion	2006–2010	In 2007, *Measures for the Management of Trust Companies* and *Measures for the Management of the Collective Trust Schemes of Trust Companies* ("the two new regulations") were revised	Private equity trust Bank-trust cooperation Government-trust cooperation Sunshine private placement fund trust REITs QDII Public interest trust
Innovative breakthrough	2010 till now	In 2010, the CBRC promulgated the *Management Measures on Net Capital of Trust Companies* and the supporting *Circular on Matters Concerning Net Capital Calculation Standards of Trust Companies*	Bank-trust WM Specialized private equity investment REITs Industrialization/infrastructure trust Private banking WM Multi-asset-type trust

Notes: REIT, real estate investment trust; WM, wealth management.

3 Lower risks and higher returns: Compared with individual WM efforts, trust companies conduct professional portfolio management for individuals. This avoids the myopia of individual investment. Meanwhile, compared with other financial institutions, trusts have a wide scope and flexible ways to invest. All of these reduce investment risks and increase expected investment returns.

4 Legal and institutional safeguards: "One law, two regulations" defines the basis of trust WM, providing a reliable and clear legal framework under which trust WM can operate, which further enhances investors' confidence in trust WM. Regulatory authorities are well-positioned to strictly regulate the trust industry. They further define the trust company as an institution that "manages the assets with trust," which provides a regulatory safeguard for the trust industry's sustainable development.

Market scale

After the re-registration of trust companies in accordance with the *Measures for the Management of Trust Companies* since 2002, especially over the past few years, the business of trust companies has grown rapidly. From 2007 to 2012, the trust industry's AUM increased sharply. In 2007, the AUM of the trust industry was under RMB 1 trillion. Then it topped RMB 1 trillion, RMB 2 trillion, RMB 3 trillion, and RMB 4 trillion successively in 2008, 2009, 2010, and 2011. In 2012, it reached a further RMB 7.47 trillion (see Figure 3.1).

By the end of the third quarter of 2013, the AUM of 67 trust companies was RMB 10.13 trillion, a new peak once again. In terms of the source of assets, single-investor trusts rose as a proportion, reaching 71.28%, while collective trusts make up 23.28% and property trusts 5.44%. From the trust function perspective, financing trusts make up 48.15%, investment trusts 32.67%, and service-related trusts 19.18%, similar to that in the second quarter. In terms of investment direction, the top five industries invested were industrial and commercial enterprises at 29.49%, infra-structure industry 25.97%, financial institutions 11.38%, securities markets 10.78%, and real estate 9.33%.

Risk characteristics

Risks from investment targets

Trust investment may fail in the evaluation of its investment target. Major deviation in the evaluation of the asset–liability ratios, costs, profits and losses, or other major operation factors may result in the ultimate failure of the project. Since trusts are in a non-debt legal relationship, trust companies gain profits from the returns on investment. Their profit-making mechanism is therefore different from traditional banks that reap profits from the net interest margin (NIM) between deposits and loans. Once an improper investment decision is made, banks will be responsible for the promised returns with their own capital, but trust companies only have to conduct investment pursuant to the trust contract and carry out investments with reasonable care and prudence. Therefore, they have no responsibility to compensate for the failure of the invested projects.

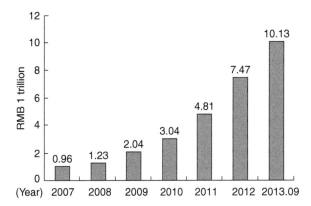

Figure 3.1 Trust industry AUM.

Liquidity risks

The liquidity risks of trust WM mainly reflect in the payoff of trust plans upon maturity. When trust companies invest trust funds in low-liquidity assets, the value of underlying assets may not be realized upon maturity. Such assets may depreciate and suffer losses if liquidated. Then, the only solution is that the trust companies make advance payments with their own capital or negotiate with clients to prolong the term of the trust. Otherwise, liquidity risks are likely to arise. Besides, in the case of non-capital trust, liquidity risks may arise as well. If the trust documents state that the client can be paid with the underlying asset upon maturity, then trust companies will have no liquidity risks. However, practically, many clients require cash payments upon maturity, likely resulting in liquidity risks.

Management risks

Poor decision-making by the trustee or unreasonable managerial structure may lead to the failure of the invested project. The return of investment may therefore not live up to expectations. The success of a trust scheme is closely related to its manager's ability. Managers need to be aware of the current market conditions and relevant policies, but they also need to make forward-looking, sound decisions. Moreover, management risks also include incomplete internal management structures and incompetent operations management. These problems undermine the proper operation of investment projects and thus cause the actual returns to deviate from expectations.

Moral hazard

Such risks may arise in the case that the trustee fails to honor the trust agreement and conducts inappropriate management of trust assets. Trust companies may, for their own interest, violate the trust contract and unilaterally use or embezzle trust assets at the expense of clients. Such behaviors violate the basis of trust and could seriously undermine the normal development of the trust industry.

Client risks

According to the definition of trusts, trustees manage the investment pursuant to the client's guidelines. But the client may not be investment savvy, may give poor investment guidelines, and thus may agree to a subpar trust plan. It is expressly specified in the trust document that trustees (i.e., trust companies) assume no responsibility for losses arising from investment in accordance with the contract and client's guidelines. While such losses shall be assumed by the client, it nevertheless is a violation of the clients' primary purpose to preserve and appreciate their wealth. It damages the reputation of trust companies and harms both the parties.

Incomplete legal frameworks

As provided in Article 2 of the *Trust Law* of China, clients "entrust," not "transfer," the property right to trustees. However, no conclusions have been made regarding whether or not the ownership of trust assets is transferred. Besides, the trust registration system is not yet established, so there is no solid protection of the trustees' right to trust assets. These deficiencies as such may not cause serious problems in trusts with fund assets but may have a negative influence on trusts based on real assets. For example, in real estate trusts, trustees cannot take action against infringement by a third person as an owner of the assets. It can only do so as a possessor. If a client violates the trust contract and transfers the trust assets to a third person after the registration proceedings are completed, the trustee cannot guard against the third person as the owner; he/she can only sue the client for a breach of contract. Besides, with regard to all activities conducted in the name of the owner, for example, opening a bank account, purchasing stocks, paying taxes, and so on, trustees may be faced with difficulties as a practical matter and face ownership risks.

Operational principles

The trust relationship is a special legal relationship among the client, trustee, and beneficiaries. It is centered on the transfer of trust assets, management of trust assets, and distribution of trust returns (see Figure 3.2).

The investment style of trust may be debt or equity investment, or mezzanine investment between the two.

The first type is debt investment. In this investment model, the trust company issues trust loans to a specific company after raising capital from the purchasers of trust products (clients). Besides, if the trust capital is invested in the equity of the company (or some other types of rights), and other major stockholders of the company (or a third party) promise to repurchase such rights with fixed prices, this investment model is essentially a debt investment.

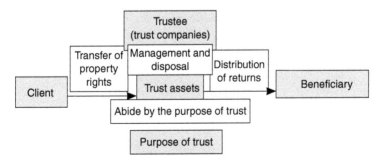

Figure 3.2 Map of business relationship of trust financing. Note: It is the "self-benefit trust" if the client and the beneficiary are the same person; if not, then it is the "trust for a third person's benefit."

The second type is equity investment. In this investment model, the trust company invests capital raised by trust plans in the equity of a company. It becomes shareholder of the company and exercises pursuant rights. Compared with debt investment, the equity investment allows the trust company to nominate directors to the board of the target company and thus influence the operation of the latter and supervise its daily operations. Also, there is no cap on the returns from equity investment. If the invested company is in good operation and finally goes public, the returns will far exceed those of debt investment.

The third type is mezzanine investment. The mezzanine investment is a mixture of the debt and the equity models. Take convertible bonds as an example. Although trust capital invests in the company by means of debt, the debt can be converted to stocks under certain preset circumstances. Preferred stock is another example. Although trust capital invests in the company by means of a type of equity, a series of preferred dividends and principal guarantee mechanisms are specified. The most significant advantage of the mezzanine model lies in its flexibility. As a practical matter, the capital demands, the pre-existing condition of equity arrangement, and the risk conditions determine that neither debt nor equity investment will provide the solution to the investment target. To meet the risk preference of both the capital users (investment target) and the capital providers (trust fund), a mezzanine model may be adopted. Alternatively, a hybrid of debt and equity may be used.

Trust businesses of trust companies include money trusts (whose assets are funds), movable property trusts, real estate trusts, negotiable securities trusts, other property trusts, or property rights trusts. Of these, money trusts dominate. Depending on the number of clients, money trusts can be divided into single-investor trusts and collective trusts.

With respect to the investment target, trusts can be divided into infrastructure trusts, real estate trusts, securities investment trusts, bank-trust cooperation trusts, and PE investment trusts.

Shadow banking determination

Trust WM is a typical credit intermediary business. In terms of its current operation, however, it does not satisfy the four characteristics of shadow banking or will not cause systematic risks and regulatory arbitrage. Therefore, it is not shadow banking in a true sense. The detailed reasons are as follows:

No leverage

Trust companies are not allowed to operate with debt or to seek bank financing. They manage wealth on behalf of clients, and the returns that investors receive are generated from the trust assets. Besides, the overall size of trust industry is limited, and the financial market in China is still under development. Trust companies operate with relatively simple product structures. All these suggest that trust WM will not cause systematic risks to Chinese financial market.

Liquidity risks controlled through net capital regulation

According to the *Trust Law* and *Measures for the Management of Trust Companies*, most of trust WM have fixed terms. Upon maturity of a trust product, the trustee bears the obligation to pay returns to the beneficiary only to the extent allowed by the trust asset (see Article 34 of the *Trust Law*). To ensure that trust companies have sufficient capital and keep liquidity available, the CBRC specifically formulated *Measures for the Management of the Net Capital of Trust Companies* (No. [2010]5 of the CBRC) to implement net capital management for trust companies and expressly stipulate the minimum standard of net capital, risk management standards, and calculation standard of risk capital so as to prevent liquidity risks.

No credit risk transfer instruments such as credit derivatives

The Chinese financial market is still under development, and non-bank financial institutions like trust companies in China have not involved themselves in credit derivatives such as credit default swap (CDS). China's asset-ABS is still in a pilot stage, and trust companies act only as trustees in the ABS. The *Measures for Supervising and Administrating the Pilot ABS by Financial Institutions* (No. [2005]3 of the CBRC) prescribes the qualifications of a trust company's engagement in this business in details, and all issuances of ABS must be approved by the CBRC.

Simple business models and no credit intermediary chain

The assets of trust companies in China are independent from those of the trust plans, and different trust plans are independent from one another, without cross-trading. The capital is mainly invested in companies that are part of the real economy, with an investment style of "buy-and-hold." Therefore, the business structure is simple, and there is not a credit intermediation chain.

Some trust WM has features of shadow banking but is under strict regulations

Liquidity transfer and credit conversion exist in bank-trust cooperation, negotiable instrument trusts, and non-standard pooled fund, and they may lead to regulatory arbitrage. However, CBRC promulgated in the *Notice on Further Regulating Bank-Trust Cooperation WM* (No. [2011]7 of the CBRC) that banks are required "to transfer off-balance sheet assets of bank-trust cooperation onto balance sheets" and "trust companies to hold back risk capital at a rate of 10.5% for bank-trust cooperation loans that the bank has not yet transferred onto the balance sheet." In 2012, CBRC promulgated in the *Notice on Bill Trusts and Other Related Issues by Trust Companies* (No. [2012]70 of the CBRC) that "trust companies shall not engage in any form of commercial paper/bill transfer/assignment with commercial banks." In 2013, the State Council issued *Notice of the State Council on Further Reinforcing the Regulation of Shadow Banking* (No. [2013]107 of the State

Council), ordering that "trust companies shall not develop business with shadow banking characteristics such as non-standard pooled funds." The stipulations above timely regulated trust business that may have been risk-prone and cause regulatory arbitrage.

Development trends

We have seen a recent return to the origin of trusts, including a transfer from focus on commercial trust to private trusts. With regard to the origin of trust, it emerged as a mechanism under which it manages affairs under the client's trust. But in recent years, trust companies in China have been engaged primarily in commercial trusts and conducted few private trusts. In the era of multiple-asset management in which banks have intensively developed WM businesses, trust companies need to explore new business models. Trust companies should leverage their institutional advantages in WM, transforming from institutions primarily engaged in trust loans into those that provide wealth and asset management services to clients with high net worth, becoming professional wealth and asset management institutions for various types of capital.

Another trend is the exploration of active management businesses with professional expertise. In some countries and regions, special funds management is operated by trust institutions. For example, the pension funds of Hong Kong and annuity trust and charitable trusts of Japan are all managed by trust companies. We could learn from their experience to develop asset management trusts such as trusts for social security, pensions, property management fees, and charity. This approach may provide trust companies with new opportunities for further development. Trust will also follow the national macroeconomic policies and seize the opportunities afforded by urbanization.

The new urbanization is a forward-looking strategy made at the Third Plenum of the eighteenth Party Congress. As an important part in the capital market, trust companies should grasp the opportunities of urbanization and new rural construction. They should make contributions to new urbanization while stimulating the development of related trust businesses. Land transfer has become one of the hot topics following the Third Plenum. Trust companies can give their licenses to full play to facilitate rural land transfer under the trust mechanism. CITIC Trust and Beijing Trust set up a good example in setting up land transfer trusts.

International comparison

Modern trusts originated in the United Kingdom reached their heyday in the United States and were improved in Japan. They reached China much later. Trust WM abroad is more developed than that in China. Research on the development and current condition of overseas trust WM can provide a key reference point for trust WM in China.

The current development of trust business in the United Kingdom

Trusts are not as developed in the United Kingdom as those in countries such as the United States and Japan. At present, the British financial trusts are 80% individual trusts. Corporate trustee businesses are mainly operated by banks and insurance companies, and only a small proportion is run exclusively by trust companies. Even more, over 90% of trusts set up by banks are from four major commercial banks, namely, RBS, HSBC, Barclays Bank, and Lloyds Bank.

In terms of operational business, the British trust industry still focuses on traditional trusts, namely individual (private) and charitable trusts. Individual trusts are mainly wills, including asset management, will implementation, legacy management, financial advisory, and advisory services regarding the management, use, investment, and tax payment of individual wealth. Charitable trust mainly refers to a situation in which people entrust the funds donated or raised to the trustee and then instruct the trustee to employ the entrusted funds or materials for charitable causes.

Moreover, British securities investment trusts are prevalent. Pension fund trusts, investment trusts, and unit trusts are usually adopted in the United Kingdom. To safeguard participant interests, all pension plans in the country are set up and managed through pension fund trusts. Until the end of 2001, there were a total of 200,000 professional pension plans in the United Kingdom. The overall assets of these plans added up to 600 billion pounds. Investment trust companies provide possibilities for investors of small amounts to diversify investments by setting up investment trusts. The self-disciplined association of investment trust companies, the Association of Investment Trust Companies, was founded in 1932. By the end of February 2003, there were over 300 member investment trust companies. The affiliated trust funds are conventional funds and split capital funds, respectively, managing assets amounting to 26.8 billion and 8.1 billion pounds. A unit trust is an open-ended mutual investment instrument and is growing rapidly. Its first self-governing association was the Association of Unit Trusts and Investment Funds that was set up in 1959. Since February 2002, it has merged with the Fund Managers Association to create the new Investment Management Association. At present, its members include those with "full-time" and "affiliated" qualifications. Of these, the "full-time" members include 200 investment management companies, directly managing assets of over 2 trillion pounds, while the "affiliated" members are responsible for providing facilities and services for the "full-time" members.

Current development of trusts in the United States

Currently, securities investment trusts are the major institutional investors in the US securities market. Statistics suggest that there are over 8,900 mutual funds registered under the Investment Company Institute (ICI) with a net capital of approximately US$ 6.3 trillion, representing over 90 million individual investors. Such numbers do not include assets in alternative forms of securities investment trusts such as closed-end funds, ETFs, and unit investment trusts (UIT).

Currently, trust businesses in the United States can be divided into three categories, namely, individual trusts, corporate trusts, and individual-and-corporate hybrid trusts, according to the client's legal status. Individual trusts include living trusts and wills. Entrusted trust institutions deal with asset-related affairs and all the after-life affairs on behalf of clients including asset management, asset disposal, appointing or acting as the guardian, manager, and legal person of private accounts. Corporate trusts mainly focus on stock and bond issuance, asset management, company establishment and restructuring, merger and acquisition (M&A), and liquidation on behalf of both private and public institutions. Individual-and-corporate hybrid trusts include employee share ownership trusts (ESOTs), annuity trusts, charitable trusts, and so on. In addition, many new trust investment instruments have been developed in the United States, such as money market mutual funds (MMMFs), cash management accounts (CMAs), common trust funds (CTFs), and financial leases. Trust capital can also be invested in short-term instruments in capital market by means of certificate of deposit (CD), commercial paper (CP), and Treasury bills (TBs). As the new technology revolution occurs, the trust industry of the United States diversifies its business in order to adapt to market changes and satisfy investor demands for WM.

The current development of trusts in Japan

At present, the main players in the Japanese trust industry are trust banks. Trust banks mainly engage in the following businesses: money trusts, loan trusts, pension trusts, property establishment trusts, securities investment trusts, negotiable securities trusts, debt trusts, movable property trusts, real estate trusts, land trusts, charitable trusts, special grant trusts, wills, and others. Besides the aforementioned businesses, Japanese trust banks engage in intermediary businesses like real estate, securities brokerage, and execution of wills.

The growth trends of the aforementioned businesses are as follows: money trusts and securities investment trusts have relatively stable market shares; the market shares of pension trusts is rising on a yearly basis; while market shares of loan trusts and other capital trusts are declining on a yearly basis.

According to the trust WM development of the United Kingdom, the United States, and Japan as stated earlier, it is obvious that the trust business varies in different countries due to diversified cultures and traditions. For example, in the United Kingdom, individual trust businesses (private trust and charitable trust) are dominant and corporate trust make up a small proportion, securities investment trusts have large shares in the United States, Japanese trust products are innovative, and most of these are money trusts.

On the other hand, despite all the differences, trust businesses in these three countries have significant common features. First, various trust products have already become an effective way to do wealth and asset management. Second, trust has an intersecting relationship with other financial institutions. Third, with a strict regulatory mechanism for systemic risk management, trust products have no features of shadow banking. Last, foreign trust WM industries show some common trends in their development: diversification of trust functions, homogenization between trust institutions and other financial institutions, and internationalization of the trust business. There are various types of foreign WM businesses that cover across the three major markets. Since they are under strict regulation, they tend to be reasonable business forms in which systemic risks are unlikely to occur. Foreign trust businesses do not constitute shadow banking, and it reflects the maturity of their trust business, indicating a direction for the development of Chinese trust WM. With the growing number of high-net-worth individuals in China and an increasingly sophisticated asset and WM market, the trust WM business in China will return to its original and primary business purposes. The trust WM business could therefore learn from the business models of foreign WMP to get on a stable and sustained development path.

Securities and asset management business

Historical development

Wealth management businesses at securities firms are called asset management businesses. A securities firm's core business includes asset management, brokerage, investment banking, and proprietary trading. The asset management business of Chinese securities firms originated in 2000. CSRC issued the *Circular on Regulating the Entrusted Investment Management Business of Securities Firms* in 2001, laying a foundation for the subsequent development of the asset management business. In 2003, regulators issued and implemented the *Circular on Issues Relevant to Securities Companies' Engaging in Collective Entrusted Investment Management Business, Trial Implementation Measures for the Client Asset Management Business of Securities Firms* and other rules that further standardized the asset management business.

In 2005, Everbright Securities issued the first approved securities collective asset management product. From 2005 to 2007, the development of collective asset management products remained tepid. After simplified approval procedures and other beneficial policies were released in 2008, the collective asset management business saw a steadily increasing AUM. In 2012, this business grew explosively with 116 newly issued collective asset management products and 103 billion shares in total.

After 2008, securities firms launched the managed accounts business, the growth of which gradually exceeded that of the collective asset management business. Fixed-income products then became the first choice among client-specific asset management business. With reinforcing cooperation between banks and securities companies, banks turn on-balance sheet assets to off-balance sheet assets through their managed accounts business to satisfy the regulatory requirements for capital adequacy ratios (CARs) and still provide more loans to clients when there is an insufficient bank credit quota. The managed accounts business has become one of the most important channels of corporate financing from banks. In 2011, the scale of the managed accounts business has exceeded that of collective asset management business. From October 2012, with the promulgation of the *Measures for the Administration of the on Client Asset Management Business of Securities Firms*, the business has undergone a series of changes including a shift from an approval system to a registration system. This led to the significant expansion of the business in 2012.

Development incentives

Economic growth and societal wealth

Economic growth and the resulting accumulation of societal wealth are the main factors driving the development of asset management business of securities firms.[4] Asset management products are closely related to the development of the macro economy, and the scale of the asset management market positively correlates with the economic development. From 2002 to 2012, Chinese urban disposable income per capita grew together with the national economy. For most of the time during this period, the growth rate of Chinese urban disposable income per capita was higher than that of the national economy. The rapid growth in urban disposable income per capita and wealth accumulation laid a solid foundation for the development of the Chinese securities asset management industry.

Investor willingness

Investors in asset management products of securities firms mainly include institutional (e.g., banks) and individual investors. For the latter, deposit interest rates offered by traditional banks are strictly limited and non-competitive, which makes it difficult for them to satisfy people's demands for WM.[5] The asset management business offered by securities firms with a market-driven rate of return is an alternative asset management choice for individual investors. Compared with asset management products provided by trust companies, securities firms limit the investment scope of their products to only those on securities markets with sufficient liquidity. Their products are more flexible and have a lower investment threshold.

Institutional investors are certainly attracted to these products' rates of return, which are higher than banks' deposit rates. Securities firms can accept both cash and alternative financial assets such as funds and bonds as the investment assets for the client-specific asset management products, which expands the universe of possible choices for institutional investors. For the time being, banks are the most important institutional investors in such business. Banks can spin off their risky assets into an off-balance sheet investment in the client-specific asset management business of securities firms to obtain credit quotas, refinance, and reduce regulatory capital.

Borrower demands

For enterprises with demands for financing, securities firms provide client-specific asset management businesses as a significant source of funding and an effective supplement to bank loans. Securities firms charge lower transaction fees than trust companies when they cooperate with banks, which results in lower financing costs for borrowers.

Direction of regulatory policies

Development and transformation in regulatory policies and measures are important impetus to the growth of security asset management business. On October 19, 2012, CSRC officially issued the revised *Measures for the Administration of the Customer Asset Management Business of Securities Firms, Detailed Rules for the Implementation of the Collective Asset Management Business of Securities Firms,* and *Detailed Implementation Rules for Client-Specific Asset Management Business of Securities Firms* (referred to as "one law, two regulations" in the security industry), to relax restrictions on the asset management business of securities firms. This replaced the approval system of collective asset management plans with a registration system and indicated a direction for the development of securities firms' asset management business. On July 19, 2013, the Securities Association of China (SAC) officially issued the *Notice on Matters Relevant to Regulating Cooperation between Securities Firms and Banks in Engaging in Client-Specific Asset Management Business.* Such policies, laws, and regulations both regulate the business to reduce risks and relax restrictions on it. This measure reflects the policy orientation to "deregulate and encourage innovation" and pushes the development of securities companies' asset management business.

Market scale

The asset management business of securities firms grew quickly in 2012. Securities firms in China issued a total of 216 collective asset management products in 2012, much more than the 109 issued in 2011. Over the same period, the number of securities firms in the asset management business increased from 48 in 2011 to 83 in 2011.[6] According to data provided by SAC, the total AUM of securities firms was only RMB 281.9 billion at the end of 2011, but that of only 114 securities firms reached RMB 1.89 trillion by the end of 2012. To break this down further, collective management plans exceeded RMB 200 billion AUM and client-specific asset management exceeded RMB 1.6 trillion AUM, but that of special asset management was much smaller at RMB 3.5 billion. The asset management business of securities firms increased over RMB 1.5 trillion within only 1 year, especially after October 2012 when the new regulations for the business were enacted. By June 30, 2013, the total AUM of securities firms was RMB 3.42 trillion, already exceeding AUM of the fund management companies and an 80% increase over the RMB 189 million at the end of 2012.[7]

The scale of the asset management business (outstanding) of securities firms over the years is shown in Table 3.3.

Table 3.3 List of asset management business scale of securities firms (stock)

		2007	2008	2009	2010	2011	2012
Collective asset management products	No. of products (product)	26	42	82	157	275	435
	AUM (RMB 100 million)	788.09	511.54	928.71	1,121.76	1,502.56	2,052.09
Special asset management products	No. of products (product)	–	19	18	11	13	19
	AUM (RMB 100 million)	–	79.76	42.67	10.63	10.37	34.39
Client-specific asset management products	No. of products (product)	–	22	36	46	48	83
	AUM (RMB 100 million)	–	327.55	511.94	740.27	1,305.75	16,847.28

Source: SAC.

Risk profile

Asset management business of securities firms mainly has the following risk profile:

Investors assume risk themselves

Regulators explicitly stipulate that investors shall invest in the asset management products at their own risk, and securities firms must not guarantee principal or any minimum return. However, for collective asset management products, securities firms can specify the revenue-sharing ratio and responsibilities for loss in asset management agreements. Securities firms may purchase certain shares of their own asset management products and promise in relevant agreements that such capital from securities firms shall be used to compensate investment losses, if any, in subordination to that from other subscribers. Such operation is equivalent to credit enhancement for the products by securities firms with their own capital, which is called implicit principal protection.

Credit risks widely exist

The actual return of some asset management products may not reach the expected rate of return, and the products have resulted in losses for investors. This has been due to inadequate management capacity and professionalism in securities firms, as well as the longstanding depression in the Chinese domestic stock market. The performance of the money market and bonds has historically been better than that of equity-related products in China.

Low liquidity risk

For collective asset management products, investment is limited to stocks, bonds, funds, stock index futures, and other specified financial products. Such products generally feature high credit ratings and strong liquidity, so there is no maturity transformation and fewer liquidity risks arise from maturity mismatch. However, we note that the investment scope of client-specific asset management (or the managed accounts) business is broader than that of the collective asset management business. The underlying assets of the former are not guaranteed with high liquidity. In some projects, land use rights are used for financing as an underlying asset. Therefore, such kind of products may have maturity mismatch.

They lack high leverage

Investors assume sole responsibility for profits or losses, and securities firms are only responsible for asset management. Such products do not lever up the investment. However, for some structured products, securities firms invest their own funds in subordinated tranches to provide credit enhancement for other investors. With such a structure, securities firms may assume losses for all investors while gaining some extra returns in addition to their asset management fees when the products makes a profit. Such operation is equivalent to leveraging companies' own funds and thus should be strictly regulated.

Regulatory arbitrage exists

There are many business opportunities in the cooperation between banks and securities firms, and regulatory arbitrage in security asset management products mainly exists in the managed accounts business. Banks may transfer assets on- and off-balance sheet to gain more credit quotas as well as higher incomes than the normal lending business. The dramatic rise in the scale of the managed accounts business at the end of 2012 was mainly due to such cooperation between banks and securities firms.

Incomplete data

There are two main reasons for the lack of data on over the counter (OTC) transactions and double counting. First, compared with products traded in open market, the failure to disclose complete information has resulted in some difficulties in data collection for OTC transactions. Second, in the business of bank-securities firm cooperation, clients may have purchased asset management products through WM plans issued by banks, which results in double counting in both banks and securities firms' products.

Shadow banking determination

In essence, shadow banking is a system parallel to the traditional banks. It engages in credit intermediary activities and is with business forms and risk characteristics similar to those of commercial banks but with no or insufficient regulation. As a result, the kinds of institutions similar to banks are likely to cause systemic risk and regulatory arbitrage. According to this definition, the relation between asset management business of securities firms and shadow banking is as follows:

1   Securities firms' asset management business has characteristics of shadow banking in a broad sense.

 The client-specific asset management business may be used as business channel, but the actual function of securities firms' collective asset management business is similar to that of bank's deposit and loan business, as both absorb capital from the general public and make profits through management on behalf of clients. If we set aside the high minimum purchase threshold and limited investment scope, securities asset management products provide an alternative to banks' deposit and loan business, so it has some characteristics of shadow banking in a broad sense.

2   The asset management business of securities firms is under strict supervision and does not escape the regulatory system.

 The outflow and use of funds of an asset management product are explicitly specified and disclosed to investors upon their purchase. For example, funds from collective asset management products can only be invested in the securities market. Therefore, the business model is quite different from that of the conventional deposit and loan business of commercial banks.

3   Most of the business has no maturity mismatch.

 The underlying assets of asset management products of securities firms are mainly securities such as stocks and bonds with liquidity only inferior to cash deposits. Additionally, many asset management products are open-ended with considerably strong liquidity.

4   They lack high leverage.

 There may be certain leverage in some securities firms that purchase subordinated tranches of structured products with their own capital. Other than such cases, there is basically no leverage in the asset management products of securities firms. It prevents risk in such products from spreading to other companies or industries in the case of low liquidity or losses, that is, the risks are not contagious.

In conclusion, security asset management products provide market-driven interest rates for investors to satisfy their demands for asset management. Although different from the conventional deposit and loan business of banks, such products provide capital users financing channels beyond bank loans. They are strictly supervised, and the overall scale and development trend have depended and will depend significantly on regulatory policy. Though certain leverage exists in some structured products, it is generally low, and risks are under control. Therefore, the asset management products have characteristics of shadow banking in a broad sense but do not cause systemic risks, so they are not shadow banking in a narrow sense.

Operational principles

After many years of development, the issuance of asset management products by securities firms already displays a comprehensive system and stable procedures. Some asset management products are structured with credit enhancement mechanisms that design manager-subscribed subordinated tranches and provide risk reserve funds. The main reasons for such credit enhancement mechanism are profit sharing and increased issuance. Securities firms involved in collective asset management plans can obtain management and incentive fees from their asset management services and also share profits from investments. During a depressed securities market, such schemes allow securities firms use their own capital for credit enhancement. This offer of a limited guarantee for investors allows them to raise the issuance volume.

The current asset management products issued by securities firms have the following characteristics: the rate of return is market-driven; there are more detailed descriptions and requirements concerning the investment horizon, investment scope, and asset allocation; and asset management products vary greatly due to different underlying assets. The differences between asset management business by securities firms and the deposit and loan business of traditional commercial banks are shown in Table 3.4.

Development trends

After the explosive growth of securities asset management business, some changes are found in its development trend.

More rapid product innovation

In 2012, securities firms have issued many innovative asset management products. Some of these new products resulted from ideas that securities firms took from competitors in other industries such as fund management companies and trust companies. Others resulted from securities firm cooperation with other financial institutions such as private equity (PE) firms.

Table 3.4 Comparison between financing business of securities firms and the deposit and loan business of traditional banks

	Asset management business of securities firms	*Deposit and loan business of traditional banks*
Rate of return	Completely market-driven and determined by securities firms and other stakeholders	The deposit and loan interest rates are strictly regulated by government policies
Scope of investment	Limited by the regulatory authority. For example, collective asset management products can only invest in securities with high credit and strong liquidity such as bonds, stocks, and funds, and the investment scope of asset management business also includes bank deposits	The scope of loan purpose is theoretically broad and almost unlimited in practice
Risk	Clients assume investment risks, and securities firms shall not guarantee principal or any minimum return in any form	Have fixed deposit and loan interest rates, supervised by regulators, with lower risks
Information disclosure	Collective asset management products are not required to disclose information regularly, client-specific asset management products disclose in accordance with the asset management agreements	The loan purposes are not disclosed to depositors
Threshold	Minimum purchase threshold is required	Generally no minimum quota
Bankruptcy disposal	Assets entrusted by clients are bankruptcy remote from those of the issuing securities firms and trustees	According to the Bankruptcy Law, individual depositors will have first priority in payment from the bank
Asset forms	Not limited to cash. For example, the entrusted assets in client-specific asset management businesses may be cash, bonds, assets-backed securities, securities investment funds, stocks, financial derivatives, or other financial assets approved by the CSRC	Cash

Acceleration of AUM expansion

There may be some disadvantages in securities asset management products when compared with competitors such as trust companies and fund management companies. For example, asset management products may have limited investment scope and no asset isolation mechanism such as those offered by trust plans. On the other hand, there are also advantages for security asset management products, such as lower investment thresholds, lower fees for joint deals with banks, and strong liquidity. Regulatory authorities have encouraged the securities asset management business, at the same time as cooperation between banks and trust companies has been more limited by government policies, which has to some extent restrained the explosive growth in trusts. Accordingly, there may be more room for the development of the asset management business by securities companies.

More comprehensive regulatory system

In February 2013, CSRC promulgated the *Interim Provisions on the Management of Publicly Offered Securities Investment Funds by Asset Management Institutions* (hereafter referred to as *Interim Provisions*) that came into effect on June 1, 2013, and corresponded to the *Securities Investment Fund Law* that came into effect at the same time. Brokers, PE funds, and insurance companies are allowed to engage in public fund business by the *Interim Provisions*, but securities firms are no longer allowed to launch collective asset management plans with over 200 investors. Hence, the large collective products from securities firms are to be replaced by publically issued investment funds.

Fund wealth management business

Historic development

Funds are a collective investment scheme operated by professional managers. They can be divided into funds offered through public and non-public offerings. Public investment funds (mutual fund or public fund) are raised from general retail investors, strictly supervised by regulatory authorities, and strictly limited in terms of investment scope and asset diversification. Based on their investment scope, investment funds can be divided into stock, bond, hybrid, index, and money market funds; based on their investment strategies, they can be divided into growth, balanced, income, and guaranteed funds; and based on their fund structures, they can be divided into single, series, and umbrella funds. In 2007, public funds grew explosively, and the NAV of total funds soared to RMB 3.2 trillion. But due to the global financial crisis and influenced by the stock market, the NAV of the public funds plummeted below RMB 2 trillion in 2008. From 2008 to 2012, though fund issuance steadily grew, the stock market was sluggish. Therefore, the NAV of funds fluctuated rather than growing with the increase in fund issuance volume.

A non-public fund is raised directly from specific group through a non-public offering, mainly including social security funds, enterprise annuity funds, asset management services for specific clients (managed account service), and privately placed funds (private fund).

The investment manager, who is appointed by the National Council for the Social Security Fund, manages a social security fund. On December 13, 2001, the Ministry of Finance and the Ministry of Labor and Social Security published the *Tentative Measures on the Administration of Investments by the National Social Security Fund.* At the end of 2002, six fund management companies—China Southern Asset Management, Bosera Funds, China AMC, Penghua Fund, Changsheng Fund, and Harvest Fund—became the first batch of social security fund investment companies. Bank of China and Bank of Communications were the custodian banks. In 2004, three fund management companies—E-fund, Guotai AMC, and China Merchants Fund—became the second batch of social security fund investment companies entrusted within Chinese territory. In 2010, seven fund management companies—Dacheng FMC, Fullgoal Fund, ICBC Credit Suisse, Guangdong Development Fund, Haifutong Fund, 99fund, and Yinhua Fund—became the third batch of social security fund investment companies.

Enterprise annuity funds are supplementary pension funds set up according to the law, to manage both the principal and returns from enterprise annuity plans. Starting from May 2004, China implemented the *Measures for the Management of Enterprise Annuity Funds.* In 2005, the first batch of companies were qualified as enterprise annuity fund management institutions. In 2007, 24 more companies officially became the second batch of enterprise annuity fund management institutions. The revised *Measures for the Management of Enterprise Annuity Funds* that came into effect on May 1, 2011, relaxed regulatory constraints on annuity investment. For example, the ratio of stock investment became capped at 30% of the net fund capital.

The specific client asset management business (or managed account service) refers to activities where funds raise capital from or are entrusted as wealth managers by specific investors. They invest this entrusted capital on behalf of such investors, with investor assets in the custody of custodian. In August 2011, CSRC promulgated the *Trial Measures for Fund Management Companies to Provide Asset Management Services for Specific Clients* (No. [2011]74 of CSRC) and two supporting principles for contracts[8] that integrated the existing five laws and regulations.[9] On September 26, 2012, No. 83 Order of the China Securities Regulatory Commission released the revised *Trial Measures for Fund Management Companies to Provide Asset Management Services for Specific Clients*, stipulating that fund management companies should set up specific subsidiaries and develop specific client asset management business through specific asset management plans. After that, the CSRC promulgated the *Tentative Provisions for the Administration of the Subsidiaries of Securities Investment Fund Management Companies.* As of March 2013, nearly 20 such asset management subsidiaries have been approved.

A private fund is sold to specific group through private placement. Private funds in a broad sense include PE funds in addition to (privately placed) securities investment funds. The operation model of PE fund is equity investment, which is to acquire shares of (non-listed) private companies through capital investment or share transfer and gain profits through value appreciation or share transfer. Compared with public funds, private funds have more flexible asset allocation, less information disclosure, and more focus on performance. The *Law on Securities Investment Funds* issued at the end of 2012 first brought private funds into China's regulatory framework.

Development incentives

The development of fund WMPs is mainly influenced by the macro environment, investor demand, and regulatory policies.

The macroeconomic situation, in particular the development of the stock and bond markets, directly impacts the issuance of WMPs, which is key to the historical development of public funds. Besides, the development of pan-asset management industry has led to fierce competition. In February 2013, the CSRC promulgated the *Tentative Provisions for the Engagement in the Public Securities Investment Fund Management Business by Asset Management Companies*, prohibiting securities companies from issuing collective asset management plans with over 200 investors and specifying that the new plans would be replaced by their public investment fund business. Since then, all the securities companies, private funds, and insurance institutions were allowed to distribute funds through public offering, which was no longer the exclusive business of fund management companies. The competition in the public investment fund business will become increasingly fierce.

Willingness and demand of investors, most of whom are individual (retail) investors, are undoubtedly important factors for fund development. First, funds are one of the most important channels for WM. Funds have restrictive investment constraints, while WMPs of securities companies are a bit looser. Securities companies' WMP can even invest in funds. The minimum fund subscription is as low as RMB 1,000 for public investment funds, but the minimum for trust plans is RMB 1 million. Fund investment can have fixed terms and fixed principal, which are suitable for medium- to long-term continuous investment. The purchase and redemption usually takes 2–3 days. The capital can be redeemed at any time. On the other hand, the maturity for collective WMPs of securities companies and trust plans is mostly 2–3 years, with a blackout period after purchase. Second, asset management business for specific clients has little requirements for information disclosure, more flexibility on asset allocation, and no constraints on net capital for fund companies, all of which offer apparent advantages for fund companies to develop channel businesses that are attractive to banks.

Development and changes in regulatory policies and measures are further important factors that stimulate the fund WM business. Both issuance and operation of funds are strictly supervised and thus transparent. It is specified in the *Measures on the Regulation of Information Disclosure of Securities Investment Fund* that came into effect in July 2004 that those responsible for fund information disclosure shall make the required information disclosure in national newspapers, the official websites of fund managers, as well as fund custodians and other media appointed by the CSRC within the required time. They shall also guarantee that investors can refer to or copy publicly disclosed information and materials within certain period, in compliance with the fund documents. Fund managers should make announcements regarding the NAV and net asset value per share (NAVPS) of the fund at least once a week and disclose the NAV and NAVPS on the last market trading days of the midyear and the whole year. In addition, fund managers should disclose the NAVPS and the accumulative net value per share through websites, sales networks, and other media on the day after each trading day.

Market scale

Until the end of 2012, there were already 73 fund management companies in China that managed 1,174 different public investment funds. According to data from AMAC, until December 31, 2012, the AUM of the whole industry totaled RMB 3.622 trillion. Among that, private investment funds (social security fund, enterprise annuity fund, and specific client asset management business) totaled RMB 756.452 billion or 20.88% of the total, and public funds (closed-end fund and open-end fund) totaled RMB 2,866.1 billion or 79.12% (see Table 3.5). In 2012, the AUM of the whole industry grew by 30.53% yoy, of which private investment funds grew by 28.79% and public investment funds by 30.99%.[10] The proportions of NAVs for various funds at the end of 2012 are shown in Figure 3.3.

Table 3.5 Distribution of scale of fund capital at the end of 2012

Type	Approximate proportion of net value at the end of the period (%)
Public investment fund	79
Enterprise annuity fund	5
Social security fund	10
Asset management business for specific clients	6
Total	100

Source: Asset Management Association of China and Asset Management Research Center of Finance Research Institute of Chinese Academy of Social Sciences.

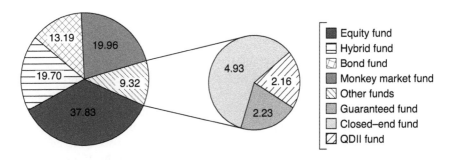

Figure 3.3 Proportions of net values for funds of various types at the end of 2012 (%).

Risk characteristics

Fund WMPs usually have the following risk characteristics: investors bear it, some credit risk exists, low liquidity risk, no high leverage, and some regulatory arbitrage.

Investors should assume investment risks, and the funds provide no guarantees on principal or minimum returns. It is common that the final incomes of fund products fail to reach the expected rates of return or incur losses. Especially impacted by the depressed stock market since 2012, the rates of return on funds have been generally low.

For the specific client asset management business developed by fund company subsidiaries, there may be credit risk due to defaults by counterparties. Not constrained by net capital, fund management subsidiaries are not required to map their business scale with net capital and risk capital (such mapping is required for trust companies and securities firms). If there is any loss in the investment, fund companies find it difficult to make an effective response with their own capital.

A public fund can only invest in listed securities such as stocks and bonds, making itself a high-liquidity financial product. For open-ended funds, the subscription and redemption generally requires 2–3 days. Open-ended funds can be sold at any time and are highly liquid. Even for the specific client asset management business, there is a matched funding structure, that is, the tenor of the investment matches that of the product. Therefore, the fund WMPs have no maturity transformation and low liquidity risks from maturity mismatch.

Since investors undertake investment risks and fund management companies provide only asset management services, the funds do not enlarge the investment, and problems arising from the funds are not contagious in a financial crisis. However, different from securities firms and trust companies, regulatory authorities do not require fund company subsidiaries to match their business scale with their net capital and risk capital, which makes these subsidiaries grow their AUM as much as possible without consideration of capital constraints. Under extreme circumstance, they are completely unable to hedge risks.

Through a channel business, banks may transfer assets or debts off-balance sheet through the specific client asset management business to enlarge banks' credit appetite or lending quotas and obtain returns beyond those of the traditional lending business.

Shadow banking determination

1   Public, social security, and enterprise annuity funds have no characteristics of shadow banking, but the specific client asset management business of fund company subsidiaries has the characteristics of shadow banking in the broad sense. These funds are strictly limited in the scope of investment and are subject to the principle that investors ultimately bear investment risks. Therefore, they do not have the characteristics of shadow banking. While the specific client asset management business has an extensive investment scope, it is quite similar

to trust products and may become a sort of alternative for bank deposits as well as the loan business, so it has such shadow banking characteristics.

2 Both public and private funds are strictly supervised and regulated, so they do not have the characteristics of shadow banking.

3 Fund WMPs have no maturity mismatch. Most of their underlying assets are listed securities such as stocks and bonds, with liquidity second only to cash deposits. The funds are also open-ended, highly liquid, and without blackout periods, so investors can easily cash out at any time.

4 Fund WMPs do not have high leverage. However, with the development of the specific client asset management business, the asset under management can be expanded almost to its utmost without considering capital constraints. In this respect, there may be some possibility of high leverage.

In conclusion, public, social security, and enterprise annuity funds have no characteristics of shadow banking. The specific client asset management business developed by fund companies' subsidiaries may have shadow banking characteristics. But with strict regulation, the asset management business does not have maturity mismatch. Moreover, there is no high leverage when we take a look at the overall scale of fund WMPs; hence, fund WMPs are not shadow banking.

Operational principles

Compared with the deposit and loan business of traditional commercial banks, fund WMPs are different with respect to rate of return, investment scope, investment risks, and information disclosure (see Table 3.6).

Table 3.6 Comparison between funds and deposit and loan business of traditional banks

	Funds	*Deposit and loan business of traditional banks*
Rate of return	The rates of return are influenced by market trends. Fund companies and other stakeholders determine rates of return on specific client asset management plans	Interest rate of deposits and loans are strictly limited by national policies
Investment scope	Strictly limited by regulatory authorities, the public investment fund allocates all investment on listed securities. Investment scope of specific client asset management business is more extensive.	Theoretically, the scope of loans is extensive, almost without any limits
Investment risk	Clients themselves assume risks. There may be negative returns.	With definite interest rates for deposits and loans and under the national regulation, there are fewer risks

	Funds	Deposit and loan business of traditional banks
Information disclosure	Public funds are more transparent in information disclosure, while the information of private funds remains confidential.	The loan flow will not be disclosed to depositors
Entry barrier	There is a (low) minimum amount for subscription.	Generally without a minimum

Development trend

The development trend of funds' WM business includes the following two aspects: fierce competition and much potential for the specific client asset management business.

On June 1, 2013, as the new *Law on Securities Investment Funds* was officially implemented, the securities companies' asset management collective WMPs of over 8 years were replaced by securities companies' public investment fund products. Securities companies, private funds, and insurance institutions are allowed to issue public investment funds under certain conditions, ushering in an era of large-scale public asset management in China.

Meanwhile, the fund distribution channels in China are expanding. In the open-ended fund sales in the past, sales channels of commercial banks dominated, and fund distribution channels were simple. In the revised *Measures for the Administration of Sales of Securities Investment Funds* and *Tentative Provisions on the Administration of Sale Settlement Capital of Securities Investment Funds* that came into effect in October 2011, entry barriers for fund distribution institutions were relaxed, making it possible to expand fund distribution channels from a regulatory angle. In the long run, the fund market is expected to distribute over multiple channels.

As stipulated by the CSRC, the investment scope of the specific client asset management business includes, "equity, debt and other property rights that are not listed on securities exchanges" and "other assets recognized by the CSRC," in addition to cash, bank deposits, stocks, bonds, securities investment fund, bills of the central bank, non-financial enterprise debt financing tools, asset-backed securities, commodity futures, and other financial derivatives. Therefore, the investment scope of the specific asset management business is very broad, its investment approaches are diversified, and its business models include quasi-securitization tools such as small loan and credit assets transfer, real estate, financing lease, and stock-pledged repo. Therefore, it is possible to hedge for the conditions inherent to a depressed stock market.

The specific asset management business, especially specific asset management plans, is characterized by little information disclosure, flexible asset allocation and no constraints on net capital of the fund management companies (the regulatory authorities require fund subsidiaries that develop specific asset management business to have registered capital no less than RMB 20 million, without a mapping for net capital and risk capital). All of the above provide absolute advantages to the specific asset management plans of fund company subsidiaries when they are engaging in the channel business. It is predictable that with public funds impacted by the stock market, the specific asset management business will have larger room for development.

International comparison

The fund management business has a history extending hundreds of years into the past. It originated in the United Kingdom and enjoys widespread success in the United States. Investors favor investment funds because they feature professional WM, investment diversification, high transparency, and good stability. Over the past few decades, funds grew much faster than other financial products globally, which have already become the most important investment products for the general public. Fund management occupies an important place in the global asset management industry. According to data from the ICI, until the end of 2012, the NAV of mutual funds operated globally was approximately US$ 26.8 trillion, of which, the United States made up US$ 13 trillion, nearly half of the total amount worldwide. China ranked tenth in the world, making up 1.6%, or 1/30 of the United States and 60% of Japan, slightly higher than Germany.

The fund management industry is more mature abroad. Based on underlying assets, funds can be divided into securities investment funds (with stocks and bonds as underlying assets), futures funds (with futures as underlying assets), monetary investment funds (with foreign currencies as underlying assets), gold investment fund (with gold as underlying assets), funds of funds (FOF, with PE and VC funds as underlying assets), real estate investment trusts (REITs, with real estate as the underlying assets), trust of trusts (TOT, with trust plans as underlying assets), hedge funds (aka arbitrage funds, taking advantage of various arbitrage opportunities), and others. However, China lacks many of these types of funds. Public investment funds in China are securities investment funds only, and private funds are mainly focused in securities investment and equity investment.

The United States has the most advanced modern financial industry in the world. Equity funds in the United States mostly invest in US stocks. Since the 1990s, large fund management companies have kept expanding their product lines to satisfy investor demand, and the number of equity funds rapidly increased. Based on investment strategy, equity funds can be divided into value, balanced, and growth funds. Based on the market value of stocks invested, equity funds can be divided into large-cap, medium-cap, and small-cap funds. Currently, there are over 10,000 domestic equity funds in the United States, of which large-cap equity funds make up nearly 50%. In large-cap funds, balanced funds are the major players. Among all medium-cap and small-cap equity funds, growth funds outshine others. Value funds are always a minority in small-cap, medium-cap, or large-cap equity funds.

Insurance wealth management business

Historical development

By issuing institutions, insurance WM is mainly divided into two major categories: WM business of insurance companies and WM business of insurance asset management companies.

WM business of insurance companies

The WM business of insurance company deals with WMP developed from the traditional life insurance created by life insurance companies, including participating insurance,[11] investment-linked insurance,[12] and universal life insurance.[13] China Life Insurance issued the first participating insurance in China in 2000. Over the past couple of years, participating insurance developed rapidly. Ping An Insurance issued the first investment-linked insurance in 1999. Since then, investment-linked insurance was much favored in the capital market and was soon recognized by the market, thanks to the booming capital market and the brand new investment ideas. According to statistics from the CIRC, the premium income of investment-linked insurance in 2001 was RMB 10.6 billion, up 542% on yoy basis. During the second half of 2001, China suffered a bear market that brought disaster to investment-linked insurance. Clients started to make complaints and cancel insurance policies. This crisis started in investment-linked insurance business. From 2002 to 2005, Chinese insurance institutions that were still new in their product development had experienced an "insurance cancellation crisis," and market share of investment-linked insurance dropped year by year.

At the end of 2006, the Chinese stock market started to recover, and investment-linked insurance became popular again. It finally ended its four consecutive years of shrinkage since 2002. In 2007, investment-linked insurance closely linked to the capital market became extremely popular owing to the impressive performance of the capital market. However, from 2008, the capital market entered a downward cycle, and investment-linked insurance went with it. In 2009, the premium income of investment-linked insurance was RMB 14.79 billion, down 65.2% on a yoy basis. In 2010, the premium income was RMB 15.28 billion, up only 3.3% on a yoy basis, and premium income dropped by 14.1% on yoy basis in 2011.

China Pacific Insurance issued the first universal life insurance in 2000. Just like investment-linked insurance, universal life insurance is closely linked to the capital market. During the first 2 years after issuance, the sales of universal life insurance grew rapidly due to the bullish stock market. But after 2002, there was a downturn in the capital market, and sales plummeted. From 2005, as the capital market entered a new upward drive, universal life insurance became popular once more. Once again, in 2008 as the stock market declined, sales went down with it. In 2009, the premium income of universal life insurance dropped by 27.3%; in 2010, it grew by 6.5%, only to drop by 8.3% in 2011 yoy.

WM business of insurance asset management companies

Insurance asset management companies are financial institutions approved by relevant authorities and registered by law to manage entrusted insurance capital. The first insurance asset management company in China, PICC Asset Management Company Limited, was founded in 2003. Before 2010, regulatory authorities were strict in approval of insurance asset management companies, and large insurance companies set up all these insurance asset managers. Since 2010, regulatory authorities have relaxed the restriction on the establishment of insurance asset management companies by medium- and small-sized insurance companies.[14] At present, over 70% of insurance companies have set up independent asset management departments to conduct the direct investment business.

Insurance asset management products are securities investment funds issued by insurance asset management companies in accordance with the *Law of Insurance of the People's Republic of China, Law of Securities of the People's Republic of China, Tentative Provisions on the Administration of Insurance Asset Management Companies*, and other laws and regulations. The CIRC adopts a registration process for the issuance of such products.[15] The first insurance asset management product, Guo Kai Hu Tong investment product was set up by Hua Tai Asset Management in 2006 but was a small issuance. Only seven products were issued by 2012, all of which were issued during 2006 and 2007.

Development incentives

Development incentives for the WM business of insurance companies

Compared with traditional guaranteed life insurance policies, participating policies do not provide a guaranteed insurance interest. They are thus an effective means for insurance companies to avoid interest rate risk and to ensure stable operation. In this context, Chinese life insurance companies have adopted participating insurance.

As the Chinese economy rapidly grows, individual wealth accumulates and demands for investment are increasing. Financial institutions like banks and funds have successively developed abundant new WMP to absorb individuals' financial assets. Consumers may get better investment opportunities through deposits or other investment tools, while traditional life insurance companies cannot survive by only relying on the conventional insurance business. Life insurance companies should develop WM insurance products. In this context, Chinese life insurance companies have successively launched investment-linked and universal life insurance with professional WM services.

Development incentives for the WM business of insurance asset management companies

As subsidiaries of insurance companies, insurance asset management companies have two development motivations for the WM business. The first is to facilitate business development of insurance companies, which satisfies the demands for insurance capital preservation and appreciation. As national wealth increases, Chinese citizens are increasingly aware of insurance. Insured assets keep expanding, and the demands for insurance capital's preservation and appreciation become stronger.

On the other hand, the development of insurance company WM business requires professional investment management, but the investment of insurance capital tends to be conservative due to its risk profile. It is difficult to reach the investment target through other external financial institutions within an incomplete financial system. It is these conditions that have led insurance companies set up insurance asset management companies dedicated to the investment and operation of insurance capital.

Another reason is that they enter the asset management industry to meet their own needs for development. As professional asset management companies, insurance asset management companies are solely responsible for insurance capital. Such an investment model is subject to the development condition of insurance companies and faces increasing competition from other financial institutions that are also allowed to manage insurance capital.

Market scale

Market scale of WM business of insurance companies

By the end of 2011, the premium income of participating insurance reached RMB 766.25 billion, making up as much as 80.2% of the life insurance business. Participating insurance became the most important type of life insurance product. With respect to investment-linked insurance, according to the Annual Report on Accounts of Investment-linked Insurance of China in 2012 released by HuaBao Securities, the assets under investment-linked insurance at the end of 2011 was RMB 84.3 billion; universal life insurance has no publicized data yet.

Market scale of the WM business of insurance asset management companies

Until the end of 2012, there were already 16 insurance asset management companies approved (excluding those in Hong Kong), 13 of which were approved to receive entrusted insurance capital (see Table 3.7).

With regard to business development, according to the CIRC, insurance institutions accumulatively issued 83 infrastructure investment plans and 11 real estate debt plans of RMB 302.5 billion until the end of December 2012. At the end of March 2013, insurance asset management companies had issued a total of 10 products, one of which was issued by PICC and two of which were issued by Taikang Asset Management. Seven of these plans were issued before 2012 and three of which were issued within the first 3 months of 2013.

Table 3.7 List of insurance asset management companies approved by the end of 2012

Insurance asset management company	Approval time	Shareholder	Qualification for capital entrustment	Registered capital	Overall scale of entrusted capital management
PICC	2003	PICC (81%) and Germany's Munich Reinsurance Asset Management Company (19%)	Yes	RMB 800 million	Over RMB 300 billion
CLAMC	2003	China Life Insurance (Group) and China Life Insurance Co., Ltd	Yes	RMB 3 billion	Over RMB 1 trillion
Ping An Insurance	2005	Ping An	Yes	RMB 500 million	RMB 982.363 billion
China Re Asset Management	2005	China Re Group and Swiss Reinsurance Asset Management	Yes	RMB 200 million	Over RMB 13 billion
Huatai Asset Management	2005	Huatai Insurance	Yes	RMB 100 million	
Taiping Assets Management	2006	China Taiping Insurance Group	Yes	RMB 100 million	Over RMB 180 billion
New China Asset Management	2006	New China Insurance Group	Yes	RMB 100 million	
Taikang Asset Management	2006	Taikang Life Insurance and China Credit Trust	Yes	RMB 1 billion	Over RMB 460 billion
Pacific Asset Management	2006	China Pacific Insurance	Yes	RMB 500 million	Over RMB 10 billion

Insurance asset management company	Approval time	Shareholder	Qualification for capital entrustment	Registered capital	Overall scale of entrusted capital management
Sinolife Asset Management	2010	Sinolife Life Insurance and Shenzhen Guoli Investment	Yes	RMB 100 million	
Sun Life Everbright Life	2011	China Everbright Group and Sun Life Everbright Life	Yes	RMB 100 million	
Union Asset Management	2011	Union Life Insurance and Zhongfa Industries	Yes	RMB 100 million	
Anbang Asset Management	2011	Anbang Assets and Anbang Life Insurance	Yes	RMB 300 million	
Minsheng Tonghui Asset Management	2012	Minsheng Life Insurance	No	RMB 100 million	
Sunlight Asset Management	2012	Sunlight Insurance Group, Sunlight Assets, Sunlight Life Insurance and Standard (Beijing) Insurance Agency Co., Ltd	No	RMB 100 million	
Zhongying Yili Asset Management	2012	Zhongying Life Insurance, Sinatay Life Insurance, StarRock Investment and Shanghai Vstone Investment Consulting Co., Ltd	No	RMB 100 million	

Source: Data publicized on websites of insurance asset management companies.

Operational principles

Participating insurance

The WM function of participating insurance is mainly reflected in dividends. As stipulated in prevailing laws and regulations, the dividends practically distributed to policyholders each accounting year by insurance companies shall not be less than 70% of the distributable profit of that year. The profit mainly comes from mortality savings, interest rate spreads, and fee surpluses. Among these, mortality savings refer to the interest arising from an actual mortality rate less than potential mortality rate; interest rate spread refers to the margin between the real rate of return on investment and potential interest rate of insurance companies; and fee surplus refers to the surplus arising from the margin between real operation and administration expenses and those forecasted. Generally, life insurance companies will not distribute all the profits each year. They distribute dividends according to their projections regarding the future economy, capital market, operating condition, and bonus guaranteed in the future. The operational principles of participating insurance are shown in Figure 3.4.

Investment-linked insurance

According to regulatory laws and rules by the CIRC, as the most powerful insurance WMP, investment-linked insurance accounts can be divided into two types: general account and investment account. The first is mainly for insurance, while

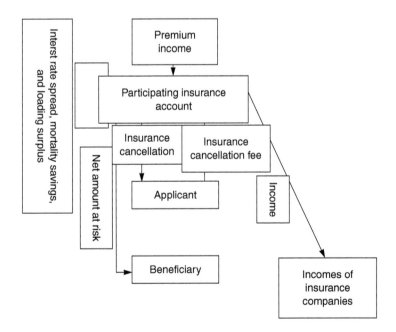

Figure 3.4 Operational principles of participating insurance.

the other is mainly for investment. The two functions are strictly separated into two types of segregated accounts. Besides, multiple accounts of investment-linked insurance are set for applicants to choose according to different allocations of underlying assets and different product risk profiles. The operational principles of investment-linked insurance are shown in Figure 3.5.

Universal life insurance

The operational principles of universal life insurance are described as follows. After original expenses are deducted from each period's premiums, the remaining amount is deposited to the policy account. Insurance companies will collect the mortality risk premium, policy management fee, asset management fee, and administration fee regularly. If the policies are cancelled before maturity, the companies are likely to collect insurance cancellation fees. Compared with investment-linked insurance that has multiple investment accounts and that enables investors to choose voluntarily and undertake risks, universal life insurance has only one investment account, and the asset allocation and investment decision-making depends on insurance companies. Applicants have no right to make their own choices. In most cases, insurance companies will not manage the policy accounts of universal life insurance separately; they put them together with premiums of other types of insurance in a common account. When determining the returns of the accounts, insurance companies must distribute the overall investment returns appropriately and allocate the returns to policy accounts of universal life insurance and accounts of other types of insurance. The value of policy accounts is calculated according to the settlement interest rate regularly released by the insurance companies. The calculated interest rate should not be less than the guaranteed interest rate. The operational principles of universal life insurance are shown in Figure 3.6.

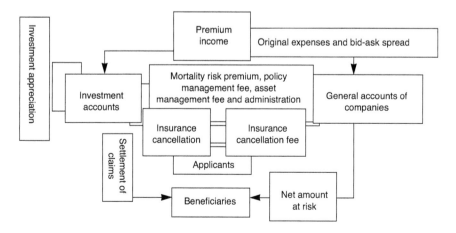

Figure 3.5 Operational principles of investment-linked insurance.

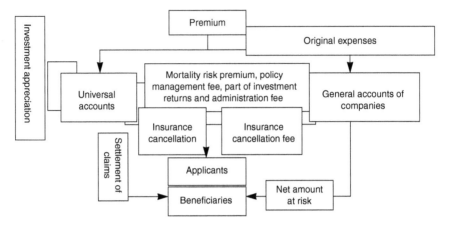

Figure 3.6 Operational principles of universal life insurance.

Shadow banking determination

The WM business of insurance companies is not shadow banking

Insurance regulators all over the world pay significant attention to regulation on participating insurance. The core of supervision over participating insurance is to guarantee the interest of policyholders and ensure that life insurance companies have sustainable operational capacity. The regulation focuses on bonus reporting, bonus distribution, information disclosure, policyholders' reasonable expectations, confirmation of fund liabilities, and other key areas. As life insurance products, participating insurance plays a function in WM. However, it is still the same as traditional life insurance products in which the participating insurance premiums paid by applicants are still the liabilities of insurance companies, and such liabilities have a long duration (generally over 5 years). Due to the investment constraints of insurance capital, "long-term liabilities and short-term assets" have always been the main characteristics of Chinese life insurance. Therefore, participating insurance has no problem of "short-term liabilities with long-term assets" that brings about maturity mismatch. On the one hand, underlying assets include abundant high-liquidity financial products like bank deposits and bonds; on the other hand, an administration fee in insurance cancellation is usually stipulated for participating insurance. This restrains the ratio of insurance cancellation and results in a low liquidity risk for participating insurance. Participating insurance does not guarantee dividends, so there will be no transfer of credit risk. Conservative investment is a basic principle in insurance asset management, so there will be no high leverage. In conclusion, participating insurance business is not shadow banking.

Investment-linked insurance is actually a securities investment fund, whose underlying assets are identical to those of securities investment funds. It is mainly invested in the stock and bond markets and can be divided into seven categories based on asset allocation: aggressive, hybrid conservative, hybrid aggressive, enhanced bond, index, money market, and comprehensive bond. In this case, investment-linked insurance has no maturity mismatch or high leverage. Although the NAV is released every day and insurance can be cancelled at any time, the underlying asset is of high liquidity, and transaction costs are generally imposed for insurance cancellation. As a result, liquidity risks are lower. Additionally, risks in investment accounts are assumed by applicants alone, so there is no credit risk transfer. In conclusion, investment-linked insurance is not shadow banking either.

Just like participating insurance, universal life insurance has no maturity mismatch, liquidity risks, or high leverage. However, as it guarantees a minimum interest rate, universal life insurance transfers credit risk. Some insurance companies started to issue short-term WMP after March 2013. Theoretically, except for the death benefit and total disability benefit, universal life insurance is the same as short-term guaranteed WMP of banks. The minimum maturity is 1 year, 3 months, 1 month, or even shorter. Also, the insurance cancellation fees are low. For example, "Wangcai No.1" of Taikang Life Insurance deducts 5% for cancellation within the first year but costs nothing for cancellation after the first year. "Good Wife's Steady Wealth Management" of Union Life Insurance deducts 3% for cancellation within the first year and costs nothing for cancellation after the first year. Once long-term financial products like infrastructure bonds are included in the underlying assets, maturity mismatch will occur in such short-term universal life insurance. But with small-scale and effective regulation, there will be no systemic risk or regulatory arbitrage. To conclude, universal life insurance is not narrow shadow banking.

The WM business of insurance asset management companies is not shadow banking

Debt investment plans are restrained by laws and administrative regulations like the *Law of Insurance of the People's Republic of China*, *Law of Trust of the People's Republic of China*, and *Law of Contract of the People's Republic of China*. Based on the principle of trust, beneficiaries hire independent supervisors to supervise the trustee's management of investment plans and related project operations. The investment scope of debt investment plans mainly includes national key infrastructure projects like transportation, communication, energy, municipal administration, environmental protection, and real estate.

Maturity mismatch is mainly caused by conflicts between the capital providers' short-term investment tenor and the capital users' needs for long-term financing. The capital source for insurance asset management companies is mainly life insurance with a maturity of 5–10 years. As for capital use, infrastructure debt investment plans have the longest maturity. By the end of 2012, net premiums of life insurance (the margin between the original premiums of life insurance and the compensation) reached RMB 740.3 billion. The life insurance capital can absolutely cover the RMB 302.5 billion debt investment plan. With respect to specific infrastructure debt investment plans, in accordance with the *Circular on the Investment of Insurance Funds in Infrastructure Bond Investment Plans* (No. [2009]43 of the CIRC), there are limits on the ratios of insurance capital invested in infrastructure debt investment plans in general and for a single infrastructure project.[16] Therefore, maturity mismatch is unlikely to affect infrastructure debt investment plans. Debt investment plans have poor liquidity without a unified product exchange or trading platform. However, as insurance companies that do not require high liquidity generally subscribe debt investment plans, there is no liquidity risk. No credit risk transfer or high leverage has been found in all issued debt investment plans.

Based on underlying assets and funding sources, among the seven asset management products issued since 2012, one was a stock type of insurance product, one was money-market type, one was equity focused, and the remaining four were bond asset management products. All the seven products lack maturity mismatch, liquidity risks, credit risk transfer, and high leverage. The three insurance asset management products issued since 2012 have poor liquidity, but can be subscribed by other eligible investors. Different capital sources result in increasing possibilities of maturity mismatch and liquidity risk. As for leverage, since the investment scope of new asset management products cover securities margin trading, stock index futures, and other leverage trading clauses, high leverage is likely to result. But with a small-scale regulation, there will not be systematic risks. In conclusion, it is not shadow banking in the narrow sense.

Development trend

After October 2012, the CIRC successively promulgated a series of new insurance regulations and new policies of insurance asset management. New insurance regulations mainly include the *Circular on Investment in Relevant Financial Products with Insurance Proceeds*, *Tentative Measures for Administration of the Allocation of Insurance Assets*, and so on; new policies of insurance asset management mainly include the *Tentative Provisions on the Administration of Infrastructure Bond Investment Plans*, *Circular on Matters Relevant to Insurance Asset Management Companies*, and *Notice on Issues concerning Pilot Practice of Assets Management Production Business by Insurance Asset Management Companies*. The promulgation of new policies regarding insurance asset management has significantly improved the policy environment of the industry. On the one hand, these new policies on insurance asset management companies made reference to those for trust companies, brokerage (securities) firms' asset management business, and fund management companies. Accordingly, such policies allow insurance asset management companies to set up specific and collective products for eligible investors. They may also expand their investor scope from insurance companies to other eligible investors. On the other hand, the new policies also allow insurance asset management companies to expand their investment scope to "bank deposits, stocks, bonds, securities investment funds, central bank bills, non-financial enterprise debt financing tools, credit asset backed securities, infrastructure investment plans, real estate investment plans, project backed investment plans, and other assets accepted by the CIRC." This considerably broadened investment scope brings this business to the asset management market and allows them to become a credit intermediary, which means competition with trust companies, securities firms' asset management divisions, and fund management companies. As relevant supporting policies are not yet promulgated, insurance asset management products have uncertainties as to maturity mismatch, liquidity risk, credit risk transfer, and high leverage, making it possibly a kind of shadow banking. Regulatory authorities should pay close attention and reinforce supervision to mitigate risks.

Business of various financial companies

Finance company

A finance company of an enterprise group refers to the non-bank financial institution that provides financial management service for members of an enterprise group to reinforce integrated capital management and enhance the efficiency of capital use. A finance company is an independent business entity that needs to be regulated by the CBRC in accordance with relevant laws and regulations. The operation and development of a finance company is closely related to its group corporation and the member companies thereof, which fully reflect the finance company's nature of "focusing on and serving the group."

Historical development

Finance companies of enterprise groups emerged with the reform in the Chinese economic and financial systems. They is a type of non-bank financial institution with outstanding Chinese characteristics. Finance companies were set up to support the establishment of "large companies and large group companies," a strategy implemented by Chinese government during the 1980s. On May 7, 1987, the People's Bank of China approved the establishment of Dong Feng Auto Industry Finance Company, which was the birth of finance companies of enterprise groups in China.

Development incentives

Since the 1980s, along with the gradual implementation of a policy for decentralization of governmental power and sharing of profits with corporations, a special-purpose funding system of enterprises was reformed, and enterprises obtained more autonomy in their capital deployment. Due to the expanding business scope and scale of enterprise groups, member companies had certain time differences in their respective funding needs due to different geographical locations and production cycles. Since enterprises were not allowed to borrow money from one another, a group company was unable to have a unified allocation of precipitation funds, resulting in poor capital use efficiency. Enterprise groups badly wanted to have an internal financial institution to help take advantages of the differences in location, time, industrial sector, and production process to enhance capital use efficiency in the group. However, the management system and service quality of the banking industry at that time were not able to satisfy demands from large enterprise groups for optimizing their internal capital deployment, enhancing capital use efficiency and other financial issues, so various non-bank financial institutions became the main power stimulating the diversification and development of China's financial market. Under such circumstances, some of the largest enterprises and enterprise groups began to establish internal financial institutions to serve themselves.

Scale of market

By the end of 2012, there were 148 finance companies in China with RMB 2.1 trillion in total assets, RMB 1.8 trillion total debts, RMB 295.3 billion in owner's equity, and RMB 46.4 billion in profits. The average non-performing asset ratio of the industry was 0.12%, and 122 financial companies had no non-performing assets. The average CAR was 25.74%, and the average liquidity ratio was 57.31%.

Risk characteristics

A finance company has the basic characteristics of a financial institution and strong features related to the industries of the group company. According to the *Core Principles for Effective Banking Regulations* issued by Basel Committee on Banking Supervision, financial risks of the banking industry include credit risks, sovereign and transfer risks, market risks, interest rate risks, liquidity risks, operational risks, legal risks, and reputation risks. As a non-bank financial institution, a finance company is faced with the aforementioned eight types of financial risks. Furthermore, due to its association with certain industries related to the businesses of its group company, a finance company has unique risks that are influenced significantly by the operation risks of its group companies, policy risks caused by relevant industrial and regulatory policies, as well as strategic risks of their own. Due to its industrial characteristics, a finance company will be affected directly or indirectly by many factors of the group company, including the latter's industrial features and development prospects, organizational structure and operational capacity, and external business environment.

Since its service scope is limited to within the group company, a finance company is faced with low credit risks. According to regulatory provisions, a finance company can only receive deposits from or provide loans to member companies of the group, resulting in far less information asymmetry than that of banks. Besides, finance companies have great influence with regard to the capital allocation and loans of the member companies. Member companies are unlikely to default, to commit frauds, or to escape from debt. Even if they fail to pay off the loans due to financial difficulties, the enterprise group can allocate capital to pay for its membership companies.[17]

Shadow banking determination

In terms of their current business model, risk profile, regulatory provisions, and other related aspects, finance companies are strictly regulated by the CBRC.

They conduct business within the enterprise group in general, and their parent companies bear the responsibilities of final rescues. Therefore, they are unlikely to cause systemic risks and are not shadow banking. Detailed explanations are given as follows:

1 A finance company collects temporarily idle capital of all companies in the group for optimized capital deployment to meet funding needs of the member companies.[18] Internal capital is the most important funding source for finance companies. The ratio between the deposits from internal membership companies and the total amount of debts is around 90%. Regulatory authorities strictly limit the external financing business of finance companies, that is, the aggregate amount of inter-financial company borrowing and the balance of guarantees should not exceed the aggregate amount of its total capital at any time.

2 Finance companies are closely regulated by the CBRC. According to their regulatory principles, "supervise legal entities, manage risks, regulate internal control, and enhance transparency," the CBRC focuses on risk regulation and has been improving both regulations and the regulatory system for finance companies. It has successively promulgated a series of laws and regulations concerning finance companies. To reinforce routine supervision, CBRC promulgated the *Tentative Measures on the Appraisal of Risk Regulation Index of Finance Companies of Enterprise Groups* based on *Measures on Administrating the Finance Companies of Enterprise Groups* and, by integrating the functions of finance companies and focusing on risk control, specified 11 regulatory parameters including the CAR, non-performing asset ratio, ratio of short- and long-term investments and liquidity ratio, as well as five regulation indexes such as loan-to-deposit ratio and profit margin. For specific issues relating to finance companies, CBRC issued the *Circular on Reminding Risks in Securities Investment Business of Finance Companies* and *Circular on Further Administering the Entrusted Business of Finance Companies of Enterprise Groups* to put forward formal requirements for high-risk business and promulgated the *Risk Appraisal of Finance Companies of Enterprise Groups and Guidance on Classified Regulation* to preliminarily set up a risk assessment system in line with characteristics of finance companies.[19]

Operational principles

1 Loans on one's own account refer to the loans lent to member companies of the group company according to the finance company's credit lending function. Today's loan business has always ranked at the top among the asset-side business of finance companies. Since all enterprises of the group have accumulated proprietary capital and temporarily idle funds, finance companies accomplish the optimization and integration of internal resources via their financial operation and a reasonable and efficient collection and allocation of capital within the group company. Finance companies provide capital to borrowers with an

interest rate and term as agreed, including short-, medium-, and long-term loans, but not including funds related to trade finance, factoring/discounting, and discounts related to buyouts.

2 Entrusted loans refer to loans issued by finance companies under the entrustment of certain member companies. Clients provide capital, while finance companies deploy and supervise the use of loans and assist in collecting the loans repayment in pursuant to the counter-party, use of funds, size, tenor, and interest rate of the loans. No advance capital from finance companies is allowed, and clients should assume the risks. Such loans are finance companies' off-balance sheet assets.

3 Investment refers to securities and long-term equity. Regulatory authorities allow such investment when there are stable deposits of funds after the group company's business funding needs are satisfied. Limited by the regulations, however, the total amount of investment of a finance company shall not be higher than 70% of its total capital.

Financial leasing companies

Historical development

Chinese financial leasing business started in the early phase of Reform and Opening Up. In July 1981, China Leasing Co., Ltd was established (it received its financial license in 1987). The period 1981–1988 is the initial period for the development of financial leasing industry, during which seven companies were established. In light of the social credit environment at that time, there were few non-performing leasing assets, the collection rate of lease payments was high, and the industry was in a stable condition. The period from 1989 to 1995 was a period of fast, even chaotic development. During those days, companies aggressively expanded business, absorbed deposits with high interest rates, and invested much in real estate and various industries, resulting in a large amount of non-performing assets and receivables for lease payments. By 1996, there were a total of 16 financial leasing companies approved by the People's Bank of China. The period from 1996 to 1999 was a period of overhaul. Hainan International Leasing Co., Ltd, Guangdong International Leasing Co., Ltd, Wuhan International Leasing Co., Ltd, and many other companies exited the market, and the remaining companies basically maintained the status quo. After 2000, with the promulgation of *Measures on Administering Financial Leasing Companies* and the improvement of legal and tax frameworks, the financial leasing industry revived and was faced with both development opportunities and risks. Meanwhile, the regulatory authorities were considering policies and measures to revive the industry and standardize its development. After 2007, the newly revised *Measures on the Administration of Financial Leasing Companies*[20] was promulgated to introduce commercial banks and other large corporate investors with genuine strength and demands into the financial leasing industry. The industry then stepped into favorable development—financial leasing companies rapidly grew, kept high capital adequacy and low non-performing leasing asset ratios—and showed progress in professionalism and specialization. By the end of June 2013, there were 22 financial leasing companies with a total AUM of RMB 900 billion, over 40 times assets in 2007.

Development incentives

Banks played a significant role in enhancing the overall development of the financial leasing industry and stimulating the sound development of financial leasing companies. In the *Measures on the Administration of Financial Leasing Companies*, revised by the CBRC in 2007, eligible commercial banks are approved to incorporate and/or become shareholders of financial leasing companies, bringing commercial banks back to the leasing industry again after more than a 10-year hiatus. The commercial banks have significantly stimulated the development of financial leasing industry and added major momentum to the industry. The experience of the financial leasing market in developed countries suggests that over 80% market share is held by those financial leasing companies with banks or manufacturing backgrounds. Such a condition is due to the unique advantages of banks and manufacturers. Banks have an advantage in their extensive client networks, in sharing bank's intangible assets, and enjoying a low cost of funds, while manufacturers have product know-how and an ability to deal with the residuals of leasing assets.

Scale of market

By the end of June 2013, there were 22 financial leasing companies in China. In terms of their shareholder background, 12 companies have bank backgrounds, 4 with asset management companies, and 6 with non-financial enterprises. The financial leasing companies had total assets of RMB 905.4 billion, total debts of RMB 805.4 billion, owner's equity of RMB 99.9 billion, and leasing assets of RMB 846.7 billion. With respect to leasing form, direct leasing occupied RMB 250.677 billion (making up approximately 30%) and leaseback RMB 596.094 billion (making up around 70%). By function, financial leasing occupied RMB 782.107 billion (making up around 92%) and operational leasing RMB 64.665 billion (making up 8%).

Risk profile

Financial leasing companies mainly adopt financial leasing for the financing of lessees. Different from conventional leasing, financial leasing companies are generally long-term investments, 3–5 years on average, and aim to satisfy medium- and long-term financing needs for lessees. Due to characteristics of such transaction structure, financial leasing companies are faced with credit risks arising from the inability of a lessee to make the leasing payments. With respect to capital source and usage of financial leasing companies, since the tenors of assets and debt are not completely matched, financial leasing companies may have financing difficulties or inadequate liquidity and are thus faced with liquidity risks. Meanwhile, the lease belongs to the lessor, which puts the lessor at risk of market value decreases and depreciation.

Those lessors, especially those running the operational lease, are thus faced with considerable asset risks. To be specific, the main risks faced by financial leasing companies are credit, liquidity, and asset risk.

The credit risk faced by financial leasing companies mainly depends on the lessee's operating condition, profitability, industry, and the macroeconomic environment. By the end of June 2013, the non-performing asset ratio of financial leasing companies was 0.44%, and the provision coverage ratio was 359.78%. Generally speaking, credit risks are controllable and financial leasing companies have a strong capacity for risk prevention and control.

For the industry as a whole, due to limited financing channels, financial leasing companies generally lend long term and borrow short term. Assets and debt maturity are seriously mismatched. Financial leasing companies face huge liquidity management pressure. By the end of June 2013, the 1-month liquidity ratio of financial leasing companies was 67.02%.

1   Asset risk. Different from bank loans, the lessor enjoys the ownership of the lease. It thus faces certain asset risks. In the operating leasing business in particular, the lease has a high residual value and much influenced by factors like market prices and technical changes. Influenced by international financial crisis and the adjustment and transformation in economic structure, leases in some industries like airplane, ship making, and engineering machinery with concentrated leasing business of financial leasing companies face downward pressure and certain asset risks. In addition, the lack of the financial leasing registration system in China indicates that lessors can hardly secure against third parties who obtain the lease by the *Law of Property*, so they face risks arising from malicious disposal of the lease by the lessee.

Financial leasing companies run a more simple business with less operational risk. They cannot invest in stocks, bonds, futures, or derivatives, so there is almost no market risk. The cross-border leasing business, with limited volume of business, faces with limited sovereign risks.

Determination of shadow banking

1   Financial leasing companies have some shadow banking characteristics. First, as for maturity mismatch, financial leasing companies have substantial short-term liabilities, while they have plenty of medium- and long-term leasing assets. The assets and liabilities could have serious maturity mismatch. But as their financing options increased through issuing bonds, financial leasing companies can better control their maturity mismatch. The second characteristic is liquidity risk. Financial leasing companies, due to their narrow financing channels, have limited liquidity management tools and obtain capital mainly through bank loans and interbank borrowings, which results in maturity mismatch and liquidity risks. The third is hidden credit risks. When transferring receivables from financial leases to commercial banks, financial leasing companies, according

to relevant regulation, should abide by the principle of clean transfer in order to realize the actual and complete transfer of assets and risks. Transferors are not allowed to offer explicit or implicit repurchase clauses. Financial leasing companies have no off-balance sheet business, so they do not hide credit risks. The fourth is high leverage. As non-bank financial institutions, financial leasing companies usually have a leverage ratio of 11%, higher than industrial and commercial enterprises but similar to other financial institutions. The average CAR is around 12%, higher than the required 8%. With the implementation of new regulation, financial leasing companies will be subject to higher capital requirements as time goes by.

2 The CBRC has adopted prudential regulation for financial leasing companies. According to the principle of strict risk-oriented regulation and the regulatory standards of commercial banks, CBRC has set up a complete prudential regulation system to target financial leasing companies. The regulatory system effectively covers various risks in daily operation, such as credit risk, liquidity risk, market risk, and operation risk through market entry, off-site regulation, and on-site inspection to stimulate the steady development of financial leasing companies.

The CBRC regulates financial leasing companies in the following aspects: the first is regulation of market entry. The CBRC has strict regulation over the market entry for institutions, business, and senior management. *Measures on Administering Financial Leasing Companies* provided a set of systematic regulations in terms of financial leasing company incorporation, change, operation, and supervision. For example, the major shareholders of a financial leasing company must satisfy certain legal and regulatory criteria. Second, The CBRC adopts a prudential off-site supervision over financial leasing companies. To monitor CAR, new measures require financial leasing companies following the standard of 10.5% also implemented for banks. The *Measures on Administering Financial Leasing Companies* states explicitly that the concentration and relevancy ratios for a single client shall not exceed 30% of the net capital, the relevancy ratio for group client shall not exceed 50% of net capital, and the ratio of interbank lending shall not exceed 100% of the net capital.

The CBRC also requires financial leasing companies to adopt the five-class classification system for risky assets in the same manner as that for commercial banks. Additionally, the CBRC requires financial leasing companies to have adequate provisions for non-performing assets and set out clear limits for provisioning coverage, provision-to-loan, and other ratios. In daily off-site supervision, the CBRC monitors the liquidity, liquidity gap, and other ratios to actively mitigate maturity mismatch and liquidity risk. Third, the CBRC conducts ad hoc on-site inspections at financial leasing companies. According to the problems and risks detected in the off-site supervision, the CBRC makes reasonable allocation of regulatory resources, conducts high-frequency inspections for high-risk companies and low-frequency inspection for low-risk companies, sends risk warnings, and investigates illegal behaviors strictly to push financial leasing companies to operate in compliance with laws and regulations.

Under the prudential supervision of the CBRC, financial leasing companies are also covered in the unified loan limit required by the People's Bank of China. They are required to control the scale of financial leasing business. Financial leasing companies do not conduct off-balance sheet business, so there is no circumvention or arbitrage of regulations. With respect to shareholders' backgrounds, leasing companies with banking backgrounds make up around 80% of the total AUM. These companies are strictly regulated by the CBRC, and the parent bank must consolidate the subsidiary leasing company in its financial statements and reinforce the risk management of the leasing company through credit policies and client rating. Some leasing companies are even covered in the unified authorization system of their parent banks.

In conclusion, under the CBRC's strict regulation, financial leasing companies, thanks to small scale and steady operation, will not lead to systematic risks and are not shadow banking.

Operational principles

1 Direct lease. The financial leasing company, based on the lessee's and supplier's choices, leases assets from suppliers as agreed in the contract. It then collects lease payments from the lessee.

   For example, a printing firm needs to invest in advanced production equipment, but due to insufficient capital, it cannot make the purchase without loans. The printing firm applies to the financial leasing companies to lease the equipment. The financial leasing company, according to the manufacturer and equipment type chosen by the printing firm, directly purchases the equipment from the manufacturer, leases it to the printing firm and charges lease payments after the financial leasing company acquires the ownership. As the lease expires, the printing firm may purchase the production line equipment at an agreed price and acquire the ownership in the end.

2 Leaseback. The lessor (the supplier in the meantime) sells the asset to a financial leasing company and collects the sale price. Meanwhile, the lessee signs a financial leasing contract with the financial leasing company to lease back the asset in exchange for lease payments.

   For example, a machine tool manufacturer sells one of its pieces of processing equipment to a financial leasing company to recapitalize such equipment for funding. Based on the equipment's evaluation, the financial leasing company pays a price and acquires ownership. Meanwhile, the financial leasing company signs a leasing agreement with the manufacturer to lease the equipment to the manufacturer. After the lease expires, the financial leasing company transfers ownership of the equipment at an agreed price to the manufacturer.

3 Vendor leasing. In vendor leasing, a financial leasing company and an equipment manufacturer or its leasing subsidiary come into a strategic marketing alliance. For clients who need the manufacturer's products through leasing, the financial leasing company leases the equipment as a strategic alliance with

the equipment manufacturer. Both sides make arrangements for mutual benefit in aspects such as equipment price, profit distribution, lessor risk management, and lease disposal. In this way, it integrates the equipment manufacturer's client resources, marketing network, and risk management platform with the funding capacity of the financial leasing company to boost the sales for the equipment manufacturer and satisfy the manufacturer's needs for funding.

In another example, an engineering equipment manufacturer enters into a strategic partnership with a financial leasing company to boost sales and accelerate capital recovery. The financial leasing company signs a leasing agreement with the lessee, who is in a client list provided by the manufacturer, provided the lessee is qualified according to the leasing company's evaluation. The leasing company purchases the equipment from the manufacturer and leases it to the lessee. Meanwhile, the financial leasing company requires the manufacturer to provide credit enhancement such as repurchase guarantees so that if the lessee breach the leasing agreement, the manufacturer must compensate the leasing company.

The financial leasing business is similar to traditional commercial banking business in respect to its economic function. It satisfies client financing demands. Financial leasing is, however, something unique. Financial leasing integrates financing and lease, and companies obtain financing through leasing. Financial leasing companies own the lease and enjoy stronger control over the equipment, which enhances risk mitigation and reduces requirements for credit enhancement such as collateralization. Meanwhile, the more flexible repayment schedule and the higher LTV satisfy diversified demands of medium- and small-sized enterprises and other clients.

Development trends

Financial leasing has grown rapidly over the years. In particular, pilot financial leasing companies set up by commercial banks boosted development of the whole industry and enjoyed more market recognition. Currently, China is in a key phase of economic transformation and upgrading, and enterprises have abundant demands for equipment investments. As an important way of equipment financing, financial leasing helps boost the investment as well as domestic demands and enhance both technical development and the product sales. In such a macroeconomic environment, financial leasing companies have great potential and room for further development. However, in the meantime, financial leasing companies also face some challenges such as incomplete tax policies, incomplete legal environment, incomplete international accounting principles, and low market recognition. To boost the development of financial leasing companies, the policy environment needs to be further improved. Also, the financial leasing companies need to enhance their professional ability and core competency to serve the economy.

International comparison

The modern financial leasing industry originated in the United States. After decades of development, it has become an important equipment financing method worldwide. The penetration ratio of financial leasing in developed countries in Europe and America is around 20%, and financial leasing is second only to bank loans for equipment investments. With respect to shareholder backgrounds, the financial leasing companies can globally be divided into three categories: those with a banking background, those with a manufacturing background, and independent enterprises. Leasing companies with a banking background have already become the major participants in the industry owing to their parent banks' advantages in market, clients, assets, and risk management. Over 10 out of 15 major financial leasing companies in Europe have a banking background. In China, leasing companies with the banking background also act as major participants in the industry.

Auto and consumer finance companies

Historical development

When China entered the World Trade Organization (WTO) in 2001, it promised to approve foreign-owned non-bank financial institutions to develop an automobile consumer loan business without any limits in terms of market entry and company nationality. To fulfill the aforementioned commitment, a new type of institution should be added to Chinese financial institutions exclusively for the automobile consumer loan business. Since its founding in 2003, the CBRC conducted thorough research on the domestic and overseas markets and ran studies on the successful operation and risk management of overseas auto finance companies. After taking consideration of the practical condition in the domestic market, the CBRC formulated the *Measures on the Administration of Auto Finance Companies* that was officially enacted and implemented in October 2003 after approval of the State Council. This new type of financial institutions enriched the organizational structure of the Chinese financial system (Appendix). In August 2004, the CBRC approved the establishment of GMAC-SAIC Automotive Finance Company Ltd, the first Sino-foreign joint auto finance company, symbolizing a start to China's auto finance industry with diversified market competition.

China has fewer financial institutions engaging in consumer lending business than developed countries, less consumer loan participation, and fewer products. The traditional business mainly focuses on mortgage loans, car loans, and credit cards, which are insufficient to satisfy the demands for financial services from a vast amount of consumers. In particular, there is a lack of consumer finance products and service systems that target middle- and low-income consumer groups. On July 22, 2009, CBRC publicized the *Pilot Administrative Measures for Consumer Finance Companies* and initiated the approval of consumer finance company incorporations. In 2013, to implement requirements set out in *Guiding Opinions of the General Office of the State Council on Financial Support for Adjusting, Transitioning and Upgrading the*

Economic Structure (No. [2013]67 of GOSC), CBRC summarized its pilot experience over past 3 years, extensively solicited public opinions, and revised and completed the *Pilot Administrative Measures for Consumer Finance Companies* which was publicized on November 22, 2013, and came into effect on January 1, 2014.

Development motivation

It is a global trend to develop auto finance companies. At present, automobile financial service has become the core driving force and major profit contributor for the development of auto companies. Over the years, the auto industry value chain has been fundamentally changed all over the world. Due to the shrinking profits of finished automobiles, automobile financial services have become the most important link in the auto industry value chain. According to international experience, even when the production profit margin of automobile manufacturers reduces to 3%–5%, the profit margin of automobile financial business has stayed around 30%. Automobile finance does not suffer from the auto production cycle, making it a "growth support line" for automobile production. All the world's largest auto groups have their own financial platforms to provide dedicated and comprehensive financial services for their affiliated vehicle brands.

When China entered the WTO, it promised to open the auto finance market, which is a significant step. It helped to change the Chinese traditional auto industry's myopic focus only on auto manufacturing, stimulated the organic integration between auto finance and auto manufacturing, and extended the industrial value chain and its further development. The introduction of world's famous auto finance companies brings successful ideas and advanced professional managerial techniques. The integration between the auto industry and financial service makes a profound difference and boosts the development of both auto finance and the auto industry. Auto finance companies diversify competition among the consumer finance market and improve the professionalism of auto financial services. Auto finance companies promote auto sales, stimulate consumption, and boost the development of the auto industry.

Consumer finance companies

To implement the strategic guidelines of the central government to further expand domestic demand and boost economic growth, consumer finance companies encourage consumption demand and reinforce the impetus of consumption to economic growth by providing more financial services. Setting up new financial institutions like consumer finance companies is a significant endeavor. First, it helps boost the economic transformation from a simple dependence upon investment and export to a coordinated dependence upon investment, exports and consumption, so as to further implement the central government's strategic guideline of expanding domestic demands and boost economic growth. Second, it helps improve China's financial system, enriching financial institutions and boosting the innovation of financial products. Third, it helps provide alternative financial services for individual clients who have not benefited from commercial banks. It thus satisfies various demands from consumer groups and raises their living standards.

Market scale

Through its 8-year development, the AUM of auto finance companies grew rapidly, the capital quality stayed high, and profitability rose. Gradually, auto finance companies are becoming major participants in the Chinese auto finance market. By the end of December 2012, a total of 16 auto finance companies were approved to incorporate in China. The total assets in the industry were worth RMB 191.5 billion, the total debts were RMB 165.5 billion, shareholder's equity was RMB 26 billion, and after-tax net profit for the whole year was RMB 3.1 billion. The overall asset quality was in good condition. The non-performing asset ratio of the whole industry was 0.65%, average CAR was 15.27%, and liquidity ratio was 279.94%.

Until the end of June 2013, the total assets of all auto finance companies were RMB 220.2 billion, total debts were RMB 187.5 billion, shareholder's equity was RMB 32.7 billion and after-tax net profit of the year was RMB 2.4 billion. The overall asset quality is in a good condition. The non-performing asset ratio of the whole industry was 0.60%, average CAR was 16.50%, and the liquidity ratio was 201.01%.

Currently, consumer finance companies are in a pilot phase. The first batch of four pilot consumer finance companies opened in 2010, and the industry has run well. Companies keep exploring a professional consumption financial model suitable for China, innovate in company management, risk management, client cultivation, and product development, and accumulate abundant experience for promotion in other cities. After the implementation of the revised *Pilot Administrative Measures for Consumer Finance Companies* in 2013, the State Council approved another 10 cities—Shenyang, Nanjing, Hangzhou, Hefei, Quanzhou, Wuhan, Guangzhou, Chongqing, Xi'an, and Qingdao—to set up pilot consumer finance companies. In addition, according to the *Closer Economic Partnership Arrangement*, qualified financial institutions in Hong Kong and Macao are allowed to set up pilot consumer finance companies in Guangdong Province (including Shenzhen). According to the principle of "one company for one place," 12 pilot institutions can be added.

Until the end of December 2012, the total assets of the consumer finance industry were RMB 4.6 billion, total debts were RMB 3.1 billion, owner's equity was RMB 1.4 billion, and after-tax net profit for the whole year was RMB 66.4 million. This marked the first time that the industry as a whole made a profit. The overall asset quality was in good condition. The non-performing asset ratio was 0.62%, average CAR was 33.20%, and liquidity ratio was 129.32%.

Until to the end of June 2013, the total assets of all consumer finance companies were RMB 7.8 billion, total debts were RMB 5.2 billion, owner's equity was RMB 2.5 billion, and after-tax net profit from January to June 2013 was RMB 110 million. The overall asset quality remains in a good condition. The non-performing asset ratio of the whole industry was 1.15%, average CAR was 36.96%, and liquidity ratio was 600.76%.

Risk profile

Similar to other financial institutions being engaged in loan business, auto finance companies and consumer finance companies are faced with credit, liquidity, market, and operational risks.

The credit risk of retail loans issued by auto finance companies and consumer finance companies is mainly default risk arising from changes in retail clients' willingness to pay, income, and other factors. For example, credit risk in auto finance companies' dealership loans is mainly default risk arising from changes in auto manufacturing, auto sales, and economic conditions, which may cause a deterioration of dealers' business conditions. As non-bank financial institutions engaging in the consumer lending business, these two types of finance companies are more sensitive than banks to the industry concentration ratio and market fluctuations in specific industries. However, they do have an edge on professional risk management and financial service ability due to the support from manufacturers (for auto finance companies) or the close partnership with retailers (for consumer finance companies). For the time being, they have fairly good quality assets and sufficient provision, and credit risks are under control.

For liquidity, mainly finance through debt maturing is in 1 year, but auto finance companies and consumer finance companies mainly extend retail loans with a tenor of 2–3 years. This does lead to maturity mismatch between assets and liabilities to some extent. Nevertheless, the overall liquidity risk in this industry is still at a low level and is controlled mainly by sufficient bank financing reserves and strict daily liquidity supervision. Furthermore, retail loans have stable repayment cycles and thus bring steady cash flows. The liability of this industry is also different from that of bank deposits. It has specific paydays and is active borrowing. When facing financing difficulties, the companies could adjust their credit rating scale to deal with the maturity mismatch issue. As medium- and long-term direct financing channels such as financial bond issuance and assets securitization have expanded, the two types of finance companies will further improve their financing structure and alleviate their potential liquidity risk arising from the maturity mismatch.

Market risk mainly consists of interest rate risk due to the lack of foreign business. As most auto finance and consumer finance companies issue floating rate loans with a repricing interval of less than 1 month, but external financing is basically fixed-interest rate interbank borrowing, there is a mismatch in interest rate interval between interest-earning assets and interest-bearing liabilities. However, with a small interest rate repricing gap, the interest rate risk is low.

With respect to operational risk, the two types of finance companies have kept their operational risk under control due to effective corporate management and internal control, as well as refined risk management. As business expands, operational risk is on the rise, which has been led to concern by the companies and regulatory authorities. According to *Administrative Measure on the Capital of Commercial Banks (Trial Implementation)* implemented from January 1, 2013, the two types of finance companies should set aside operational risk reserves to better cover potential losses from operational risk.

Characteristics of shadow banking

Although such companies have characteristics of shadow banking with respect to maturity mismatch, liquidity risk, and leverage due to the lack of stable medium- and long-term financing channels, they are under the strict prudential risk-based supervision by the CBRC. This is similar to that carried out with commercial banks, so they are not shadow banking. To be specific: With respect to maturity mismatch and liquidity risk, as stated above, the two types of finance companies engage in retail loans with a tenor of 2–3 years, while their liabilities business is mainly bank financing with a term around 1 year. They lack stable medium- and long-term financing sources. Therefore, there are potential liquidity risk and maturity mismatch between assets and liabilities. Nevertheless, the risks are generally at a low level, and liquidity risk will be under more effective control with the diversification of financing sources.

These two types of finance company comply with the same CAR requirement as non-core commercial banks do, but upon more prudent supervision in routine regulation. As a result, the leverage level of these finance companies is significantly lower than that of commercial banks.

With respect to hidden credit risk, the business model of these finance companies precludes the concealment of credit risk, unlike banks. As stated above, as professional financial institutions, they have effectively controlled the credit risk of the related loan business with professionalism and careful management. With respect to the effectiveness of regulation, for the time being, the CBRC adopts prudent risk-based supervision for auto finance and consumer finance companies, carries out strict off-site monitoring and on-site inspection polices for corporate governance, internal control, CARs, leverage ratios, credit and concentration risk, liquidity risk, market risk, operational risk, and other risks. It also conducts regular risk assessment with reference to relevant standards for commercial banks. For example, the major indices/ratios for monitoring auto finance companies include: CAR no lower than 8%, core CAR no lower than 4%, credit balance of a single borrower no higher than 15% of the auto finance companies' net capital, credit balance of a single group client no higher than 50% of the auto finance companies' net capital, credit balance of a single shareholder together with its affiliates no higher than the contribution amount of the shareholder in the auto finance company, and the fixed assets for its own use no higher than 40% of the auto finance companies' net capital. Major indices/ratios for monitoring consumer finance companies include: CAR no lower than 10%, inter-bank borrowing ratio no higher than 100% of total capital, loss reserve ratio no lower than 100% and investment balance no higher than 20% of total capital. Monitoring indices/ratios for both types of finance companies include non-performing loan ratio, loan loss reserve adequacy ratio, provision coverage ratio, provision-loan ratio, liquidity ratio, liquidity gap ratio, and interest rate risk sensitivity.

Operation mechanism

The main business of auto finance companies include dealers' auto inventory loans (financing provided by auto finance companies for dealers to purchase vehicle inventory for sale), individual auto loans (loans issued by auto finance companies for individuals and institutions to purchase cars) and auto finance leases (auto finance companies purchase cars as required by the lessee and lease the cars to the lessee for use).

First, we examine the steps involved in dealer auto inventory loans:

- Approval prior to loan issuance, including collection of information related to the dealer.
- Lending officials conduct on-site information collection and verification.
- Inquire and verify relevant information through loan records and the credit reference system of the People's Bank of China.
- Analyze dealer financial data by inputting dealer's key index in the credit rating system to score the dealer.
- Refer to the qualitative analysis result and complete the dealer's credit assessment report.
- The credit committee (or the board of directors) makes final decision on the credit quota according to committee's authority.

For controls during the lending process:

- Dealer applies for car purchase to the manufacturer
- Manufacturer receives application and sends relevant information to the auto finance company through the system
- Finance company runs a check on the dealer's credit quota in the loan management system
- System decides to release loans automatically if the dealer's request is within its available quota.

For post-lending management:

- According to agreement, the dealer repay through a dedicated repayment system on the second day after car is sold.
- Auto finance company releases the original credit quota upon repayment.
- Auto finance company checks the inventory (frequency depends on the dealer's rating and the risk condition).
- In the case of late repayment, fraud, or other material misbehaviors, the auto finance company will penalize the dealer accordingly, for example, reduce the credit quota, increase the proportion of cash deposit, or even terminate the credit.

Now we turn to individual car loans:

- Client examines stock at a dealer.
- Decision to purchase a request loan.

- Financing insurance manager trained by the auto finance company submits loan application form and identity information to the company through an online application system.
- Finance company verifies information through a comprehensive credit system.
- Applicant is graded, and system makes decisions on credit with telephone interview or on-site investigation and gives feedback to the client through the dealer.
- Upon client agreement, manager signs loan contract and sends the video of contract signing to the auto finance company.
- Company verifies client information and releases the funds to the dealer.
- Client obtains the car from the dealer.
- The dealer assists the client with the mortgage registration.
- For all the pledged cars, at least the following three types of insurance are required: vehicle damage insurance, third-party liability insurance, and robbery and theft insurance.
- The client repays auto finance company as agreed in the loan contract, and the finance company has set up departments exclusively responsible for the post-lending verification, management, and collection.

Third, we look at automobile financial leasing. The business flows are similar to those of individual car loans, but the difference lies in car ownership. In the automobile financial leasing business, the auto finance company retains ownership of the car. After the company purchases the car and leases it to the lessee, the lessee must make the lease payments on time to the company. For the time being, due to the lack of financial leasing car registration system in China, no Chinese auto finance companies currently engage in this business.

On the other hand, consumer finance companies mainly issue individual consumption loans. The individual consumption loan of consumer finance companies is similar to the individual car loan of auto finance companies in its business pattern. The only difference is that the individual consumption loans of consumer finance companies are mainly credit loans without pledged collateral or other guarantees.

Development trend

At present, the GDP per capita of China has already exceeded US$ 6,000, which is solidly in the middle-income category. There is great room for a rise in consumption. More people also accept the idea of consumption on credit. As the Chinese economy develops in a continuous and sound way, the income distribution and social security system is continuously being improved, so citizens' consumption level keeps rising. China's consumer finance market has promising prospects for further development. Auto finance companies and consumer finance companies will continue their rapid growth. Since these companies satisfy consumers' diversified needs for consumption credit and have increasing shares in China's credit market, they will be an important force in years to come.

International comparison

The basic business scope and pattern of Chinese auto finance companies are similar to those of main auto finance companies in the rest of the world. Both of them issue dealer's auto inventory car loans, individual car loans, automobile financial leasing, and other products. While both cannot take public deposits, they have distinct differences with respect to financing channels. The capital market in countries in Europe and the United States is developed, so the financing channels for auto finance companies are mainly direct financing such as bill issuance, bonds, and asset securitization. In China there are prudent, strict stipulations on the loan issuance of auto finance companies, the asset securitization is still in the pilot phase, and Chinese auto finance companies still finance through interbank borrowings. With respect to regulation, as non-bank financial institutions, Chinese auto finance companies are under strict supervision by financial regulatory authorities similar to those for commercial banks, while in other countries such as the United States, such finance companies are not subject to such strict regulation.

Chinese consumer finance companies are similar to the main consumer finance companies in the rest of the world in the business pattern for the time being. But since Chinese consumer finance companies are still in a pilot stage, they have a narrower business scope than that of foreign companies and are not allowed to provide housing loans, car loans, and individual business loans. Differences in financing channels and regulation are similar with the condition of auto finance companies stated earlier.

Conclusions

As analyzed earlier, bank WM, trust WM, securities WM, funds WM, insurance WM, and financial companies (finance companies, financial leasing companies, auto finance companies, and consumer finance companies) have characteristics of maturity transformation, transfer of liquidity, credit risk transfer, and high leverage to different extents, but regulatory institutions have formulated a set of regulatory measures such as net capital administration, risk capital control, strict information disclosure, and approval and registration of product issuance. Regulators also promulgated a series of timely rules, regulations, and standards to respond to market demands and set out regulatory measures with clear targets customized to various business sectors. For example, for finance companies, auto finance companies, financial leasing companies, and consumer finance companies, the CBRC applies regulatory means similar to those that apply to banks and sets out stipulations regarding capital adequacy and other ratios. For trust companies, the CBRC applies regulatory policies stricter than those adopted by other regulatory authorities overseas. It adopts regulation for net capital and disapproves any liability. There is no operational leverage. With respect to the practical operation effect, bank WM, trust WM, securities WM, funds WM, insurance WM, and financial companies are under the strict, systematic supervision of the CBRC, CSRC, and CIRC and are in a stable operation. They do not pose systemic risk to Chinese financial markets. Therefore, they are not shadow banking in the narrow sense.

Notes

1 The data are quoted from *China Securities Journal*, January 29, 2013.
2 The data are quoted from *Financial Times*, August 5, 2013.
3 The data are quoted from *Financial Times*, August 1, 2013.
4 See Section 3 of the *Report on the Development of China's Security Industry (2013): Review in the Development in 2012 and Prospective of Asset Management Business of Chinese Securities Firms.* www.sac.net.cn/was5/web/pdfbook/jsp
5 For example, until February 2013, the annual interest rate paid by commercial banks to depositors was only 3%, while the consumer price index (CPI) during the same period rose by 3.2%, suggesting bank deposits cause shrinkage in real individual assets.
6 See Sub-Report III of the Report on the Development of the China Securities Industry (2013): the Review and Outlook on the Development of Assets Management Business of China's Securities Firms in 2012, http://www.sac.net.cn/was5/web/pdfbook.jsp
7 Data are quoted from SAC website http://www.sac.net.cn/hysj/zqgsjysj
8 *Guidelines on the Content and Format of Asset Management Contracts of Fund Management Companies for Individual Clients* and *Guidelines on the Content and Format of Asset Management Contracts of Fund Management Companies for Designated Multiple Clients.*
9 *Trial Measures for Fund Management Companies' Asset Management Services for Designated Clients, Provisions on the Relevant Issues Concerning the Implementation of the Trial Measures for Fund Management Companies' Asset Management Services for Designated Clients, Provisions on Issues Concerning the Asset Management Services Provided by Fund Management Companies for Several Specific Clients, Guidelines on the Content and Format of Specific Client Asset Management Contracts and Guidelines on the Content and Format of Asset Management Contracts of Fund Management Companies for Designated Multiple Clients.*
10 10Data are quoted from the website of AMAC, www.amac.org.cn/tjsj/sysj
11 1Participating insurance is the type of insurance in which policyholders share operating results with insurance companies. Insurance companies distribute the divisible surplus, the margin between practical operating results and the prices, among policyholders in a certain proportion. Applicants can have the insurance benefits stipulated in the conventional policies and also share in the operating results of insurance companies.
12 Investment-linked insurance is a new type of life insurance product issued by insurance companies. It integrates guarantee and investment functions. It is closely related to the capital market and keeps pace with it. The development of investment-linked insurance is challenging because of fluctuations in capital markets.
13 Universal life insurance is a new type of life insurance product issued by insurance companies that is between participating insurance and investment-linked insurance. It also integrates guarantee and investment functions. It is better than the participating insurance yet inferior to the investment-linked insurance with respect to the investment function; with minimum return guaranteed, it is one kind of savings product.
14 Before the new insurance regulation was enacted in 2012, as professional asset management institutions set up by insurance companies and supervised by the CIRC, insurance asset management companies engaged in entrusted management of insurance capital of the group companies and third-party insurance companies, issuance of infrastructure bond investment plans, and asset management products for subscription of the group companies or parent companies, and investment-linked insurance management service for insurance companies. Insurance asset management companies generally purchase stocks and funds for groups and medium- and small-sized insurance companies in the management of the insurance capital business entrusted by the group companies and third-party insurance companies.
15 The financing products independently issued temporarily by insurance asset management companies are only bond investment plans and insurance capital management products. Bond investment plans refer to financial products with professional management institutions such as insurance asset management companies as the trustee, and in accordance

with *Trial Measures for the Administration of the Indirect Investment of Insurance Funds in Infrastructure Projects* (No. [2006]1 of CIRC), *Guidelines for the Administration of the Indirect Investment of Insurance Funds in Infrastructure Bond Investment Plans (Trail Implementation)* (No. [2007] 53 of CIRC) and other regulatory rules, that issue beneficiary certificates to clients (inbound insurance companies, insurance group companies and insurance holding companies), raise capital to invest in infrastructure projects through loans, and pay the prospected returns and redeem principal as agreed.

16 The balance of bond investment plans of life insurance companies generally should not exceed 6% of the overall assets at the end of the previous quarter. The corresponding figure for asset insurance companies is 4%, and the investment balance of single bond investment plans should not exceed 40% of assets of investible bond investment plans. Shares of a single bond investment plan invested in A-type or B-type enhancement should not exceed 50% of the issuance amount of the investment plan. Shares of a single bond investment plan invested in C-type enhancement should not exceed 40% of the issuance amount of the investment plan. Total shares invested by insurance companies of the same group in single bond plans issued by affiliated professional management institutions should not exceed 60% of the issuance amount of the investment plans.

17 As stipulated in Article 8 of *Measures on Administrating the Finance Companies of Enterprise Groups*, when applying for the establishment of a financial company, the board of directors of parent company shall promise, in writing, to increase the capital fund in light of the practical needs to solve payment issues when such emergency happens to the finance company. This is stated clearly in the articles of association.

18 As stipulated in *Measures on Administrating the Finance Companies of Enterprise Groups*, financial companies are allowed to operate 15 items of business: (1) financial and financing consulting, credit verification and relevant consulting, and agency business for member units; (2) to assist member units in receipt and payment of trading funds; (3) approved insurance agency business; (4) guarantees for member units; (5) entrusted loans and investments among member units; (6) bill acceptance and bill discount for member units; (7) internal transfer settlement among member units and related settlement and liquidation plan design; (8) to absorb deposits of member units; (9) loans and financing rental for member units; (10) inter-financial company borrowing; (11) to issue bonds of financial companies as approved; (12) to sell corporate bonds of member units as agent; (13) equity investment in financial institutions; (14) investment of negotiable securities; and (15) consumption credit of products of member units as well as credit and financing rental of the buyer.

19 Regulation index of finance companies are as follows: capital adequacy ratio shall not be lower than 10%; non-performing asset ratio not higher than 4%; non-performing loan ratio not higher than 5%; asset impairment allocation adequacy ratio not lower than 100%; loan impairment allocation adequacy ratio not lower than 100%; liquidity ratio not lower than 25%; self-owned fixed asset ratio not higher than 20%; short-term securities investment ratio not higher than 40%; long-term investment ratio not higher than 30%; borrowing fund not higher than 100%; guarantee ratio not higher than 100%.

20 Referring to the experience of developed countries, the CBRC revised *Measures on the Administration of Financial Leasing Companies* in 2007 to set up a system of main contributors. It is expressly specified that new financial leasing companies shall have main contributors who can only be eligible banks, leasing companies, manufacturers, and eligible financial institutions approved by the CBRC. In this way, institutions with genuine strength and demands are introduced to the leasing industry, laying a solid systemic foundation for the sound, rapid growth of the industry.

4 Research on quasi-financial institutions and their businesses

Regulation by ministries, commissions, and local governments

In addition to the financial institutions and businesses regulated by the "Three Commissions," we need to pay close attention to the quasi-financial institutions and their businesses regulated by the People's Bank of China (PBOC), the Ministry of Commerce, the National Development and Reform Commission, other government agencies, and local regulators. Such quasi-financial institutions include mainly pawn companies, guarantee companies, financial leasing companies, private equity (PE) companies, small loan companies, and financial asset exchanges.

Pawn companies

Historical development

In China, pawning is an old industry with a history of over 2,000 years. "First we have pawning, then banking emerges." Pawning may be the earliest type of financial institution in Chinese history. Historical records indicate that the organized pawn industry started during the Southern and Northern Dynasties. Thereafter, we may find relevant records about pawn in the literature of every dynasty. Throughout history, we found that temples originally organized the pawn business as a charity intended to help the poor and to provide disaster relief. Then it became a for-profit industry favored by the government and businessmen. In the Tang Dynasty, in addition to the temple-run pawn business, the pawn industry may be classified into governmental and private pawning. The economic prosperity of the Tang Dynasty set up a foundation for the development of this industry. Thereafter, the continuous development of commerce in the Song, Yuan, Ming, and Qing Dynasties led to the unprecedented prosperity of the pawn industry. At the time of the late Qing Dynasty and the early Republic of China, the emergence of modern financial institutions restricted the development of the pawn industry to certain extent, and the pawn business gradually lost its mainstream status, taking a new place as a supplement to modern financial institutions.

The 1950s witnessed the socialist transformation from capitalist industry and commerce. The Chinese pawn industry followed the new government policy of joint ventures between public and private businesses and then disappeared in mainland China soon after. After China's Reform and Opening Up, the focus of the party and government shifted toward economic development. As the commodity economy and market economy gradually developed, there were growing needs for small loans. On December 30, 1987, the Chengdu Huamao Pawn Service Firm was established in Sichuan province, which took the lead in restoring the old pawn business. Subsequently, pawnshops became available nationwide. According to statistics, during the 8 years, from 1987 to 1995, over 3,000 pawn companies were established under the approval of different governmental agencies in various regions.

From 1987 to April 1996, the pawn industry showed signs of disordered development and chaotic mismanagement under multiple and duplicated regulatory frameworks. On May 30, 1995, the Ministry of Public Security (MPS) issued the *Measures for Security Administration of Pawn Industry* (No. [1995]26 of the MPS). On April 3, 1996, upon the approval of the State Council, the pawn industry was put under the regulation of the PBOC nationwide, and the PBOC issued the *Provisional Measures for Administration of Pawn Industry* (No. [1996]3 of the PBOC), which specified clear regulations for the pawn companies' capital requirements, pricing, loan rate, fees, maturity, business scope, and other areas. Based on such regulations, the PBOC cleaned up and overhauled the pawn industry nationwide; 1,154 pawn companies survived this process.

In August 2000, the State Council recognized the need for the financial system reform and transferred the regulatory authority for the pawn industry to the State Economic and Trade Commission (SETC). Since then, pawn companies lost their qualification as financial institutions and were classified as "special industrial and commercial enterprises." The SETC issued the amended *Measures for Administration of Pawn Industry*, which simplified the administrative approval procedure and enlarged the business scope of pawn companies. Its major terms included the following:

1   permitted pawn companies to operate pawns for mortgages and the sale service, verification service, evaluation service, and consulting service relating to the terminated pawn items, within a limited price range;
2   permitted pawn companies to operate with debt and to establish branches;
3   lowered barrier of entry;
4   classified registered capital requirements into two categories, increasing flexibility;
5   abolished the provision that individual shareholder can hold no more than 25% of a pawn company's total shares.

In 2003, after the dissolution of SETC, the incorporation approval and daily regulation of pawn companies were transferred to the Ministry of Commerce. On February 9, 2005, the Ministry of Commerce and MPS jointly issued the *Measures for Administration of the Pawn Business* (effective on April 1, 2005), which was composed of 9 chapters and 73 articles. After its implementation, China's pawn industry entered a new stage of fast and healthy development. Thereafter, the number of pawn companies increased, industrial power was further enhanced, business scale rose, and business structure adjusted continuously with the nation's economic development. The pawn industry's contribution to the society and economy, with its function of providing "fast, easy, and short-term" loans to small- and medium-sized enterprises (SMEs), became increasingly evident.

Development incentives

In China, pawn refers to a loan with interest and maturity secured by pledged assets. Theoretically, it is legitimate usury. The pawn industry's revival in the 1980s was mainly due to its change of business model from that of traditional pawn business. In order to adapt to the needs of development of the market economy, pawn changed its service continuously from the early form of personal items pledge to the present form of service mainly targeting SMEs. In particular, they offer financing to SMEs for their production and operation. Currently, the main businesses of the pawn industry include two aspects, that is, pawn of personal items and SME financing. The personal items pawned[1] mainly include golden and silver jewelry and certain luxuries, mainly to meet individuals' urgent personal needs; meanwhile SMEs and private sectors prefer pawn financing for its flexibility and convenience in providing small-sized loans. They have become the main customers of the pawn industry. Specifically, development of the pawn industry is mainly based on market demand, low entry barriers, market recognition, and high profits.

Market demand

It is the fundamental reason for the fast development of the pawn industry. The customers historically were mainly individuals, but now have changed to SMEs, so the service provided has changed from meeting individual needs to meeting production and operational needs of enterprises. The industry has provided an alternative financing venue for SMEs. The pawn industry has great growth potential under the current, generally adverse business environment for SME financing.

Low entry barriers

Compared to financial institutions that provide financing, pawn companies have low barriers and easy entrance. Article 8 of the *Measures for Administration of The Pawn Industry* requires a minimum registered capital of RMB 3 million for a pawn company, RMB 5 million for a company conducting real estate pledge and pawn business, and RMB 10 million for a company conducting property rights pledge and pawn business.

Recognition by the market

At present, main businesses of pawn companies include personal item pawn and SME financing. Compared to bank loans, pawn financing has the advantages of smaller size, less financial requirements, and relatively lower credit criteria of clients. This has not gone unnoticed by SMEs. The personal items pawn mainly refers to pawn of golden or silver jewelry and certain luxury goods for individuals with urgent needs for cash. Therefore, it is easily accepted.

High profits

Pawn financing business conducted by pawn companies is short term and charges a high interest rate. This may bring considerable profits to pawn companies, which attracts many enterprises and individuals to enter the industry and expedites its fast development.

Market size

Since the restoration of the pawn industry, there was a slowdown of development when the economy went down, and the industry went through a cleanup and overhaul. In general, however, the industry's market size has increased continuously. At the end of 2012, there were 6,084 pawn companies in China, an increase of 16.2% year on year (yoy); total registered capital of the industry was RMB 99.42 billion, an increase of 27.5% yoy; number of employees in the industry was 53,000, an increase of 23.7% yoy; pawn balance was RMB 70.61 billion, an increase of 29.5% yoy; total annual revenues is RMB 11.88 billion, an increase of 19.4% yoy.[2]

At the end of first half year in 2013, the entire national pawn industry had issued RMB 163.52 billion pawn loans, an increase of 24.9% yoy. At the end of June 2013, there were 6,833 pawn companies nationwide, with total assets of RMB 122.87 billion, and a pawn balance of RMB 67.39 billion, increases of 12.4%, 31%, and 29.9% yoy, respectively.[3]

Risk characteristics

According to the business characteristics of the pawn industry, the main risks are loan quality, collateral asset valuation, and asset disposal.

1   *Risks related to loan quality.* The main function of the pawn business is to provide short-term loan to SMEs and individuals and earn commission and interest. When the pawn industry is small, the collateral consists mainly of personal items, and the risk is low. However, when the pawn business is large and gradually takes SMEs as its customers, risk and profit margins increase together. In practice, the pawn companies cannot control the loan purpose of their clients. Therefore, there may be risks behind every single loan. Furthermore, pawn companies generally have limited funding sources, so the single failure of a borrower in an amount of 1 million or 10 million could bring crisis to the whole company. Thus, pawn companies generally look for enterprises with sound credit, sufficient collateral, and strong competitiveness. Similar to banks, the pawn companies will engage in post-lending loan tracking and monitoring for large transactions to prevent and mitigate risks.

2   *Risks relating to collecting pawned assets (risks relating to valuation and market forecasting failure).* Society, technology, and markets are always evolving. Knowledge and forecasting of market trends, the maturity, and the pawn price will all have significant effect on the redemption and sale of terminated pawn assets.[4] Collection of pawned assets has various risks depending on different types of pawned assets. Business relating to pawned precious metals and jewelries involves such risks as counterfeits, safeguarding risk, and price fluctuation. That of real estate pawn involves the risks of ownership and valuation. Securities pawn mainly involves the risks of policy change and market fluctuations. Businesses related to transportation, telecommunication devices, and mechanical products involve the risks of fast upgrading and the risks in product distribution, among others.[5]

3   *Risks relating to sale of terminated pawned assets (recovery of funds).* Generally speaking, terminated pawned assets at a pawn company operating for 3–5 years accounts for 20%–30% of its working capital, with some even accounting for 50%–80%. Termination of pawned assets is an inevitable phenomenon in practice. The level of difficulty involved in sales of terminated pawn assets depends on two factors: the amount of pawn loans and the supply and demand of the pawned assets in the secondary market. If supply exceeds demand in the secondary market, which can cause the price of pawned assets to decrease, or if the pawned assets' valuation is too high, the sale proceeds of the pawned assets may be insufficient to repay its principal and interest. Some pawned assets cannot even be sold, so the funds given to the borrower cannot be recovered. The pawn then becomes a bad debt.

Determination of shadow banking

At the present stage, from the perspective of relevant legal schemes and operational practice, the Chinese pawn industry has the credit intermediary function of connecting capital supplier and capital users. In this sense, the pawn companies have the characteristics of shadow banking in a broad sense. However, such characteristics at the present stage will not affect the stability of the financial system, so the pawn industry does not fall within the shadow banking in a narrow sense. The reasons are as follows:

1   The asset/liability mismatch in the pawn industry is relatively minor. According to the *Measures for Administration of The Pawn Industry*, the capital used by pawn companies for lending comes from two sources: shareholder's equity and bank loans. Pawn company assets are pawn loans secured by the collateral of the pawned assets, which have the characteristics of "small amount, short term, fast, and flexible." In 2012, China's pawn industry reached an overall business volume of RMB 2.371 billion for both new and renewal transactions; the average transaction volume was RMB 117,000, and 49% of such transactions

were within a 30-day duration. Therefore, there is barely any term mismatch between assets and liabilities in the pawn industry.

2 There are basically no problems relating to liquidity transfer of pawn companies. Since the capital lent to borrowers mainly come from shareholders, pawn companies basically have no bank-run risks.

3 Pawn companies have no problems relating to credit risk transfer. At present, pawn companies are defined as "special industrial and commercial enterprises." Like other industrial and commercial enterprises, pawn companies cannot obtain implicit credit guarantees from banks.

4 Pawn companies have low leverage. According to the *Measures for Administration of The Pawn Industry*, leverage ratio of a pawn company cannot exceed 100% of its net asset value. In practice, the leverage ratio is even lower. As of March 2013, bank loan balance of the whole pawn industry was RMB 5.98 billion, a decrease of 5.4% yoy, which accounted for quite a low level at 5.9% of the industry's overall registered capital.

Operating principles

Compared with financial institutions, the operating principles of pawn companies are relatively simple. The pawn companies lend their own capital or bank loans to individuals or small enterprises upon the pledge or mortgage of pawned assets and then collect the principal and interest within a specified period. In practice, a pawn loan has the following characteristics: short term, small amount, fast, and flexible.

A pawn loan is generally for 10 days, a half month, or 6 months at the longest, which is much shorter than the maturity of a bank loan. A pawn loan is mostly issued in small amounts, which is determined by the capital strength and risk aversion of pawn companies. The less the pawn amounts are, the more transactions they do, and the more dispersed their risks are. Such is the operating characteristics of pawn business, which is also a reason that the pawn business is different from other financial loan activities. The procedure of pawn is convenient, its process is clear, and its decision is fast, professional, and efficient, which can fully satisfy clients' urgent needs. Finally, it is flexible. Financing through pawn is known to be fast, convenient, and flexible, which mainly appears as follows: diversity in pawned assets, flexibility in loan tenor, and adjustability of interest rate.

In substance, money provided by a pawn company is a type of loan. It is consistent with the loan business of traditional banks in this aspect. However, it has the characteristics of being "small amount, short term, fast, and flexible." As for clients, pawn financing becomes their urgent financing channel due to the above characteristics when they cannot obtain bank loans on short notice. Thus, pawn companies are supplements to the traditional bank financing.

According to the *Measures for Administration of The Pawn Industry*, pawn companies may obtain loans from banks, just like other industrial and commercial enterprises. In this aspect, the pawn companies intersect with the traditional banking system.

Development trend

In the recent years, the pawn industry developed fast and played an increasingly important role in social financing; helped the development of SMEs; met urgent needs of individuals, households, and entrepreneurs, and in overall economic development; benefited people's livelihood; created jobs; and maintained social stability.[6] Stable and continuous development of the social economy, continuous and prosperous needs of social capital, and active capital circulation will provide broader development space and opportunities for the pawn industry. Compared with mature foreign pawn markets, the Chinese pawn industry is still in the development stage of low level and small size and thus faces greater development opportunity. As indicated by information released by the National Pawnbrokers Association (NPA) in the United States, the United States has about 20,000 pawn companies with 80,000 employees. It provides direct pawn services for more than 34 million people (accounting for about 12% of the total US population).[7]

While we see great market prospects derived from needs for small-amount financing, we also need to be aware of the market competition of pawn companies in providing small-amount financing. Such competition comes from two sources: traditional bank SME loans and small/microloan companies. Traditional banks are becoming more innovative in providing customized SME loans. In order to alleviate SME difficulties in financing, the banks have gradually lowered credit requirements, improved guarantee venues, and provided a variety of financial instruments for SMEs. All of these have squeezed the market space of the pawn business. Second, small loan companies also present competition for pawn companies. Since the business scope of small loan companies and pawn companies is basically the same, and the conditions for establishing small loan companies are more favorable, the procedure easier, and the prospect broader, small loan companies' fast development also squeezes the market space of pawn companies.

In order to meet market financing needs and cope with competition, pawn companies need to work on new sources of funding beyond shareholder's equity and a small quantity of bank loans. Securitization of pawned assets, equity financing, and debt issuance by large pawn companies are possible new sources of funding. Certainly, such a change of funding sources and increased quantity would change the industry's overall risk profiles and its effect on the financial system, which also requires change in regulatory approaches.

International comparison

The pawn industry exists in most countries and regions worldwide. From a global perspective, the pawn industry and its management have different characteristics in each country.

In the tenth and eleventh centuries, as the European business and handicraft industry developed, currencies in part of the cities of Western Europe became unprecedentedly active and usury prevailed. Jewish people in Western Europe converted certain parts of self-owned capital into usury capital and established pawnshops. These were the earliest pawn operators in Western Europe.

English pawnshops include private pawnshops and public pawnshops established by the church or the government. The first pawnshop was established in 1361 by Michael, the Bishop of London. Since the 1980s, the English pawn industry has been reforming its operating model to adapt to the changing business environment. For instance, by adopting chain operation, the pawn companies provided quality service to attract clients and linked the sale of common goods with the disposal of terminated pawned assets. This made the pawn industry one of the fastest developing businesses in the services industries. The NPA of the United Kingdom had only 300 members in 1999, but this grew to 800 in 2004. At present, the United Kingdom has more than 1000 pawn companies and branches, including two listed companies. Due to its nature of business, the pawn industry is part of the financial services and commerce industries, and pawn companies are classified as SMEs. The regulator of the English pawn industry is the Office of Fair Trading under the Department of Trade and Industry. The NPA of the United Kingdom is an industry self-regulatory organization (SRO), and the National Advisory Board, the Trading Standards Bureau, and courts participate in regulatory and advisory functions.

The American pawn industry started much later than those in Europe. At the end of the eighteenth century, pawnshops emerged in many cities in the United States. In the middle and later nineteenth century, the American pawn industry approached prosperity, but its real rise was after 1980s. After more than 10 years of fast development, the pawn industry in the United States has become the largest in the world. The current number of pawn companies in the United States is more than 15,000, equivalent to half of the number of its commercial banks, and over twice the number of savings and loans banks. The American pawn industry pushed the pawnshops' roles to their limits through four operating models: sale, auction, consignment, and retail. American pawn companies provide convenient services to their clients. The clients may conduct pawn transactions with the pawn companies and obtain money from pawn companies through pledge or guarantee of items or property rights. The clients may also trade goods, purchase the terminated pawned assets in pawn companies, while selling their items to pawn companies on a consignment basis.

In the United States, chain operation is widely deployed in the pawn industry. The industry consists of single stores, chain stores, and incorporated chain operation companies. The chain operation strategy helps many pawn companies in the United States, especially the large- and medium-sized pawn companies in expanding their market shares. This significantly raises their operating efficiency and maintains their superior competitive positions. The US regulation on the pawn industry is divided into federal and state levels. On the state level, the state government is responsible for regulating the pawn industry, and every state has its own statutes with local considerations. On the federal level, the federal government mainly regulates the pawn industry with the same federal regulations for the entire financial services industry, including the Equal Credit Opportunity Act and Fair Credit Reporting Act.

Guarantee companies

Historical development

Guarantees are a link in the credit chain. They are the inevitable results of social and economic development. The guarantee industry has widened its business scope and expanded its product lines in line with the development of economy and society. After several decades of development, the Chinese guarantee industry has reached every corner of economy and social life. It also plays an important role in the nation's economic system. The guarantee industry includes financing guarantee companies and non-financing guarantee companies based on the purpose of the guarantees they issue. Financing guarantee companies refer to limited liability or joint stock companies that are established to engage in the financing guarantee business. As a guarantor, a financing guarantee company makes pledges to the banks and other creditors. When the guaranteed party does not perform its financing obligations to creditors, the guarantor will need to step in to bear the contractual guarantee liability. For the purpose of this book, the guarantee companies referred to herein will be limited to financing guarantee companies that provide credit guarantees.

The development of Chinese guarantee industry may be divided into exploratory, rapid development, and standardization stages.

The first stage is the beginning and exploratory stage. In 1993, the SETC and the Ministry of Finance jointly established the first national and professional guarantee company in China upon approval by the State Council. In June 1999, based on extensive investigations, the SETC issued the *Guidelines on Establishing Pilot Credit Guarantee System of Small-and-Medium-Size Enterprises (SMEs)* (No. [1999]540 from SETC), which provided for industry-specific regulations in terms of guiding principles, business models and systems, guarantor's sources of funds and roles and functions, cooperative banks, risk control and the division of roles and responsibilities, internal supervision and external regulation, and organizational implementation. The pilot program of China's SME credit guarantee industry preliminarily entered into a normal operating stage, and various supporting policies were promulgated. During such period, the number of guarantee companies was small, and its source of capital was mainly governmental funds.

The second stage is that of rapid development. After 2000, governmental agencies issued a series of policy incentives and supported the development of the guarantee industry. In 2008, as SMEs suffered extraordinarily due to the financial crisis, the government enhanced its support for the guarantee industry, and a great amount of private and foreign capital flooded in. The number of guarantee companies grew explosively, while at the same time many controversial or nonconventional practices emerged.

The third stage is that of standardization and scientific development. In order to regulate the development of guarantee companies, on March 8, 2010, seven Ministries and Commissions[8] jointly issued the *Provisional Measures for Administration of Financing Guarantee Companies* (No. [2010]3 of CBRC), which provided the industry clear regulations for guarantee companies' nature of business, market positioning, and operational rules. These included requirements for incorporation and business operation, regulatory frameworks, and legal responsibilities of guarantee companies. Subsequently, an overhaul of guarantee companies was carried out widely, and the industry stepped into a stage with standardized operation and scientific development.

Development factors

The rapid development of guarantee industry in the recent 10 years was directly linked to the full implementation of the roles and functions of guarantors:

1   The guarantee industry provides professional services and solutions to meet the needs for risk management in economic activities. The industry assumes and manages risks in economic activities with its professional expertise, and applies credit-enhancement for economic entities that lack credit. Thus, risk identification and management capability of guarantee companies became key factors for their survival and development. In the past 10 years, especially in the recent 3 years, with the guarantee industry's regulatory framework being increasingly comprehensive, guarantee company risk management has been gradually enhanced. There is therefore now a solid foundation for the fast development of the industry.

2   The guarantee industry provides credit products and promotes the expansion and deepening of credit in the modern economic system. The development of the market economy provides the guarantee industry more space for growth. The modern economy is credit-related, and guarantee companies specialize in the management of credit products. Supported by its own credit and professional risk management capability, a guarantee company provides credit enhancement or credit rating service to certain entities that lack credit, enabling such entities to obtain credit support for business survival and development.

3   The guarantee industry may alleviate stresses in indirect financing and promote financial innovation. Through credit guarantees, a bank mitigates its information asymmetry. It adds additional risk protection for loans and reduces their credit risk and management costs. Meanwhile, the borrowing enterprise obtains the necessary capital for its survival and development thanks to credit enhancement provided by the third-party guarantor. This process to some extent relieves the pressure on indirect financing.

4   The guarantee industry helps to alleviate the financing difficulty faced by SMEs. The establishment and development of the SME credit guarantee systems play an active role in relieving financing difficulty, enhancing the credit of SMEs, promoting the healthy development of SMEs, increasing employment, and growing the tax base.

Market size

The market size for the guarantee industry has grown quickly since the industry's beginning, which is reflected as follows:

First, the number of guarantee companies is continuously increasing. At the end of 2010, there were 6,030 national financing guarantee entities, among which 1,427 (23.7%) were controlled by the state and 4,603 (76.3%) were controlled by private and foreign capital. At the county (city) level, 3,284 (54.5%) were registered. Guarantee companies with registered capital of RMB 100 million or more accounted for 40.4% of the total financing guarantee entities, and there were 29 with registered capital of RMB 1 billion or more. At the end of 2011, there were 8,402 legal entities in the national financing guarantee industry, an increase of 2,372 or 39.3% yoy, among which 18.7% were state-owned and private or foreign capital controlled 81.3%, and the percentage of private and foreign controlled companies increased by 5%. At the end of 2012, there were 8,590 legal entities in the national financing guarantee industry, an increase of 188 or 2.2% yoy. The growth rate decreased by 37% yoy, among which 1,907 entities (22.2%) were controlled by the state and 6,683 entities (77.8%) were controlled by private and foreign capital.

Second, the total assets of guarantee industry grew rapidly. At the end of 2010, the total asset of the industry was RMB 592.3 billion, and the net asset was RMB 479.8 billion. At the end of 2011, the total asset was RMB 931.1 billion, an increase of 57.2% yoy. Total net asset was RMB 785.8 billion, an increase of 63.8% yoy. At the end of 2012, the paid-in capital was RMB 828.2 billion, an increase of 12.2%. The total reserve funds reached RMB 70.1 billion, an increase of 25.2% yoy.

Third, the balance of outstanding guarantees continues to increase. At the end of 2010, the outstanding amount was RMB 1.2 trillion, an increase of 64.6% in just one year. By the end of 2011, the outstanding amount was RMB 1.9 trillion, an increase of RMB 537.4 billion over 2010. By the end of 2012, the outstanding amount for the whole industry was RMB 2.2 trillion, a yearly increase of 13.5%.

Fourth, the number of banks and SMEs served by the guarantee industry increases continuously. At the end of 2010, the number of banks (including branches) cooperating with the financing guarantee entities was 10,321, an increase of 27.1% yoy; the total loan balance of financing guarantees was RMB 893.1 billion (excluding the guaranteed financing loans of small loan companies), an increase of 60.9% yoy; and the number of entities that borrow with guaranteed financing loan was 166,000, an increase of 48.9% yoy. The balance of guaranteed loans provided for SMEs was RMB 689.4 billion, an increase of 69.9% over 2009. This accounted for 77.2% of the total amount of guaranteed financing loans. The number of SMEs that have received financing guarantees was 142,000, an increase of 58.3% yoy. This accounted for 85.5% of all entities borrowing with guaranteed loans.

At the end of 2011, 15,997 banks (including branches) had cooperative relationship with financing guarantee entities, an increase of 32.6% yoy. The balance of guaranteed loans was RMB 1274.7 billion, an increase of RMB 326.9 billion or 39.8% yoy. With an increase of 16,000 or 9.6% yoy, 181,000 entities had guaranteed loans.

The outstanding balance was RMB 1,274.7 billion (excluding guaranteed financing loans of small loan companies), an increase of 39.8%, among which the balance of guaranteed loans of SMEs was RMB 985.7 billion, an increase of 40.5%. This accounted for 77.3% of the balance of guaranteed loans.

By the end of 2012, there were 8,590 legal entities in the national financing guarantee industry, an increase of 188 or 2.2% over 2011. However, the growth rates decreased by 37%; 1,907 or 22.2% of them were controlled by the state, and the rest, a vast majority, were controlled by private or foreign capital. The paid-in capital totaled RMB 828.2 billion, the guarantee reserve fund RMB 70.1 billion, and the outstanding guarantee amount was RMB 2.2 trillion. The number of banking financial institutions that cooperate with financing guarantee entities reached 15,414, an increase of 10.3% yoy. The guaranteed loan balance was RMB 1.46 trillion, an increase of 12.3%.[9]

Risk characteristics

The guarantee industry conducts the business of "managing risks." Thus, risk taking is an apparent behavior of guarantee companies. The risks of guarantee industry mainly come from the debtor of the guaranteed loan/security, especially credit risks.[10] After the guarantee company provides a guarantee, the debtor may be unable and fully repay the loan on time. Therefore, the guarantee company must repay the loan, a repayment under guarantee. If the guarantee company finally fails to recover the funds repaid under guarantee, it will suffer losses.

The guarantee industry has relatively high risk tolerance. The guarantee is an intermediate activity between banks and enterprises where the guarantor provides guarantee and thus enhances the credit level of the guaranteed entity. The involvement of the guarantee company makes the lending relationship between the commercial banks and enterprises, a relationship among three parties: the commercial bank, the enterprise, and the guarantee company. The guarantee company enhances the confidence of the banks in SME loans and facilitates such SME lending. At the same time, it diversifies the risks of bank loans. The safety of bank assets is then guaranteed at a higher level. However, SMEs look for guarantees from the guarantee companies because their credit is not sound enough and does not fully meet banks' credit criteria. The involvement of guarantee companies enables SMEs to obtain loans. The guarantee companies also assume the risk of SMEs that have poor credit.

Risks assumed by the guarantee industry may lead to contagion. The guarantee industry is a key link in the credit chain, and the credit risk of both the guarantee companies and those they guarantee may be transferred to the financial system through such guarantees provided to banks. According to provisions of the *Provisional Measures for Administration of Financing Guarantee Companies*, the financing balance of a guarantee company may not exceed 10 times its net asset value. Namely, a guarantee company's leverage ratio may reach 10 times. Such a leverage ratio may in fact increase the probability of credit risks being transferred into the rest of the financial system.

Determination of shadow banking

The guarantee industry is a link in the credit chain and a means or vehicle to spread credit risks. A guarantee itself does not have certain shadow banking characteristics such as term or liquidity mismatch. Thus, under the present business model, the guarantee industry alone should not be shadow banking. However, if the guarantee industry's clients are within the shadow banking definition, the guarantee industry may become an important link in the shadow banking system. In other words, whether the guarantee industry has the nature of shadow banking is dependent upon the nature of financial institutions it serves, the financial business it involves, and financial products it guarantees.

When a guarantee company provides guarantees for on-balance sheet loans of banks, the guarantee company provides credit enhancement. Such credit enhancement may magnify the credit supply on the bank's balance sheet. However, such supply itself is the basic business of banks, not that of shadow banking. Thus, the guarantee company is not shadow banking.

When a guarantee company provides guarantees for off-balance sheet loans of financial institutions, whether such financial institutions are commercial banks, trust companies, or other entities providing similar business, the guarantee company still provides credit enhancement. The guarantee company may become an important link in the shadow banking activities if the relevant lending activities of such entities are classified as shadow banking.

In summary, the guarantee company by itself is not shadow banking, and whether it has the nature of shadow banking is dependent upon the nature of the relevant financial institutions, products, or business. However, as the guarantee company expands credit and spreads risks, it is necessary to regulate it properly to prevent systemic risks and protect financial stability.

Operating principles

According to the provisions of the *Provisional Measures for Administration of Financing Guarantee Companies*, a guarantee company may conduct the following business: financing guarantee, non-financing guarantee, and investments with its own capital.

The basic operating principle of the financing guarantee business of a guarantee company is as follows: the guarantee company and the banks agree that when guaranteed borrowing entities such as SMEs fail to perform repayment obligations owed to creditors, the guarantee company will bear the guarantee liability according to the contract, while the guaranteed SMEs pay fees to the guarantee company. If the guaranteed SME breaches the obligations owed to the banks and other financial institutions, the guarantee company shall perform such obligations instead. After the guarantee company makes a repayment to the lender, it may recover such payment from the guaranteed enterprise.

The non-financing guarantee business mainly includes guarantees for litigation preservation, guarantees for bidding, guarantees for prepayment, guarantees for project performance, guarantees for final payment, and other guarantees business for performance, which has basically the same operating principles as the financing guarantee business. The difference is that the beneficiaries of such guarantees are non-financial institutions, and the guaranteed debt comes from factors other than financing.

According to Article 29 of the *Provisional Measures for Administration of Financing Guarantee Companies*, a guarantee company may use its own capital to invest in government debt, bonds, debt financing instruments issued by large enterprises, other fixed income financial products with high credit ratings, and other approved investments. There should be no conflicts of interest between the guarantee company and such "other investments," and the amount should not exceed 20% of the company's net asset value.

Development trend

Guarantee companies are a key component of China's credit system, but their development is relatively incomplete, especially for that of SMEs. In the present and near future, guarantee companies play an irreplaceable role in diversifying financial risks of the banking system and relieving the difficulty of financing SMEs. Therefore, the guarantee industry will have great potential in the future. Specifically, the guarantee industry has the following development trends in the future:

First, guarantee companies are gradually growing stronger and take more advantage of scalability. At present, there are large numbers of guarantee companies in China, and the strength of the overall guarantee industry has increased somewhat over the past several years. However, these guarantee companies are not very strong on an individual basis. Such a guarantee industry consisting of "numerous and small" companies is not very well suited for guarantee businesses involving financial markets, such as the guarantees for bonds.

Second, guarantee companies should be professionalized. At present, guarantee companies engage in guarantee businesses in almost all types of business, and they do not differentiate their clients in different industries. As each different industry has its unique risk profile and business models, effective risk management depends on a deep and focused understanding of the industry concerned. Therefore, industry-specialized business models should be adopted for the guarantee companies in the future.

Third, the policy-driven and commercial guarantee businesses should be appropriately separated. This is already common in the foreign guarantee industry. The former refers to guarantee business with risks that are too high to be proper for commercial institutions to operate. Normally, the guarantee business for SMEs is deemed to be policy driven. While current regulations in China make no such distinction, local governments sometimes provide subsidies to guarantee companies serving SMEs. It is necessary to make such distinction by the enterprises or business models in the future.

International comparison

There are guarantee systems and guarantors in most major countries and regions. The guarantor can be generally divided into two types: policy-driven and commercial guarantee companies.

The American policy-driven guarantee institutions can be divided into two categories: one is the United States Small Business Administration providing guarantee for SMEs. Its business scope and operating model are dictated by the *Small Business Act, Small Business Investment Act, Small Business Economic Policy Act*, and *Paperwork Reduction Act* and other legislation. The other category is the housing financial guarantee organizations serving residents, such as Federal Housing Administration and Veterans Administration to provide guarantee service for resident loans for housing purchases.

Commercial guarantees are well developed in America. American companies that conduct the guarantee business are mainly insurance companies and professional guarantee companies. Many large insurance companies have guarantee departments to provide services such as guarantees/insurance for employee integrity and performance. On the other hand, guarantee companies, such as municipal bond guarantee companies and financial securities guarantee companies, specialize mostly in the bond guarantee business. In addition, there are some professional guarantee companies that specialize in guarantees such as those for construction and transportation contracts.

In European countries, guarantees and insurance are not strictly distinct. A guarantee is considered to be a type of insurance, and the two are not distinct from each other in nature, except for some difference in operating models. Generally, guarantees provide credit to particular clients and thus have a narrower market focus, greater responsibility, and higher risks. Insurance comes in many different forms and therefore has broad market coverage and relatively low risks. The main businesses of European guarantees or insurance are

- general credit guarantees, including those for export credit, import credit, bidding, maintenance service, license, and tariffs;
- performance guarantees, including those for construction contracts, contracts for supply of goods, repayment contract, inter-bank repayment, and loans (though the business volume is small);
- employee integrity guarantee/insurance, including guarantee for damages for any loss incurred by the company due to serious violations or theft of company's assets and properties by staff, individual employees, key personnel, or key employees.

Insurance markets in most European countries are already well developed. There are close connections between guarantee/insurance companies and reinsurance companies or banks. Each guarantee company or insurer purchases insurance from one or more reinsurance companies, and the reinsurance companies and insurance companies tend to be each other's closely connected shareholders. For operations, the risk appetite of guarantees depends on the capacity to purchase reinsurance. Where the purchased amount of reinsurance is greater, the risk taken by the insurance company is smaller. Otherwise, the insurance company would need to take on greater risks.

Financial leasing companies

Financial leasing integrates financing, leasing, trading, and technology servicing. There are three major participants in China's financial leasing market: financial leasing companies under China Banking Regulatory Commission (CBRC) regulation, Sino-foreign joint venture financial leasing companies, and pilot domestic financial leasing companies approved by the Ministry of Commerce. The three participants all provide financial leasing services, but they are defined differently: the financial leasing companies under CBRC regulation are non-banking financial institution, while the latter two leasing companies are non-financial institutions (as known as leasing companies providing financing), classified as industrial and commercial service enterprises. Since we have analyzed the financial leasing companies regulated by CBRC in Chapter 3, here we focus on the latter two kinds of financial leasing companies.

Historical development

The development of financial leasing industry in China may be divided into five stages:

The first is the start-up stage (1981–1986). At the beginning of the 1980s, China's domestic economy experienced very difficult times and lacked resources and capital. The state urgently needed to introduce foreign capital to purchase advanced foreign equipment to upgrade domestic enterprises' equipment. Under such a background, in April 1981, CITIC Group and Japan Oriental Lease Company (now known as ORIX Corporation) jointly established the first Chinese Sino-foreign joint venture leasing company, China Oriental International Leasing Company. In July 1981, CITIC Group and a domestic organization established the first Chinese financial leasing company, China Leasing Co. Ltd, which marked the beginning of leasing industry in China. Subsequently, more and more companies received the financial leasing license and established financial leasing companies. Since financial leasing was at an exploratory stage, its functions were not fully realized and the growth of financial leasing business was limited.

The second is the fast development stage (1987–1996). During that period, as the Reform and Opening up grew fast, financing needs increased and new financial leasing companies flourished. Especially, from 1994 to 1995, five financial leasing companies were established, and the business scale of financial leasing expanded greatly. By the end of 1996, the total assets of the industry amounted to nearly RMB 14 billion. However, the total registered capital of financial leasing companies was a little more than RMB 600 million, and capital adequacy ratio was generally low. Thus, while financial leasing enjoyed fast development and contributed a lot to the domestic economy, it also laid potential danger to the subsequent development.

The third is the risk explosion stage (1997–2000). With large adjustment of exchange rate, lack of risk management tools, poor management, and deficient system, the potential danger laid at the previous development stages of financial leasing industry exploded fully at this stage. The operation of most financial leasing companies went into trouble due to difficulties in funding and difficulty in collection of leasing revenues. In 1997, Guangdong International Leasing Co. Ltd., Hainan International Leasing Co. Ltd., and Wuhan International Leasing Co. Ltd. went bankrupt one after another due to insolvency. Due to the same reason, China Huayang Financial Leasing Co. Ltd. also declared bankruptcy in 2000.

The fourth is the initiation stage of system construction (2001–2006). During this period, in order to make up the historical limitations, the system construction of four pillars in the financial leasing industry—laws, accounting principles, regulation, and taxation—was initiated. As early as June 30, 2000, the PBOC issued the *Measures for Administration of Financial Leasing Companies* (No. [2000]4 of the PBOC). The *Enterprise Accounting Principles: Lease* (Ministry of Finance) became effective on January 1, 2001, and was subsequently amended into the *Enterprise Accounting Principles (No. 21): Lease* that became effective on February 15, 2006. Significantly, during the 2 years after 2005, relevant regulators carried out the so-called second cleaning up of the financial leasing industry.

The fifth is the new development period of China's financial leasing industry and China's leasing industry (2007 until now). On January 23, 2007, CBRC amended the *Measures for Administration of Financial Leasing Companies* (No. [2007]1 of CBRC). Subsequently, the construction of tax policies and regulatory system sped up. According to the *Measures for Administration of Financial Leasing Companies* amended by CBRC, domestic commercial banks were permitted to reenter the financial leasing industry. Based on the amendment, from November 2007 to the end of 2009, six banks including ICBC, CCB, Bank of Communications, CMBC, CMB, and CDB established their respective financial leasing companies one after another. The entry of commercial banks was expected to promote the social status and influence of the financial leasing industry in China, which might clear out the capital bottleneck, and improve the development environment of leasing market.

Development incentives

The development of financial leasing companies is based on their unique role and status in the economic and financial system.

1 Financial leasing promotes the integration of production and financing. On one hand, financial leasing relieves the difficulty in asset selection for the lessor; on the other hand, it also solves the capital shortage for the lessee that conducts asset investment. Thus, it is an effective financial mechanism that connects closely the capital provider and the capital user. As for China, financial leasing helps enhance financing efficiency for the overall economy and solve the problems of excessive production and excessive production capacity. Financial leasing also provides effective approaches to solve the problem that financial development is "detached" from real economy and provides new tools to implement the macro-control of economy and finance.

2 Financial leasing further perfects the financial structure. Indirect financing prevails in China for a long time, and supply of the equity capital is severely insufficient, which results in an imbalance of capital structure both in the investment sector and in the production sector. The fundamental solution is to develop capital market vigorously. However, we should not limit our vision to the capital market. Instead, we should focus on creating a mechanism beneficial to the development of equity capital. Financial leasing is an essential part of this important mechanism.

3 Financial leasing solves the difficulty of financing SMEs and promotes the accessibility of capital for SMEs. First, financial leasing focuses more on the future cash flow of a project and does not narrowly focuses on the historical assets and liabilities of the lessee, which enables SMEs without enough bank credit to obtain financing for long-lived assets during development. Second, it may lower the entry barrier and financing risk. Third, the maturity and accounting specifics in financial leasing contract may help SMEs to enhance their capital efficiency and lower their financial risks. At last, financial leasing may facilitate SMEs to strengthen cooperation with large-scale enterprises, to promote their vertical or horizontal cooperation, to optimize economic relations within the industry, and to accomplish risk sharing in the industrial economy.

4 Financial leasing may promote a balanced development among different regions. In the industrial structure adjustment due to an unbalanced development of economies in different domestic regions, in which part of industrial capital transfers from the eastern to middle and western regions, financial leasing may significantly help explore markets across domestic regions. During such transfer, financial leasing can reduce the excess production capacity of financial products in the eastern regions and also complement the inadequacy of capital in middle and western regions, so as to promote the economic development and finally to balance domestic economic development.

5 Financial leasing effectively promotes the implementation of "going out" (i.e., expand overseas of domestic businesses) strategy. So far, the "going out" strategy carried out in China mainly focuses on commodities exportation. Such a strategy is hard to continue domestically and also faces more and more controversies internationally. Looking at the future, we should change from commodities exportation to production and capital exportation, utilize foreign exchange reserve more effectively and diversely, and accomplish the optimization of industrial structure globally. Financial leasing is a powerful tool to implement such strategy change.

6 Financial leasing is beneficial to enhance China's financial efficiency. First, financial leasing is beneficial to resolving information asymmetry. Second financial leasing is beneficial to overcome financial suppression and promote liberalization of interest rate. Third, financial leasing can accomplish the integration and innovation of various industries and the innovation of financial products to adapt to various personalized financing needs, via structured trading arrangement of goods flow, cash flow and maturity, and other elements. Lastly,

the development of financial leasing can promote its business innovation and cooperation with banks, securities firms, trust companies, insurance companies, and other financial institutions.

Market size

By the end of 2012, there were 560 financial leasing companies in China (excluding the financial leasing companies with single project), an increase of nearly 90% yoy. Among them, there were 460 foreign invested financial leasing companies, an increase of 250 in number yoy, 20 financial leasing companies (that are under regulation by CBRC), and 80 domestic financial leasing companies, an increase of 14 in number. By the end of 2012, the registered capital of financial leasing companies amounted to RMB 189 billion, an increase of 36.2%, with an industrial capital adequacy ratio at 12.2%. As for business volume of financial leasing, by the end of 2012, the balance of financial leasing contract amounts exceeded RMB 1,000 billion, amounting to RMB 1,550 billion, while the number reached RMB 930 billion at the end of 2011, an increase of 66.7%. By the end of 2012, the business volume of leasing contracts of 20 financial leasing companies amounted to RMB 660 billion, accounting for more than 40% of the whole business volume of the financial leasing industry.[11]

Risk characteristics

Because financial leasing combines the characteristics of both monetary financing and assets leasing, financial leasing companies face both financial risks and trading risks. Due to the financial characteristics of financial leasing, the risk is exposed all over the process. As for the lessor, the biggest risk is the repayment capability of the lessee, which directly affects the operation and survival of the leasing company. If the term structure of interest rate provided by a financial leasing company is inconsistent with its own term structure of interest rate, there will be interest rate risk. If a financial leasing contract uses foreign currency, the risk will be higher. Especially when using currencies other than US dollars, the foreign exchange risk may double the financing cost of enterprises. Monetary payment may also have risks. Especially for international payments, if the payment method, date, payment term, channel, and means are not chosen properly, the risk will be amplified. In addition, as financial leasing has the characteristics of trading, there will be risks from ordering, negotiation to test, and acceptance. The aforementioned risks have two characteristics:

1   The risks borne by financial leasing are infectious. A financial leasing company does not just operate on its own capital. In addition, a financial leasing company mainly obtains financing from financial market or financial institutions, such as loans, assets securitization, financial leasing factoring, and issuance of bonds. If a financial leasing company operates at high leverage ratio, when its operation goes wrong, the risk is easily transmitted to the financial system.

2   The risks borne by financial leasing are cyclic. Leased assets are one of the components of financial leasing. The assets financed by the financial leasing generally are capital equipment that closely connect with economic cycles, such as ships, airplanes, engineering machinery, and large equipment. When the economy is in a downturn, the risks of a financial leasing company will be easily exposed.

Determination of shadow banking

A financial leasing company is a credit intermediary. According to the relevant regulations, a financial leasing company may operate at a high financial leverage. The company obtains financing from financial market or financial institutions through bonds, securitization of financial leased assets, factoring of financial leases, and loans. Then it will use such capital to purchase the leased assets for its clients and repay the financing by using the leasing incomes paid by its clients. During this process, the financial leasing company accomplishes a credit conversion and liquidity transfer.

In addition, the level of regulation by either the Ministry of Commerce or CBRC over financial leasing companies is not as strong as the regulation by CBRC over commercial banks, which leaves room for regulatory arbitrage. Thus, in this sense, a financial leasing company has the characteristics of shadow banking. However, because the volume of financial leasing business in the entire financial system is small, its impact on the entire financial system is small. While subjecting to the regulation of the Ministry of Commerce and CBRC, the financial leasing industry has not been paid adequate attention.

Operating principles

The basic operating principles of financial leasing companies depend on the types of businesses.

In respect of a financial lease, also known as a financial leasing with full repayment, the lessee chooses the equipment, which the lessor (a financial leasing company) purchases and then leases to the lessee. During the leasing period, the lessor owns leased equipment, while the lessee holds the right to use. After the lease expires, the lessee may choose to retain and purchase the equipment. During the leasing period, the lessee makes timely lease payments and records depreciation.

In respect of an operating lease, also known as a financial leasing without full repayment, a lessor leases the assets to the lessee and collects lease payments that are in an amount less than lessor's investment for the lease, with lessor keeping the residual value of the assets.

In the case of a sale and lease-back, to obtain financing, a lessee sells its assets to the lessor and leases back such assets for use while making lease payments. The lease-back may be conducted by means of financial leasing or operating leasing, which have both the functions and characteristics of full repayment and non-full repayment. The lessee, through such service, transforms its fixed assets into cash, to supplement operating cash flow or purchase new equipment.

Development trend

Financial leasing has both the characteristics of finance and trading and shows the following development trend:

1   The financial leasing has a trend to serve manufacturers. To extend their operation chain and service chain, more and more equipment manufacturers strategically build financial leasing service platform and transform their business models from simple product sales to assets management. Financial leasing companies, as a new credit sale and assets management institution, play a remarkable role in promoting equipment circulation, increasing enterprise assets, speeding up the capital turnover of manufacturer, and reducing the impact of economic cycle.
2   Financial leasing companies, as an investment platform, provide banks and various investment institutions a channel for capital allocation and investment products that have ownership protection. Through factoring, trust plans, PE, and securitization of leased assets, financial leasing effectively utilizes the capital of banks and society and supports economic development. Financial leasing companies will cooperate fully with banks, trust companies, insurance companies, guarantee companies, and other financial institutions. Financial leasing companies owned by banks have the natural advantage in cooperating with banks, in areas summarized as follows: rental factoring, serving the deposit and loan business, mixture of lease and loan—changing the assets structure, asset spin-offs—securing safe circulation, services with complementary advantages—supporting SMEs, cooperation between banking and leasing—serving governmental finance, equipment lease—meeting the needs of banks, disposal of distressed assets—promoting industrial integration, and investment with lease—supporting infrastructure construction.
3   Financial leasing serves equipment export. With the lack of stable international finance in the near future, financial leasing may effectively expand the export of China's electromechanical machinery and promote enterprises' overseas investment. Different financial leasing forms can also balance the commodities trade surplus and service trade deficit between China, Europe, and America. The development of international financial leasing business may also become a new and safe investment channel for China's foreign exchange reserve.

International comparison

In 2006, the new business volume of financial leasing in the Unite States was about US$229 billion, accounting for 27% of the entire industrial equipment investment. After 2007, the growth remained relatively stable. After the financial crisis, the investment decreased, and business was weak. In January 2009, the growth decreased by about 22%, and in February 2009, it decreased by about 40%. At the end of 2005, there were 3,200 financial leasing institutions in America. About 25% of such institutions had enterprise background, and 35% had banking background (banks conducted leasing business directly or indirectly through their subsidiaries and affiliates). Independent leasing institutions accounted for 40%. In the United States, many manufacturers built their internal leasing departments or established leasing subsidiaries, such as IBM and Dell, whose own leasing departments or subsidiaries contributed greatly to their products sale. As a whole, equipment manufacturers are very active in the US leasing market. They produce certain equipment with their technical expertise and play important roles in many areas, such as computer, airplane, and construction machinery. The main sources of funding for American professional leasing companies include commercial banks, insurance companies, and other institutional investors; issuance of shares by means of joint stock companies; issuance of corporate bonds; issuance of short-term commercial papers; and issuance of special funds.

From a legislative perspective, America has no uniform law for financial leasing, instead, there are many legal agencies regulating financial leasing. The interpretation of each agencies and courts and the precedents have important effect on the financial leasing industry. There are no specialized regulatory agencies for leasing companies that have enterprises background. In America, there is no administrative vetting and approval for access to leasing market, and there is no minimum registered capital requirement. Leasing companies are the same as general commercial enterprises in terms of incorporation. The issues of trading, taxation, credit, and bonds issuance involved in the leasing industry are regulated by different government agencies, which is consistent with the characteristics of the common law system in the United States. The financial leasing companies with banking background are regulated by the financial regulatory agencies. Specifically speaking, Office of Comptroller of Currency (OCC) regulates licensing of banks and market risks.

After a stable development in the recent years, the market penetration rate of European leasing market in 2008 reached 16%. From the perspective of market segment, the penetration rate of equipment leasing market was 23.7%, becoming the second largest venue for equipment investment and financing, following loans, while the penetration rate of real estate leasing market was only 4.6%.

In many European Union (EU) countries, such as Germany and Spain, there is no special legislation for financial leasing, and provisions relating to financial leasing can be found in several existing laws and regulations. In Germany, people categorize various leases based on the types of lease agreements and determine whether such agreement fits well with certain tax laws and lease term standards. Therefore in Germany the "financial leasing" is not based on some leasing concept. Rather, it focuses on the contractual practiced dictated by lease agreement. The royal rules of Spain do not define the scope of financial leasing assets, rather the rules require that the lease must be for commercial purposes; and the consumption goods may not be used as financial leasing assets.

In Germany, there is no clear statutory definition of financial leasing as of today and no legislation of special financial leasing law. By contrast, the regulators of Spain consider financial leasing as financial business, whose function is basically equivalent to loan. Therefore, in terms of regulation, there is no uniform standard in EU, and each country of EU makes decision according to its own situations. Though the regulatory models of Germany and Spain are different, they have one thing in common: both of them regulate only financial leasing companies with banking background.

In Germany, leasing companies with banking background are subject to regulation, and leasing companies without banking background are not subject to any regulation. German banks may directly conduct financial leasing business or may indirectly conduct financial leasing business through establishing subsidiaries or affiliates. When a bank invests in a financial leasing company and holds more than 20% of its capital, the financial leasing company will be deemed to be with banking background and will be subject to regulation of German financial regulators. For financial leasing business with banking background that is subject to regulation, including those carried out by banks directly or indirectly, and those manufacturer's leasing with affiliated banks or financial companies, German authority will carry out an "indirect supervision" according to the *Bank Act*, namely regulate the financial leasing company and its parent bank by means of consolidation of balance sheet. That is to say, once the shares held by a bank exceed 20%, all the assets and liabilities of the financial leasing company will be consolidated into the balance sheet of its parent bank. Thus, the regulator can regulate the financial leasing company indirectly through the financial regulation of its parent bank. It is notable that the consolidation will lead to the following result: the financial leasing company with banking background will not be subject to independent regulation. While the risk management of overall assets and liabilities of the parent bank is in compliance with bank's prudent regulation requirements, the financial leasing subsidiary may have some leeway in certain aspects. For instance, its capital adequacy ratio may be less than 8%, a requirement by *Basel Agreement*.

In Spain, financial leasing is deemed to be a pure financial business that is a financial product or financial derivatives similar to bank loans. Financial leasing companies, as financial institutions, are subject to direct regulation of the Bank of Spain. To carry out financial leasing business requires approval by the Bank of Spain. Although the application for and issuance of the licenses are processed through the Ministry of Economy and Finance of Spain, actually it is the Bank of Spain that conducts material review of the application documents. The Ministry of Economy and Finance of Spain just go through some procedural formality and will not change the vetting result made by the Bank of Spain. The daily regulation after approval is also conducted by the Bank of Spain. In reality, Spain does not prohibit the existence of financial leasing companies without banking background. Such companies may be knocked out due to their disadvantage in market competition, which however is totally different from legal prohibition.

Private equity companies

A PE company, also known as a PE investment fund company (a PE company), is a company that conducts business of PE investment.[12] PE investment in a broad sense includes equity investment in companies before their initial public offers, that is, the investment in an unlisted company in its seed stage, start-up stage, development stage, expansion stage, mature stage, and other pre-IPO stages. Relevant capitals corresponding to these different stages may be categorized into venture capital (VC), development investment, merger fund, mezzanine capital, turnaround capital, pre-IPO capital, and other investment, such as post-IPO PE investment. PE investment in a narrow sense mainly refers to the investment in a mature enterprise that has some scale of business and generates stable cash flow, mainly the PE investment in a later period after VC investment. Among others, the merger fund and mezzanine capital account for the largest part of such investments. In China, PE investment always refers to the latter one, which is distinct from the VC investment.

Historical development

In September 1985, the State Council approved the establishment of China's first VC firm, China New Technology Industrial Investment Co. Ltd. During the following 10 years, the State Council gradually issued a series of policies and regulations regarding the establishment of VC funds and started an exploration of PE investment in China. In the late 1990s, foreign investors began to invest in China's IT industry, and PE investment started to develop. Meanwhile, the domestic PE started and mainly invested in the VC enterprises controlled by the government. In the early twenty-first century, China's PE investment entered hibernation. After 2004, the PE investment in China entered a stage of fast development. As the overseas market revived, PE investment became active, and Sina, Sohu, and other enterprises started their acquisitions. At the same time, certain companies in consumer goods sector also attracted attention of PE investments. In 2005, the *Provisional Measures for Administration of Venture Capital Firms* (No. [2005]39 of National Development and Reform Commission NDRC)[13] was issued, which regulated the operation of VC firms. *The Partnership Enterprise Law of the People's Republic of China* was effective on June 1, 2007, which explicitly recognized the partnership form of PE investment, and solved the double taxation issue. Subsequently, PE investment played an increasingly important role in the financing of domestic enterprises, especially private enterprises.

Due to historical differences between PE markets in China and in other countries, the development of China's PE industry followed the entry of international PEs closely, and such development may be divided into three stages: infancy, initial, and start-up.

First was the infancy stage. The first investment wave was around 1992, when a large number of overseas investment funds entered China. They tended to cooperate with state-owned large enterprises that were themselves undergoing a transformation, including the Northern Industry and Jialing Group. However, because China's market economic system and modern enterprise system were still in an exploratory stage, enterprise efficiency was generally low. Due to the lack of exit channels through overseas securities markets, the first group of investment funds that entered China ended in failure, while most withdrew or dissolved before 1997.

The initial stage was second. This was around the end of 1990s, a time symbolized by Internet boom. Driven by the global Internet boom, foreign investment funds invested in many Chinese IT enterprises. Meanwhile, domestic PE funds gradually developed, which were mainly VC firms set up by the government. However, as Internet bubble exploded and the operational mechanism of domestic VC firms was not well established, a large number of investment institutions suffered.

Third was the start-up stage. The size and influence of government-led industrial funds expanded continuously. Domestic PE funds gradually grew, and a number of domestic investment firms, such as Hony Capital, emerged with excellent investment records and great market influence. Especially after the global financial crisis, PEs became increasingly localized. This period witnessed some changes in industry practice. First, there was a localization of management for foreign funds; second, governmental capital entered into PE funds, playing an important role in industrial investment funds; third, capital from private sectors participated more actively. As global economic integration intensified, foreign investment funds became active again and played an increasingly important role in the financing of domestic, especially private, enterprises.

Development motivations

Many factors have driven the development of China's PE market. We explore the key reasons for its development here, which include rapid economic growth, need for equity capital, wealth effects, and encouraging government policy.

1 Investment opportunities resulted from the fast growth of China's economy and stimulated the development of China's PE fund market. In the last 30 years, the fast growth of China's economy shows that economic development brings in great needs and opportunities for investment, which in turn provide a wide range of opportunities for the development of PE funds.
2 PE funds meet Chinese enterprises' need for equity capital. China's financial system mainly focuses on indirect financing at the expense of direct financing. Equity capital in direct financing is especially tight. PE funds are well suited to meet such needs.
3 The wealth effect brought about by the stock market stimulated the investors' drive to invest. The huge wealth-generating effect of the stock market made investors want to invest in PE funds, which facilitates their fundraising efforts.
4 The government's encouraging policy also positively impacted the development of PE funds. In the last 10 years, the Chinese government, especially local governments, paid much attention to the development of PE funds, released a series of supporting policies, and provided PE funds with support and favors

in terms of both financing and taxation. On the other hand, governments used budget funds to establish or participate in PE funds. Such measures help push the development of PE funds.

Market size

In 2012, 369 PE funds were qualified to invest in mainland China and completed their fund raising. The number of newly raised funds exceeded that of the previous year and reached the highest level in history. However, the total amount raised decreased, and only 359 out of 369 new funds disclosed their fundraising total, which in total amounted to US$25.3 billion. There were 354 RMB funds and 15 foreign currency funds. Although there are many more RMB funds than those foreign currency funds, the average size of RMB funds are much smaller than that of foreign currency funds. The investment activities of the Chinese PE market slowed down in 2012, in which a total of 680 investments were completed. About 606 of these investments disclosed their investment amount, which together totaled US$19.8 billion. Growth capital remained the dominant investment strategy, and real estate investment and PIPE also performed well. As for exit strategy, investment institutions consciously adopted other exit methods due to difficult exits and low IPO returns. There were 177 exits in 2012, of which 124 (70%) were IPOs. Increasingly, investment institutions began to adopt other exit methods, such as equity transfers, mergers, and management buyouts (MBOs).[14]

Risk characteristics

Generally, the primary risk faced by a PE fund or its investors is investment risk, namely the investors may not exit normally due to reasons including an operational failure of the portfolio enterprise, low revenue, or an investment return that fails to meet the expectation/results in a loss.

During the course of leveraged acquisition by a PE fund, if the leverage ratio is too high, it will bring risks to the PE, its investors, and financial institutions. Generally, leveraged financing will be used when it needs to obtain capital for acquiring equity, namely a leveraged acquisition. In practice, the transaction structure becomes increasingly complex as the size of leveraged loans increases and as more lenders provide financing. Such high leverage and complex acquisitions bring potential risks to both PE funds and the lenders.

The illegal operation of PE funds, such as illegal fund-raising, insider trading, market manipulation, and tunneling may also carry risks. The managers of PE funds do not always operate according to proper standards, and in practice, the illegal operation of PE funds is not uncommon. As a typical example, a PE management company in the Chinese city of Tianjin illegally raised money and committed fraud.

PE investors would generally bear all of the aforementioned business risks. However, in leveraged acquisition, risks may also spread to the lending financial institutions.

Determination of shadow banking

A PE fund invests capital raised from investors into enterprises that are capital users, so it acts as an intermediary between capital providers and capital users. Thus, PE funds are credit intermediaries. Meanwhile, PE funds are relatively less regulated in China and show some features of shadow banking.

Although PE funds have some features of shadow banking, their investors are shareholders of the fund if it is a corporation, partners of the fund if it is a partnership, or equity investors if it is a contractual fund. Therefore, when leverage is not considered, PE funds do not have term mismatch, and their liquidity is easy to manage. PE funds with features of shadow banking do not bring obvious systemic risks to the financial system and therefore are not shadow banking in the narrow sense.

Operating principles

The operating life cycle of PE funds includes the following four sections: fund-raising, selection of target enterprises, investment and management, and exit and distribution.

Fund-raising

PE's funding sources are diverse and complex, including institutional investors, enterprises, governments, wealthy individuals, and foreign investors. Since the investment duration of PE funds is relatively long, funding sources are mostly from long-term investors. As government policies become less rigid, domestic financing channel is greatly expanded, and domestic investments account for around 50% of overall funding. Most of the VC in China comes from enterprises, although its amount has decreased in the recent years, while VC from individual investors increased. Foreign capital most often comes from institutional investors.

Selection of target enterprise

The selection is based on a principle that the target enterprise must be able to create value sufficient to justify the initial investment and subsequent deployment of resources to help the company.

Investment and management

PE investments are divided mainly into VC and merger and acquisition (M&A) investments. The former invests in the start-up and growth stages of enterprises. The growth stage includes the seed, start-up, growth, and expansion stages. Investment characteristics of each stage are different. Risk is highest in the seed stage that is mainly associated with the research and development of new products and technology. Most VC investors invest in the start-up, growth, and expansion stages of enterprises. The VC investors may reap returns several times their original investment as their investment grows with the invested enterprise. M&A investment funds require absolute control of target enterprises.

Exit and distribution

There are three methods of exit for PE investment: (a) going public in domestic or foreign capital markets (IPO); (b) equity transfer, most likely via repurchases by the original shareholders, MBO, or transfer to third parties; (c) liquidation. When the enterprises operate poorly and exit problems cannot be resolved, then PE funds go through a liquidation procedure in which it distributes the revenues to the investors and fund managers as agreed.

International comparison

PE emerged in the 1960s in America. In 1976, three investment bankers at Bear Sterns, a formerly high-flying Wall Street investment bank, established an investment company that specialized in the M&A business. This became one of the earliest PE firms. By the 1980s, PE funds grew fast and institutional investors, especially pension funds, displacing funds from individuals and family investors, became the main sources of PE capital. Since 1992, the revival of the US economy had again brought prosperity to the PE industry. Despite the Internet bubble bursting, the fund-raising and investment of PE funds increased and reached their peak before the financial crisis.

There are now more than 600 professional PE investment management companies in the United States, managing more than US$300 billion of PE investment. The US PE industry is the most developed in the world. After more than a half century of development, the US PE industry has formed a standard and scientific operating mechanism.

The regulation of PE in the United States is relatively relaxed, and its regulatory approach is primarily via self-regulation. PE funds do not need to go through a strict registration and approval procedure, nor need they perform information disclosure obligations similar to those of public funds. Fund manager admission is not subject to strict regulation by Securities and Exchange Commission (SEC), once again unlike those for the public funds. PE fund regulation in the United States mainly focuses on investor qualifications and limits the numbers of investors per fund to protect the investors' interest.

Small/micro loan companies

Historical development

A small loan company is a limited liability or joint stock company that is established by individuals, enterprise, or other social organization, to operate small loan businesses. Such a company does not take deposits from the public.

In the recent years, PBOC and CBRC promulgated a series of provisional regulations regarding management of small loan companies. Among others,

PBOC issued the *Circular on Relevant Policies of Village and Town Banks, Loan Companies, Rural Credit Unions, and Small Loan Companies* (No. [2008]137 of PBOC), and CBRC issued *Several Opinions on Adjusting Admission Policies of Banking Financial Institutions in Rural Area and Better Support Construction of Socialist New Village*, and the *Provisional Regulations for Administration of Loan Companies* (No. [2007]6 of CBRC). In 2008, the PBOC and CBRC jointly issued the *Guidelines on Pilots of Small Loan Companies* (No. [2008]23 of CBRC) and thus formally established and promoted a framework for small loan companies.

Development incentives

Small loan companies are supplements to the formal financial system. Specifically, such companies demonstrated the following two features:

1 Small loan companies meet the needs of SMEs and small business owners for small loans. In order to foster development of local areas, especially that of the rural areas, special attention should be paid to the economic well-being of SMEs and entrepreneurs, because it is widely understood that SMEs and entrepreneurs are the economic foundation for the establishment and fulfillment of a socialist market economic system. The economic prosperity of SMEs and entrepreneurs will benefit local economy.
2 Small loan companies meet the needs of grass-root agricultural applicants for small loans, whose participants primarily include farmers and herders. The Chinese problem has always been one of farmers. To enrich farmers, first we need to provide start-up capital for agriculture-related businesses. Thus, to reduce the urban–rural gap, and tackle the problems of rural areas, agriculture, and farmers, it is necessary to meet farmers' urgent needs for capital. The capital outflow in the agricultural industry is severe, and many deposits are concentrated in urban cities. This is due to a shortage of capital in rural areas, which in turn contributes to an under-developed economy there. Meanwhile, for cost and efficiency reasons, formal financial institutions cannot meet the needs of such agricultural participants for small loans. With such a background, small loan companies in rural areas can fill the gap.

Market size

Since the pilot programs began, small loan companies went through a stage of rapid development. According to statistics released by the central bank, there were 6,080 small loan companies in China by the end of December 2012, and the loan balance was RMB 592.1 billion. New loan volume was RMB 200.5 billion. By the end of June 2013, there were 7,086 small loan companies in China, and a total loan balance of RMB 704.3 billion. At the end of the first half of this year, the loan balance has grown by RMB 112.1 billion. Compared with the end of 2012, the number of small loan companies increased by 1,819, grew by 34.5%. Meanwhile the loan balance increased by RMB 215 billion, or 43.9%. By the end of September 2013, there were 7,389 small loan companies in China with a total loan balance of RMB 753.5 billion. The first three quarters alone saw the loan balance grow by RMB 161.2 billion.[15]

Risk characteristics

As lending institutions, small loan company risks are primarily the credit risks of the borrowers. Since small loan companies may borrow external funds of no more than 50% of their net capital, there is a possibility that a failure of small loan companies may bring risks to the entire financial system, but such risks are quite limited.

Determination of shadow banking

Small loan companies are professional lenders that do not take deposits from the public. In terms of their operating model, a small loan company acts as a credit intermediary among its shareholders that provide capital, banks that provide the lender financing, and borrowers that use the capital. In such sense, small loan companies have features of shadow banking. However, it is worth noting that because the financing provided by commercial banks to small loan companies are very limited and that small loan companies in China at present are very small, the risks that may be transferred to commercial banks by small loan companies are quite small. They will not affect the stability of the financial system.

Operating principles

Small loan companies fundamentally are not financial institutions. Rather, they are common industrial and commercial enterprises (Limited Liability Corporation LLCs or joint-stock companies) that conduct lending business. With that in mind, the operating principles for small loan companies are as follows:

In terms of capital sources, small loan companies cannot collect deposits from the public. Their main capital sources are capital from shareholders and from no more than two banks. To the extent permitted by laws and regulations, the balance financed by small loan companies from banking financial institutions cannot exceed 50% of net capital.

In terms of operating mechanism, loans from small loan companies should stick to the principle of "small amount and diversification," and the loan balance for any single borrower must not exceed 5% of the small loan company's net capital. Although there is no upper limit, a small loan's interest rate cannot exceed the limit specified by relevant judiciary agencies, and the lower limit is 90% of the benchmark interest rate for loans issued by PBOC. There is accordingly a market-driven floating range for the loan rate. In terms of customers, small loan companies mainly serve various grass-root agricultural participants, including farmers and herders.

Financial asset exchanges

Historical development

Since 2009, when the idea and model of financial asset exchange first emerged, all regions nationwide had promoted the local establishment of financial asset exchanges. They used it as an important reason to reconstruct cities in a way to compete for status as a financial center. Since 2010, financial asset exchange venues successively opened in Beijing, Tianjin, Chongqing, Wuhan, and Lujiazui (new financial district of Shanghai). Other provinces soon followed. Thus, there was a wave of setting-up financial asset exchanges in China.

Development incentives

The popularity of financial asset exchange is mainly due to competition and high demand for financial assets:

1   The competition to become a national or regional financial center. In the recent years, major cities proposed to build international, national, or regional financial centers. An important mark of a financial center is a developed financial market. Since the establishment of stock exchanges, future exchanges, gold exchanges, and financial futures exchanges are strictly limited by the central government, and financial asset exchanges that can trade assets with various financial features became the best alternatives for local governments.
2   Large demand for domestic financial asset trading. In a financial system in which indirect financing dominates, a large number of financial assets are generated, such as loans, insurance beneficiaries, and trust beneficiaries' rights. Low liquidity is a key characteristic of such financial assets held by the financial institutions or other holders. In order to enhance the liquidity of such financial assets, trading is needed. Financial asset exchanges meet such needs.

Market size

Due to the lack of data, the annual trading volume of financial asset exchanges nationwide is unclear. However, statistics disclosed by Beijing Financial Asset exchange indicates a large market. The statistics show that the number of accumulated listed deals for the year 2012 at Beijing Financial Asset exchange was 2,896, an increase of 265.7% yoy. The accumulated listed amount was RMB 876.6 billion, an increase of 238% yoy. The number of completed deals was 1,931, an increase of 207% yoy. The completed amount was RMB 637.9 billion, an increase of 271.7% yoy. The trading volume doubled each year for two successive years. Among others, the amount of debt investment schemes at the Beijing Financial Asset Exchange was RMB 587.358 billion, through which central enterprises raised RMB 155.5 billion, and municipal enterprises raised RMB 31.4 billion.

Risk characteristics

Financial asset exchanges conduct various levels of business and may face both trading and moral risks. Many innovative financial products that are created to circumvent regulations may have compliance risks. For example, entrusted debt investment schemes on financial asset exchanges are a channel business in which the exchanges works as a channel. It is fundamentally debt investment with fixed income backed by credit. This type of business may face credit risk, risk from insufficient due diligence, compliance risk, and operating risk, as well as the risk that a channel business may bear a liability beyond their channel role due to improper transaction structure.

Determination of shadow banking

Except financial equity rights, bank credit assets traded in financial asset exchanges help banks transfer credit assets off-balance sheet. The entrusted debt investment scheme on financial asset exchanges is a kind of product in which banks issue debt investment products based on loans for corporate clients. Meanwhile banks issue wealth management products to the public to raise funds to invest in such schemes, indirectly providing financing to their corporate clients. This practice may help the bank circumvent regulation regarding the bank's wealth management products.

In summary, financial asset exchanges, through listed sale of credit assets, debt investment schemes, and other financial assets, establish a bridge between capital providers and users, so it functions as a credit intermediary. While financial asset exchanges act as intermediary, they also help financial institutions circumvent regulation or restrictions on credit or financial product volumes, thereby achieving regulatory arbitrage. Thus, the financial asset exchanges are clearly a form of shadow banking.

Operating principles

The Beijing Financial Asset Exchange and the Tianjin Financial Asset Exchange are typical financial asset exchanges. When established, Beijing Financial Asset Exchange adopted the strategic layout of "one market, four sections," with accredit assets section, state-owned financial assets section, PE assets section, and trust assets section. The Beijing Financial Asset Exchange actively explored these innovative new businesses, including credit asset trading, trust asset trading, and private equities asset trading, expanding from their original businesses in state-owned assets trading of financial enterprises and distressed assets.

From the end of 2010, due to the change of national monetary policies, the key business of the Beijing Financial Asset exchange, credit asset transfer business, nearly stopped. Meanwhile, the state-owned financial assets business, which was random and volatile, does not really constitute a financial business. Thus, since 2011, the Beijing Financial Asset Exchange has not reached considerable trading volume for these two basic businesses.

With that in consideration, the Beijing Financial Asset Exchange uses financial product innovation to withstand risks of policy changes. In the first half of 2011, it launched a product of entrusted debt investment schemes and created huge trading volumes. The Beijing Financial Asset Exchange, through continuous innovation and financial product enrichment, has gradually broken the bottleneck of the state-owned financial asset business.

Tianjin Financial Asset Exchange was jointly established by the China Great Wall Asset Management Corporation and Tianjin Equity Exchange. Since its establishment, it has conducted a traditional state-owned financial asset business and distressed assets business based on resources of its shareholders. However, the distressed asset business is not the mainstream business, as it accounts for only a very small part of financial assets and has shrunk in volume. Therefore, the trading volume of this business is not significant.

Since 2011, the Tianjin Financial Asset Exchange has been striving to break the limit of its traditional businesses and gradually carried out product innovation. It created many new products at various levels and asset types, including trusts, insurance, funds, leasing, project financing, and others. It also expanded from the original businesses into distressed financial assets deals, credit assets deals, and transfer of state-owned assets.

Summary

From the aforementioned analysis, pawn companies, guarantee companies, financial leasing companies, private equities companies, small loan companies, and financial asset exchanges all play the roles of credit intermediaries. They are subject to weak or even no regulation, and they all have characteristics of shadow banking. The relevant laws and regulations should be improved to regulate such businesses mentioned earlier, and more importantly, to prevent systemic risk.

Notes

1 Also known as "loan by pledge of personal items," a fast financing business carried out in the pawn industry targeted at individuals and SMEs. It is a pledge loan that will be completed after the items are valued by a qualified evaluator and registered legitimately.
2 See Development of China's Pawn Industry in 2012, Circulation Industry Development Department of Ministry of Commerce, http://ddscjss.mofcom.gov.cn/pawn_monitor/_news/html/2013/3/15/1363339215337.html
3 See The National Pawn Industry Keep Stable Increase in First Half of 2013, Circulation Industry Development Department of Ministry of Commerce, http://ltfzs.mofcom.gov.cn/article/ckts/cksm/201307/20130700205015.shtml
4 When the pawn period or the renewal period expires, a pawn provider shall redeem or renew the pawn within 5 days, failure of which will be deemed forfeiture of pawned assets. Sale of forfeited pawned assets means that a pawn company sells or entrusts a sales firm to sell the forfeited pawned assets.
5 See *Feasibility Analysis Report regarding Establishing a Pawn Company*, at www.cnpawn.cn/pawnners/show.php?itemid=37763

6 The business mode of modern pawn industry has changed greatly and is different from the past traditional pawn. The clients faced by the modern pawn industry has changed from individuals to SMEs, and its service has changed from meeting the individual's needs to meeting the production and operation needs of enterprises and has developed into the provision of alternative financing venues for SMEs.

7 See CRI Global Broadcasting: *Pawn becomes new financing method in Chinese society*, at http://gb.cri.cn/1321/2006/10/02/661@1242787.htm

8 The seven ministries and commissions include CBRC, NDRC, MIIT, MOF, MOC, PBOC, and SAIC.

9 See the Finance and Guarantee Department of CBRC, *Circulation on Development and Regulation of Financing Guarantee Industry in 2012*, at www.cbrc.gov.cn/chinese/home/docView/7A12AE1C49E64F65B11ED1B2B0CEF4F9.html

10 Guarantee means an agreement between the guarantor and the creditor that when the debtor fails to perform its obligations, the guarantor will perform or assume liability as agreed. The nature of guarantee is prevention of risks or spread/transfer of risks.

11 See Qiao Jiawei, the volume of financial leasing in 2012 increases large by 67%, and the capital adequacy ratio of partial companies is less than 1%, at www.21cbh.com/2013/xintuo_320/643089.html

12 From the perspective of investment method, private equity investment means the equity investment in private enterprises, that is, the non-listed companies, through the form of private equity. During the transaction implementation, such investment will also consider the exit mechanism in the future, that is, selling the equities held and profit by means of listing, merger, and MBO.

13 These measures were issued by the NDRC, Ministry of Technology, Ministry of Finance, Ministry of Commerce, PBOC, State Administration of Taxation, SAIC, CBRC, CSRC, and SAFE, effective on March 1, 2006.

14 See Annual Brief on China Private Equity Investment 2012, at China Equity Investment Website, www.86pe.cn/html/gqzx/hangyebaogao/PEbaogao/19744.html

15 See statistics from the Investigation and Statistics Bureau of the PBOC, at http://pbc.gov.cn/publish/diaochatongjisi/3172/index.html

5   Currently unregulated institutions and new businesses in financial markets

Unregulated institutions in China's financial market mainly include the new Internet finance companies, private lending, and third-party wealth management entities. New businesses in financial markets mainly include asset securitization, securities margin trading, repos, and money market funds (MMFs).

Currently unregulated institutions

New Internet finance companies

Along with the rapid development of Internet and information technology, the new Internet finance companies have challenged the traditional banking businesses. First, the third-party payment and mobile payment offer a more convenient payment method, which poses a challenge to the traditional payment and settlement business of banks. Second, the emergence of network lending platforms provides small- and medium-sized enterprises (SMEs) with a convenient and quick way of financing that requires no collateral, which threatens the traditional SME lending businesses of banks. The new Internet finance companies mainly operate Internet-based lending platforms in two models: one is an online lending model represented by Alibaba Financial, and another is the peer-to-peer (P2P) lending model represented by renrendai.com.

Alibaba Financial

Alibaba Financial mainly provides small loans to SMEs and individual entrepreneurs registered on the Alibaba and Taobao platforms.

HISTORICAL EVOLUTION

The prototype of Alibaba Financial is "TrustPass," launched in 2002. "TrustPass" is mainly a membership-based online trading service launched for SMEs engaged in domestic trade, which solves the problem of trustworthiness of e-commerce by establishing "storefronts" to sell products and advertise enterprises and products on Alibaba. In March 2004, Alibaba launched "TrustPass Index," a quantitative and comprehensive credit scoring system for both the trading parties. The statistical system provides identity authentication of "TrustPass" members, ages of archives, status of transactions, customer evaluations, commercial disputes and complaints, and other information. "TrustPass" works more like a financial intermediary. On October 18, 2003, the birth of Alipay brought major changes to financial payment methods. A buyer can prepay money into Alipay in advance, then Alipay instructs the seller to deliver goods. Upon receipt of the goods, the buyer will confirm payment, and Alipay then makes the payment to the seller. The emergence of Alipay solved the problem of online payment and established a trust mechanism between buyers and sellers.

In 2007, joined by China Construction Bank (CCB) and Industrial and Commercial Bank of China (ICBC), Alibaba provided online joint guarantee loans to member companies, under which a consortium consisting of three or more enterprises jointly applied for a bank loan without collateral, while the member companies shared risks. Alibaba provided banks with the credit records of the members who applied for loans so that banks were able to provide loans with adequate risk control. Due to great difference in the understanding of credit-related concepts among the parties, however, Alibaba's cooperation with the two banks ended abruptly in 2010. The Alibaba group then adjusted strategy and formally established the Zhejiang Ali Small Loan Company in June 2010. Subsequently, the Chongqing Small Loan Company was founded in June 2010 with registered capital of RMB 1 billion. Through these two small loan companies, Alibaba Financial provides two types of services: loan on orders and loan on credit in the three platforms, Alibaba business to business (B2B), Taobao, and Tmall. On February 21, 2012, Alibaba announced that the former Alipay was split into a sharing platform business group, domestic business group, and international business group and merged with the original Ali financial business, thereby established a sector of "Small & Micro Finance." On March 7, Jack Ma, head of the Alibaba group, announced the formation of the Ali Small & Micro Financial Service Group in an internal email, which would be responsible for the Ali group's innovative financial business geared to the needs of small and micro enterprises and individual consumers. On March 11, the Alibaba group appointed Chief Data Officer Mr. Jonathan Lu as CEO of Alibaba group, who will be responsible for all businesses except for those of Ali Small & Micro Financial Service Group. At this point, the Ali Small & Micro Financial Service Group has developed to be parallel to Alibaba group, and the financial business had already taken a very important position in the Alibaba landscape.

Within the newly established Ali Small & Micro Financial Service Group, the original Ali financial sector was officially renamed as "Innovative Financial Business Group" (hereafter referred to as "Innovative Finance"), focusing on small and micro credit. At present, there are two core business areas of "Innovative Finance." The first is their loan services, conducted mainly through two small loan companies geared to the needs of small and micro enterprises. The second is the forthcoming credit payment for individual consumers via cooperation with commercial banks.

DEVELOPMENT INCENTIVES

On the one hand, the development of Alibaba Financial was motivated by the e-commerce customer base and transaction data accumulated over many years.

Alibaba Financial's business covers areas beyond those of traditional commercial banks. Commercial banks usually grow organically with a step-by-step expansion due to the high cost and low penetration of bank branches. Alibaba's online network, however, has unparalleled advantages in terms of cost and scope, with a large number of potential customers from its online B2B and business to customer (B2C) businesses. E-commerce transactions take place in an information sharing and transparent environment, in which such transactions accumulate data. The identities and commercial activities of all traders can be stored, discovered, analyzed, and refined. Data thus become Alibaba's core asset.

On the other hand, the development of Alibaba Financial is inseparable from the Alibaba group's data technology platform. Thanks to the strong support of big data, Alibaba is able to serve small and micro credit customers and engage in businesses beyond those of traditional financial institutions. Many years of background data stored in Alipay makes Alibaba Financial capable of learning the credit rating and repayment ability of customers, in addition to monitoring customer cash flows after providing loans. It makes Alibaba e-commerce both a platform and a data collection and processing center. Monitoring the trading behaviors and traces of customers is the core work of risk prevention in finance. Normally, it is very difficult to truthfully and accurately trace customer behavior. Traditional lenders depend on collateral and guarantees when facing uncertainty of mass information related to small and micro credit customers. Since such collateral and guarantees are difficult to obtain, the commercial banks often have no choice but to abandon the huge market of small and micro credit customers.

MARKET SIZE

Alibaba Financial lent RMB 13 billion in the first half of 2012 through its microfinance business, which is composed of 1,700,000 loans. Almost 10,000 loans were closed daily on average, and the average amount of each loan is only RMB 7,000. Since 2010, when it began to run small loan business, it has lent RMB 28 billion and provided financing to more than 130,000 small and micro enterprises and individual entrepreneurs over these 2 years. However, Alibaba Financial is still a small player in terms of its loan volume, as 130,000 only accounts for about 0.3% of the 40 million small and micro enterprises in China.

By the end of 2012, Alibaba's Innovative Finance had served more than 200,000 small and micro enterprises. The average amount of the loans was between RMB 60,000 and 70,000. The average loan term was 123 days, and the actual annualized interest rate was 6.7%.

OPERATING PRINCIPLES

Alibaba's financial business was based on its unique model of "small and micro loan plus platform." Alibaba Financial provides two types of services: loan on orders and loan on credit. These services span three platforms: Alibaba B2B, Taobao, and Tmall. The total registered capital of Ali's two small loan companies is RMB 1.6 billion.

According to relevant government policies, the two companies are entitled to borrow no more than 50% of their registered capital from banks, so Alibaba Financial can lend a maximum of RMB 2.4 billion via the two companies. Recently, it launched a B2C platform to provide loans to customers of Taobao and Tmall, while a B2B platform provides loans to Alibaba customers. Such loan products include Taobao (Tmall) credit loans, Taobao (Tmall) order loans, Ali credit loans, and others. Taobao (Tmall) credit loans aim at customers of Taobao and Tmall. The maximum loan amount is RMB 1 million, and the loan term is 6 months. The customers of Taobao and Tmall can apply for unsecured loans based on their credit records. The loan interest is settled on a daily basis with a daily interest rate of 0.06%. The customers of Taobao and Tmall can also provide an invoice stating that "seller has delivered goods" to apply for a Taobao (Tmall) purchase order loan of no more than RMB 1 million and a term of 30 days. The interest is also settled on a daily basis with a daily interest rate of 0.05%. Ali credit loans aim at corporate clients registered with Alibaba, with a loan size from RMB 50,000 to 1 million and a term of 1 year. There are both revolving and fixed-term loans. With revolving loans a customer can apply for a certain amount of money as reserves; no interest on which will be charged if the money is not withdrawn. Borrowing and repayment can be conducted any time, and simple daily interest is 0.06%. With fixed-term loans, a customer may receive a one-time loan after the application, and daily interest is 0.05%.

Ali Finance's model is built on the large Ali e-commerce ecosystem. Familiarity with the operational performance of merchants applying for loans is equivalent to the possession of a detailed proprietary credit-reporting database. Based on such a database, data mining helps deal with the problem of risk control. The existing hurdle in providing loan to small and micro business is exactly this asymmetry of credit information.

In June 2013, Alipay introduced Yu'E Bao, with which a user may deposit cash for an investment return. Meanwhile, the money can be used at any time for online shopping, Alipay account transfer, and other payment functions. Transferring the balances in Alipay account into Yu'E Bao is actually like subscribing a MMF. At present, Celestica Fund is the only MMF provider for Yu'E Bao, for which it established a MMF called "Zeng Li Bao." As a brand new value-added service launched by Alipay, the third-party payment platform Yu'E Bao takes advantage of the Internet to collect "piecemeal" money. Thanks to the characteristics of a simple operational process, no limitation on minimum purchase amount, high yield, and flexibility of use, expanded with a breathtaking pace. On June 13, 2013, quasi-deposit business was launched. On November 14, 2013, there was a breakthrough of RMB 100 billion in "deposits," a new record size for a Chinese fund. As of January 15, 2014, it exceeded RMB 250 billion and 49 million customers.

RISK CHARACTERISTICS AND ANALYSIS

First, China Banking Regulatory Commission (CBRC) or the People's Bank of China (PBOC) has not regulated the small loan business of Alibaba. According to relevant rules and regulations, small loan companies are allowed to conduct loan business within the administrative area of its own county (city and district), but may not operate across regions. Currently, Alibaba can only make loans to local customers through the two small loan companies in their respective registered cities, Hangzhou and Chongqing, and shall be subject to the approval and regulation of local government finance offices.

Second, laws and regulations stipulate that Alibaba Financial may only rely on its own registered capital to make loan and may borrow up to 50% of its registered capital. The money on the books of Alipay may not be used to make loans. With the increase of loan customers, Alibaba will eventually face shortages in funding sources; at the same time, because it is not allowed to accept cash deposits, there is a much higher requirement for controlling the bad debt ratio. An increasing bad debt ratio will erode its capital, limit its ability to lend, and ultimately affect the size of its lending business.

Third, Alibaba's credit lending displays a clearly different risk control mechanism from that of supply chain finance. No collateral and no credit enhancement show a simplicity and independence in risk decision-making, which also means no recourse, and significant losses when risks emerge. Alibaba Financial declares that it has developed a new type of microfinance model through which all kinds of information on customers can be collected online. It can judge customer qualification through analysis of the data, which means an innovative microfinance mechanism whose combination of data and Internet is cost-effective and at low risk. However, the Internet and data are merely information, not assets. At present, the target customers of Alibaba Financial mainly come from its sales and purchase clientele. The customer base will be limited by the technology platform until it expands into other links in the industry chain in the future.

Fourth, the interest rate for small and micro enterprises is too high. The traditional bank interest rate is 7% per year, while the annual interest rate on Alibaba Financial's loans can reach 20%. Such high cost of funding is unbearable for customers, for either urgent or regular needs. This high interest is partly due to the relatively higher tax burden assumed by small loan companies compared to that of financial institutions.

P2P lending

P2P lending, also known as "peer-to-peer lending," is a type of private lending that uses online credit platforms as the intermediaries to bring fund providers and fund users together. P2P lending platforms rely on the power of Internet to effectively connect borrowers to lenders, creating considerable value for both borrowers and lenders. The model is mainly person-to-person information acquisition and capital flows, and it is divorced from the traditional medium in terms of credit and debt. In this sense, P2P lending is a type of financial disintermediation.

DEVELOPMENT OF THE P2P INDUSTRY

Since 2005, P2P lending models such as Zopa sprouted up in Europe and the United States, then quickly spread throughout the world. This Zopa model is widely copied *atively successful P2P lending globally includes three models: two P2P *ing platforms Prosper and Lending Club in the United States and Zopa in the United Kingdom. Prosper is a simple intermediary platform that brings capital providers and capital users together through auctions. In Lending Club, the intermediaries assume additional functions such as allocating different interest rates according to the borrower's credit ratings, matching capital providers and users via social networking platforms, and circles of friends. With Zopa, intermediaries act simultaneously as guarantors, co-claimers of loans, and setters of interest rates. Intermediaries divide the creditworthiness of borrowers into different ratings, and then lenders make loans based on credit rating, loan amount, and loan term. Borrowers are required to sign contracts and make mandatory monthly repayments to reduce risk for lenders. Zopa, the world's first well-known P2P lending platform, had successfully facilitated around GBP 290 million of loans by the end of 2012.[1]

Until April 2, 2013, Prosper and Lending Club, the two main P2P lending platforms in United States, respectively, facilitated US$447 million and US$1.521 billion in loans.[2] Although the overall market size of the P2P industry is not large, it is full of vitality and has the ability of being continuously innovative. The reasons are as follows: market segment needs; attraction of profit and low cost; low barriers to entry and no special regulation; and necessary support of Internet technologies, data mining technologies, and credit systems.

Since 2006, P2P lending platforms have emerged gradually and have had rapid development in China. P2P lending platforms in China numbered 110 in 2012. The *White Paper on the P2P Lending Service Industry in China (2013)* reveals that innovation and risk management promoted the development of P2P lending services. Compared with the traditional financial industry, the base size of P2P lending industry is not large but has grown at an annualized rate of more than 300%. Available data show a total loan balance of the P2P online business at nearly RMB 10 billion, with more than 50,000 investors. Such numbers would be greater if the uncounted offline P2P businesses were added.[3] The P2P growth mainly stems from the increasingly great market demand for individual consumption, personal investment, and wealth management, along with people's growing habit of using Internet and the growth of P2P platforms.

OPERATING PRINCIPLES

There is an intermediary within the P2P business model, that is, the P2P lending platform, which mainly provides online borrowers and lenders with information flow and matching, information evaluation, and other services that facilitate the completion of a transaction. However, it does not serve as a creditor or debtor. The services a P2P platform provides include but are not limited to the publication of information on borrowing and lending, credit assessment, legal procedures, investment advisory, recovery of overdue loans, and others. Some P2P lending platforms also provide fund custody and settlement services, still without taking roles as a "creditor or debtor." P2P lending and private lending are the same in substance, and the laws governing private lending are referenced in the P2P sector.

P2P lending in China mainly include four models: offline transaction, online and offline combination transaction, online with principal guarantee, and online without principal guarantee. For the offline transaction model, the P2P website only provides information on capital providers and capital users, while the transaction procedures and transaction processes are completed by offline intermediaries and customers in person. A typical example of this business model is "CreditEase." A typical example of the online and offline combination transaction model is Lujiazui Financial Assets Exchange, which has close connections with Ping An Bank, small loan and guarantee companies, credit guarantee insurance institutions, and other financial institutions offline. It produces standardized online products with fixed rates and duration with guarantees of principal and interest. This model is suitable for rapid accumulation of customer data and expansion of scale. However, as a guarantor's guarantee ability is restrained by capital, its development and scale could be limited. It is also unable to avoid systematic risk. In the P2P online model with principal guarantee, the online platform facilitates deals between capital suppliers and capital users based on credit rating and other characteristics of each. In case of default, the online platform promises to reimburse the capital supplier for principal and interest. Typical examples are "Renrendai," "Hongling Venture Capital," and the now bankrupt "Populace Loan," which declared insolvency only a month after establishment. In the P2P online model without principal guarantee, the capital providers and capital users conduct transactions through online auctions. In case of borrower default, the online platform will not reimburse the capital provider for principal and interest. The two P2P online lending models, with or without principal guarantee, are mainly online services providers.

RISK CHARACTERISTICS AND ANALYSIS

P2P lending platforms often lack adequate risk control ability due to their inability to obtain sufficient credit records and the absence of collateral assets. There have already been embezzlement scandals at several P2P lending platforms including Taojindai, Youyi, and Antaizhuoyue. There was a lack of sufficient monitoring and supervision of fund movements, transaction settlement, and information on bad debts at these P2P lending platforms, which even participated as a party in the transaction. These examples suggest that P2P industrial development needs to go beyond using the Internet to accumulate large amount of data to identify risks. They also need to establish standardized risk management systems.

P2P lending models allow a broad range of participants with diversified profiles and complicated debtor–creditor relationships, which display a crossover and multiline relationship between information and funding. With this scattered, wide-ranged, networked, and interconnected relationship between information and funding, regulators need to consider first the issue of public interest, which requires careful handling, and then to consider technical issues such as monitoring of fund movements and effects of macro-policy. P2P lending has a credit intermediary business model and risk characteristics similar to those of commercial banks, but the lack of regulation or adequate regulation in P2P lending will likely cause systemic risk and regulatory arbitrage. P2P lending accordingly has the characteristics of shadow banking.

Private lending

Drifting outside the financial system, private lending refers to the financing among natural persons, legal persons, and other social organizations, such as non-financial institutions. Chapter 12 of the *Contract Law* ("Loan Contract") provides that borrowing money and the repayment of both principal and interest are under the protection of law. Therefore, the law would protect private lending that reflects real lending relationships. According to the *Several Opinions of the Supreme People's Court on Trial of Borrowing Case by the People's Court* (No. [1991]21), the borrowing disputes between natural persons, natural person and legal person, and natural person and other organizations are treated as cases of lending, which guarantees the legitimacy of private lending. However, private lending should also follow some special laws and regulations. For example, the lending rate shall not exceed four times the benchmark interest rate published by the PBOC. On November 22, 2013, the sixth meeting of the 12th Standing Committee of National People's Congress of Zhejiang passed the *Wenzhou Private lending Management Ordinance* (implemented as of March 1, 2014) to regulate three types of private lending including private lending, targeted debt financing, and targeted collective funding. This is China's first local regulation, as well as the first special regulation on private lending, the promulgation of which will provide guidance on the private lending reform nationwide.

Overall status

According to the *Report on China's Regional Finance Operation in 2004* issued by the PBOC, private lending generally fits into four categories based on the counterparty, financing purpose, and interest rates. The first is collaborative lending with low interest rates. The borrowers are mainly natural persons who have a close relationship with the fund provider. The funds are mainly used to meet urgent life needs of life, and the scale of the financing is small. Mostly, there is either no interest or low interest rates. The second is fiduciary loans with relatively high interest rates. The borrowers are mainly individuals and SMEs. It is based on the relationship and the reputation, and funds are mainly used for production needs. The interest rate is primarily agreed upon based on the creditworthiness of borrowers or determined by the relevant market. This type of lending, based on credit trading with high interest rates, is most common in private lending. The third category is private lending via intermediaries, including private lending facilitated by formal intermediary organizations and the private lending relying on unofficial intermediaries. In recent years, illegal financing institutions such as underground banks, funding clubs, and Rotating Savings and Credit Associations (also known as ROSCA) have greatly decreased. However, alternative funding operation channels have appeared via new types of private lending organizations such as information consulting companies, township enterprises, and investment companies that operate a financing model similar to bank fiduciary loans. Brokers have also begun to provide guarantees for both borrowers and lenders. Fourth, there is convoluted company-led direct financing. Due to the insufficiency of systematic, formal, successfully operated venture capital funds in China, many small- and medium-sized private enterprises and individual entrepreneurs often directly raise funds from the public in the form of "margins," worker's funds, operations in partnership, and absorbing non-local capital investment to maintain or expand the scale of production and operation.

Practical reasons for the existence of private lending

Private lending alleviates information asymmetry due to its geographical advantages and its unofficial resources. Private lending is established on the basis of geopolitical relations, blood relationships, personal networks, commercial networks, and other social networking relationships. Therefore, the credibility and economic status of borrowers are sufficiently recognized and accepted by their private lenders, and access to information is more convenient and cost-effective. In addition, private lending can use a variety of informal information channels to solve the problem of information asymmetry at a low cost.

Adequate supply of private capital is the main reason for the existence of private lending. The rapid development of the non-public economy requires corresponding multi-level capital markets and diversified forms of financing. Money suppliers have incentives to seek higher returns through private lending in the absence of legitimate investment channels.

Insufficient supply of loans by the formal financial sector is another reason. In the recent years, borrowing demand from small and micro enterprises has been very strong. However, due to incomplete and defective credit records, it is often impossible for them to obtain financing from formal financial institutions. It may also be that the amount obtained from formal financial institutions is insufficient, so they must resort to private lending.

Market size

In early May 2008, the PBOC and CBRC jointly organized a survey on private lending among 7,500 SMEs, 11,000 natural persons, pawnshops, guarantee companies, and other intermediaries. The estimated amount of private lending was then about RMB 2.5 trillion, accounting for about 8% of the loan balance of financial institutions at that time. In two regions, private lending was relatively active and the interest rates were relatively high: one was China's eastern regions such as Jiangsu, Zhejiang, Guangdong, and Fujian, where numerous SMEs were located; the other was areas with rich mining resources including Inner Mongolia, Shanxi, Yunnan, and Xinjiang.

Main risks and shadow banking

1   Financing intermediary risk. Small loan companies, pawnshops, consignment stores, and other quasi-financial institutions operating "over the line" sometimes participate in private lending in disguised form, gathering scattered and idle social funds to lend to bigger customers, all of which magnify the financing risks and disturb the financial order.

2   Ponzi schemes. High interest rates of private lending and possibility of being caught in "Ponzi schemes." It is common for private lending to use high returns to lure in capital with interest rates much higher than bank deposit rates. However, high interest rates are difficult to be covered with an enterprise's operating profits, and some debtors with weak financial strength can only use the money from new investors to pay interest and principal to old investors, creating the illusion of earning money and catch many investors in "Ponzi schemes."

3   Legal risks. The entry barriers for private lending are low. The majority of private lending is loans on credit, with the signature of a promissory note or written contract as a main operation form. Such simple borrowing procedures lead to weak binding forces and set hidden obstacles to proper dispute resolution. Sometimes there is only an oral agreement. If dispute occurs in this case, it becomes very difficult to determine the true lending relationship between the parties.

4   Risk transfer and shadow banking. When the economy is in a downward cycle or there is a shortage of capital in the market, the risks of private lending are more likely to be spread and transferred to the banking system through various channels. First, some enterprises or individuals obtain lower interest funds from bank loans, bills, and credit cards and then lend the money to others at higher interest. Second, bank staff may participate in private lending, even usury, directly or as an intermediary to make a profit. Third, guarantee companies and others may illegally engage in intermediary activities like private lending, which is beyond their authorized business scope and endangers the safety of funds from the banks they work with. Fourth, some borrowers and lenders use banks as the financing platform for their private lending, so they may transfer losses resulting from borrowing disputes to banks by taking advantage of bank's internal control deficiencies. High interest rates and poor standardization of private lending magnify such financing risk transfer and disturb financial stability. Accordingly, private lending is a form of shadow banking in a narrow sense.

Third-party wealth management companies

Overall status

The so-called third-party wealth management companies (WMCs) refer to intermediary financial advisers independent of commercial banks, securities firms, and other financial institutions. Third-party WMCs are not financial institutions, producers, or direct sellers of financial products. They independently provide consumers with financial advice and intermediary broker services.

Third-party or independent financial advisors first appeared in Europe, the United States, and other developed countries in which relatively mature market systems have been established. In May 2006, as the first Chinese financial advisor, Beijing Youxian Wealth Management Firm began its operation, marking the official entry of the financial advisory business in China. At present, the third-party financial advisory is still in its infancy stage in China. Third-party WMCs shall be registered in the form of company (or partners) and are under the general supervision of the administration for industry and commerce.

The main characteristics of the third-party WMCs:

1   Relatively independent status. Third-party WMCs mainly provide wealth management and asset allocation advices, in addition to professional financial planning according to customer needs and changes in the market, to help clients manage risks and obtain greater returns. Judging from the history of WMCs in developed countries, the main source of income for third-party WMCs is service fees from clients. This ensures its independence and professional judgment and avoids a direct conflict of interest with financial institutions.
2   Diversity of business. In the regulatory environment that separates financial sectors, third-party WMCs have the advantage to provide a variety of cross-sector financial products and advisory services, which can be more comprehensive than the services provided by banks, securities firms, and insurance companies. In addition, some third-party WMCs also provide alternative investment services like real estate and art.
3   Customized services. Third-party WMCs provide comprehensive financial planning, strategies, and schemes. These focus on tailored and customized services. Third-party WMCs shall focus on their customer's best interests and optimized value, act for the customer's benefit, and meet the diversified needs of customers.

Main business and revenue model

The basic model of third-party WMCs starts from a customer's selection and engagement of an independent financial adviser. The customer then should conduct analysis on his/her own financial situation and risk tolerance with the help of the financial adviser. Finally, after setting up customer's financial goals, the financial advisor helps the customer choose different asset allocations and investment tools to achieve such goals.

First, the common profit models of third-party WMCs include financial planning and advisory services, for which the incomes are from membership fees, advisory fees, and relatively stable service fees, which can also help to maintain WMC's independence and objectivity. Second, they may collect sales commissions from the distribution of financial products. Domestic third-party WMCs also engage in recommendation and distribution of trust products, "sunshine private funds" (collective trust plans investing in listed securities and managed by external third-party money managers that are not regulated financial institutions) and securities investment funds, and so on. Third-party WMCs take the role of intermediary and broker. They collect subscription fees in agreed proportion or performance returns from trust companies, private equity funds, and others in accordance with the agreement. Third, fees generated from providing investment management services. Some third-party WMCs provide both advisory and investment management services.

Risk status and main problems

First, a third-party WMC plays a role to help its clients overcome their disadvantage in understanding and use of information provided by the financial institutions, and to help its clients avoid risk while obtaining returns. In line with the purpose of their set-up, the third party WMCs should not deal with their client's funds directly. After a WMC recommends financial products to their clients, the clients can establish direct relationships with the providers of such products. Therefore, a typical third-party WMC does not have common characteristics of shadow banking.

Second, moral hazard may exist. WMC services usually end right after the sale of the products. Such a commission-driven mechanism and business model are more likely to lead the sales manager at WMC to emphasize returns while hiding risks and selling the products that do not match client's risk tolerance.

Third, there are three negative effects on banks and other formal financial institutions: The first is the reputational risk. Some third-party WMCs arbitrarily use words like "bank custody for funds" in their marketing materials or claim that they have closely worked with commercial banks for product design and selection to enhance their credibility and take advantage of commercial bank's reputation. When there is a loss, the bank's reputation may be compromised. The second is the risk to client's private information. In order to find qualified and high net worth clients to buy products, third-party WMCs may collect name lists and other information of qualified clients from commercial banks and other formal financial institutions. The third is the risk of improper movement of funds. Some WMCs engage in movement of large amounts of funds with clients. If client investments suffer losses, banks and other formal financial institutions may have joint and overlapping liabilities, as well as the operational risk related to their staff who are involved in the fund movement.

Summary

With the development of information technology, some Internet companies have become involved in the financial intermediary business. However, for technical and other reasons, they are currently not under strict regulation. In addition, private lending is a typical form of shadow banking which is also free from regulation at present. It is necessary to pay close attention to these businesses and introduce timely, relevant regulations and policies to reduce systematic risk.

New businesses in the financial markets

Asset securitization

Asset securitization refers to the process of segregating certain assets with low liquidity but stable cash flow through a structured arrangement and issuing securities backed by such assets. The basic process is as follows: a sponsor will entrust its property or property rights to a trust company or other relevant institutions so that the trust company or the relevant institutions may set up a special purpose vehicle (SPV). With a true-sale, sponsors transfer accounts receivables, bank loans, and other property or property rights into the SPV as underlying assets. The SPV will issue securities backed by these underlying assets in open markets. The cash flow and related rights and interest generated from the underlying assets are the legal support for the returns, rights, and interests of the issued securities. The SPV is the core of asset securitization. An SPV can take the form of a company (special purpose corporation, SPC) or a trust (special purpose trust, SPT). The purpose is to ring-fence the underlying assets from the sponsor.

Business model

China's asset securitization currently has two models: securitization of credit assets supervised and regulated by CBRC, and the special asset management plan (SAMP) from securities firms that are supervised and regulated by the CSRC.

SECURITIZATION OF CREDIT ASSETS

This is a type of structured financing activity in which financial institutions in the banking industry will serve as sponsors and entrust credit assets to a trustee. The trustee will issue asset-backed securities (ABSs) to investment institutions in the form of ABSs, and investors are paid with the cash generated from such assets. This structure can be divided into the following parts: underlying assets; credit enhancement, consisting of internal enhancement (senior and junior tranches, the excess interest income, and credit triggering mechanism), external enhancement (insurance and external guarantees), and risk retention; off-balance sheet treatment of credit assets, which means when the sponsor has transferred almost all (usually 95% or more) of the risks and rewards associated with credit assets, such assets can be removed from the account and balance sheet of the sponsor, with however at least a 62.5% risk reserve for the 5% retained risk; trading market, which refers to the national interbank bond market where issuance and trading take place; and approval authority, which refers to the CBRC and PBOC, as shown in Figure 5.1.

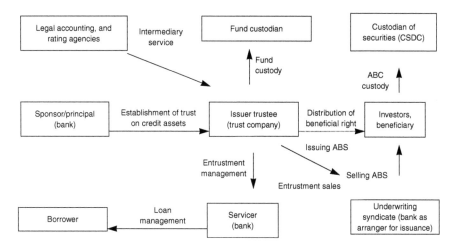

Figure 5.1 Business model of securitization of credit assets.

SPECIAL ASSET MANAGEMENT PLAN FROM SECURITIES FIRMS

Security firms use a SAMP as an SPV to issue this ABS, which relies on the cash flow generated from the underlying assets or portfolio to support its payment to investors, with a structured arrangement for credit enhancement from securities firms. The key factors include underlying assets, which refer to accounts receivables, credit assets, beneficial rights of a trust or infrastructure property, commercial real estate assets, and others; credit enhancement, for which more external credit enhancement is needed for SAMP than for the securitization of credit assets; trading market, which refers to the stock exchange, the quotation and transfer system among institutions of the securities industry association, over-the-counter markets, and other trading places approved by the CSRC; and approval authority, which refers to the CSRC, as shown in Figure 5.2.

Market size

In January 2004, the State Council issued the *Several Opinions on Promoting Capital Market Reform and Stable Development* (No. [2004]3 of the State Council), which recommended that China "actively explore and develop asset securitization products"; in August 2005, the CSRC approved the first enterprise asset securitization pilot project: the China Unicom CDMA Network Rental Income Plan. So far, 11 SAMPs have been issued successfully.[4] In May 2009, the CSRC issued the *Guidance on Enterprise Asset Securitization Business Pilot of Securities Firm (Trial Implementation)*. On March 15, 2013, the CSRC issued the *Regulations on Management of Asset Securitization Business of Securities Firms* (No. [2013]16 of the CSRC), which made asset securitization part of the normal business of securities firms rather than pilot programs. In 2005, the pilot programs for securitization of credit assets were officially launched. As of June 2013, the cumulative issuance of credit ABSs was US$89.6 billion. In the first round of pilot programs from 2005 to the end of 2008, 11 large- and medium-sized financial

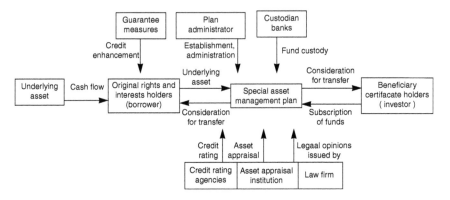

Figure 5.2 Business model of special asset management plan from securities firms.

institutions issued 17 transactions worth RMB 66.7 billion. Since 2011, when the State Council approved further pilot programs, six institutions issued six transactions totaling RMB 22.8 billion.[5] In August 2013, the State Council decided to further expand the asset securitization pilot programs.

Determination of shadow banking

Asset securitization has maturity or maturity transformation, liquidity transformation, credit risk transfer, and high leverage. Asset securitization is an important way to trade assets and liabilities between banks and non-banks, and it is also a potential source of systematic risk. It is thus shadow banking. A detailed analysis is as follows:

MATURITY TRANSFORMATION

The underlying assets of ABS mainly consist of creditor rights or property rights like mortgages, credit assets, and accounts receivables, some of which have longer maturity (e.g., the longest maturity of mortgage loans is 20–30 years) and some have shorter maturity. The issuer is usually allowed to replace some of the underlying asset pool of ABSs after issuance. Maturity terms of ABSs and those of underlying assets are often different, so it has a function of maturity transformation.

LIQUIDITY TRANSFORMATION

Liquidity transformation is the most important feature of asset securitization. In general, the underlying assets of the ABSs have weak liquidity due to long duration, large scale, poor asset standardization, and other factors. Collateralized with assets of weak liquidity, a sponsor produces standardized securities, which are sold in the open market to obtain highly liquid cash. Investors subscribe such ABSs and may trade them on the open market at any time in accordance with relevant regulations. Liquidity transformation of low-liquidity underlying assets is accomplished by securitization. It is worthwhile to mention that at present the re-securitization (securitization of ABSs) is forbidden in China. Assets, property rights, or creditor's rights with stable cash flow and clear ownership must back the ABSs.

CREDIT RISK TRANSFER

Generally, senior and junior/subordinated tranches will be structured within an asset securitization transaction, or an external guarantee mechanism will be introduced. First, in the design of a structured deal with senior and junior tranches, senior tranche investors have extra protection because the assets and earnings of junior tranche investors support the senior tranches' principal and returns. With its assets and credit, an external guarantor provides guarantees to decrease the likelihood that securities investors must take a loss. Through embedded structured arrangements or external guarantee, asset securitization restructured the credit risk exposure of the underlying assets.

LEVERAGE RATIOS

Leverage is not allowed for ABSs in China. However, the arrangement in its transaction structure has an effect of leverage, as investors of different tranches bear different risks and enjoy different returns. A key factor of such leverage is that a sponsor would keep the most junior tranche in a securitization deal, so the risks of underlying assets are not completely transferred away. Nonetheless, the sponsor may invest the money raised from the transfer of underlying assets to further expand business, effectively making asset securitization play a certain leverage role.

CONNECTION BETWEEN BANKS AND NON-BANKS

Commercial banks sponsor credit assets, and commercial banks in China are required to hold a certain percentage of the lowest level ABSs. In addition, China's commercial banks are the most important investors in various ABSs, holding more than 90% of ABS assets. Some ABS are even subscribed entirely by commercial banks. Therefore, ABS does not transfer risks and assets to non-banks. Instead, commercial banks can release capital in the process of asset securitization and further expand the credit business. Asset securitization is thus an important source of systematic risk.

Securities margin trading and repurchase (repo)

Margin trading

According to Article 2 of the *Measures for the Administration of the Securities Margin Trading Business of Securities Firms* (No. [2006]69 of the CSRC), issued by the CSRC in August 2006, the securities margin trading business means the business of lending money to customers for the purchase of listed securities or lending listed securities to customers for sale, with receipt of collateral.

In November 2011, the CSRC revised the *Measures for the Administration of the Securities Margin Trading Business of Securities Firms* (No. [2011]31 of the CSRC; hereinafter referred to as the "*Measures*"). The Shanghai Stock Exchange and Shenzhen Stock Exchange also amended the trading operation rules according to the revised *Measures*.

BUSINESS INTRODUCTION

According to the provisions of *Measures*, securities margin trading can be divided into financing transactions (borrowing cash) and securities loans (borrowing securities). In a financing transaction, investors borrow funds to buy securities from securities firms using funds or securities as collateral and repay with interest within a prescribed time limit. In a securities loan, investors borrow securities from securities firms using funds or securities as collateral for short-selling, that is, first selling the securities and then later buying back the same security to give back within a prescribed time limit, paying a certain borrowing cost for the securities loan. The core of margin trading is "financing," and the core of "financing" is that investors shall provide collateral, pay the financing costs, and return the money or securities borrowed within a prescribed time limit. Therefore, securities margin trading is also called securities credit trading.

MARKET SIZE

As of December 31, 2012, 74 securities companies engaged in the securities margin trading business, and 500,000 margin accounts were open. On January 31, 2013, stocks eligible for securities margin trading on the Shanghai Stock Exchange rose from 180 to 300. On the Shenzhen Stock Exchange, stocks eligible for securities margin trading rose from 98 (i.e., those eligible for being included in Shenzhen 100 index) to 200. By then, stocks eligible for securities margin trading in Shanghai and Shenzhen together reached 500. In April 2013, several securities firms adjusted the threshold of the "two financings" (i.e., either borrowing cash or securities) to require such customer to own at least RMB 10,000 in an account active for 6 months or longer. A reduction in the threshold of "two financings" should increase the trading activity in securities markets. On April 25, 2013, for example, the financing balance in the two exchanges was RMB 167.5 billion, and the securities loan balance was RMB 248 million. The financing purchase amount was RMB 11.1 billion, and the securities loan sales amount was RMB 1.8 billion on that day. The total number of the stocks purchased through financing was 489, and 453 stocks were sold by securities loans.

DETERMINATION OF SHADOW BANKING

Securities margin trading has the characteristics of leverage, although it basically shows no characteristics of liquidity transformation, credit risk transfer, or maturity transformation.

First, securities margin trading has the typical effect of leverage. The leverage ratio of securities margin trading depends on the margin ratio. At present, the margin ratio of securities margin trading shall not be less than 50% in China. Therefore, the leverage ratio of securities margin trading will not exceed two times. According to relevant regulation, securities companies engaged in margin trading shall open a special account for the securities loan in its own name in the securities registration and settlement organization. The account is used to record the securities that are held by securities firms for lending to customers and to record the securities returned by customers. According to the regulation, securities firms are prohibited to lend securities they do not hold to customers. Securities firms can only act as a broker and a fund/securities supplier in securities margin trading, so the leverage ratio of securities margin trading will be somewhat controlled. At the same time, a relevant regulation also provides that "customers may enter into contract for securities margin trading with only one securities firm, and borrow funds and securities from this one securities firm." This provision further limits the leverage ratio of securities margin trading.

Second, there is an association between securities margin trading business and a commercial bank's business. In China, an application to conduct securities margin trading must be subject to a higher threshold and a more restrictive approval process. As the securities firms carrying out the securities margin trading business are generally the borrowing members in the interbank market, it is also likely for the securities firms to establish a credit relationship with a commercial bank through the issuance of the securities firm's corporate bonds. Therefore, securities margin trading and commercial bank face relevant risks. Such risks are managed, however, through the control of capital amounts and the number of securities that can be provided to customers for margin trading. Usually, such amount cannot exceed a certain portion of the securities company's net capital.

Repurchase (repo) business

A repo is a common investment and financing business in the financial markets. The underlying assets of repos include bonds, bills, and other assets.[6] According to convention in China, the repurchase of exchange-traded bonds was generally expressed as the "repurchase business," and the repurchase of notes and other assets was generally expressed as the "purchase and resale business." The repos discussed in this chapter refer to the repurchase of bonds. Repos can be divided into repo and reverse repo depending on the sponsor's position as borrower or lender of money. Repos can then be divided into pledged repo and buyout repo depending on the different disposal approach of the bond in the repo transaction.[7] Institutions short of funds may employ repos to quickly get money into the bond market by pledging the bond without losing the ownership of the pledged bonds; institutions with surplus funds may employ reverse repo to lend money.

The bond repo business is very active in the interbank market. It is an important business for the liquidity management of financial institutions and the allocation of assets and liabilities through short-term financing. In a bond market with considerable depth and scope, high credit rating bonds are easy to sell, with high liquidity and low price fluctuation. Treasury bonds are the main underlying assets of the repo business. The repo rate is also a key benchmark rate in a country's financial market, whose stability is an important indicator of the stability of a country's financial market.

DEVELOPMENT AND EVOLUTION

The bond repo business, long practiced internationally, began in China around 1991. Since 1993, the main provincial capital cities had established securities trading centers. Due to the lack of strict regulation, in 1994 and 1995, fictitious transactions of treasury bonds became increasingly serious, in addition, a "proportional pledge" of treasury bonds was practiced in some places, with many traders short selling with blank checks instead of custodial receipts for actual collateral. The result was serious short selling and false repo problems. In the first half of 1997, the Shanghai and Shenzhen exchanges saw significant price increases partly due to massive bank fund flows into the stock market through the exchanges' bond repo.

In June 1997, with the consent of the State Council, the PBOC issued the Notice of the People's Bank of China on Suspension of Securities Repurchase and Bond Transactions on Stock Exchanges by Commercial Banks (No. [1997]240 of the PBOC), which requires commercial banks to exit the Shanghai and Shenzhen stock exchange markets, transfer all their bond holdings to China Central Depository & Clearing Co. Ltd. (CCDC), and conduct their bond transactions through the trading system at nation's interbank lending/borrowing center.

On June 16, 1997, the center began to deal with interbank bond repo transactions, and the national interbank bond repo market was formally put into operation. In 2000, PBOC issued the *Measures on Administration of Bond Trading in National Interbank Bond Market*, providing that the non-bank financial institutions and non-financial institutions could also participate in the interbank bond repo transactions in order to conduct their bond repo financing and liquidity management in the interbank bond market. In 2004, the buyout repo business was launched in the interbank bond repo market.

MARKET SIZE

The interbank bond market is the main part of China's bond market. Take the data at the end of June 2013 as an example: the bond custody balance of interbank transaction market was RMB 23.5 trillion, accounting for 93.9% of all bonds. The remaining bonds were exchange-traded bonds, over-the-counter (OTC) traded bonds, and other bonds, accounting for 2.6%, 1.6%, and 2.6% respectively. Therefore, without undue bias of the research conclusions and constrained by data availability, all the following statistics for bond repo transactions come from interbank bond transaction data.

The main trading model of interbank bond repo is pledged repo. In June 2013, for example, the delivery volume of pledged bond repo in interbank bond market was RMB 12.1 trillion; the funds delivered was RMB 11.9 trillion in 4.5 million transactions, and the delivery volume and the funds delivered of buyout repo were RMB 282.8 billion and RMB 287.218 billion, respectively.

Among the bond traded, high credit-rating bond (including government bonds, central bank bills, policy bank bonds, government-backed institution bonds, and commercial bank bonds) are the main collateral of pledged repo, accounting for 87.2% and 87.3% of the total delivery volume of bonds and delivered funds. The proportion of bonds with credit risks is relatively small in the Chinese bond repo business.

Commercial banks are the main investors of pledged bond trading. In June 2013, for example, commercial banks accounted for 79.78% and 56.34% of the trading volume of repo and reverse repo; securities firms, insurance companies, and funds were also important investors of bond repo. All the three accounted for 13% and 15% of the trading volume of repo and reverse repo, while the trading volume of non-financial institutions' bond repo was small. Although individuals were allowed to participate in bond repo transactions, there was almost no volume.

SHADOW BANKING CHARACTERISTICS OF THE REPO BUSINESS

The irregularities of the bond repo market at its early stage are mainly shown in the following aspects: first, the bond market was decentralized. There was no centralized custodian and no exchange of the bonds in various markets. Second, the practice of "proportional pledge" in the absence of a guarantee mechanism resulted in a prevalence of fictitious transactions and thus enormous risks. After regulations for the repo business were properly implemented, the practice of "proportional pledge" was stopped and the repo business no longer had the characteristics of leverage. The phenomena of liquidity transformation, credit risk transfer, and maturity transformation are also insignificant in the repo business. The risks of repo transactions concentrate on the traded bonds. The transmission effect of risk between banks and non-bank institutions is also small. The shadow banking characteristics of repo business are as follows:

Leverage ratio   Pledged bond repo must be subject to pledge registration,[8] and an unregistered repo contract is invalid. Both sides are not allowed to dispose or use the pledged bonds during the repo transaction period, and both sides shall not engage in repo transactions with borrowed or leased bonds. The agreement of buyout repo signed by both parties in fact is a bond sale and purchase agreement. Both parties must have sufficient bonds and funds at the time of delivery, cannot switch the underlying bonds, and must use cash delivery or execute early redemption during the repo period. These strict rules for bond trading helped to control the leverage ratio. Registration of pledged bonds guarantees the safety of the pledged bond repo transaction. Moreover, the borrower in the buyout repo business obtains ownership of the bonds. If the seller fails to repurchase the bonds according to the repurchase agreement, the seller automatically loses the ownership of the bonds.

Liquidity transformation   Nearly 90% of the bonds traded in the bond repo business are high credit-rating bonds registered with CCDC, which have good liquidity and low price fluctuation.

Therefore, while the borrower in a repo transaction executes a switch between bonds and money, both parties' purposes for engagement in repo transactions are for asset and liability management and short-term investment, rather than liquidity transformation.

Maturity transformation   According to relevant regulation, all kinds of bonds can be targets of pledge or buyout in repo transactions. The remaining terms of the bonds are usually longer than the repo contract. In other words, the term of the repo contract is generally shorter than bonds, which implies a function of maturity transformation.

Credit risk restructuring   In pledged bond repo, both parties shall not dispose or use the pledged bonds or engage in repo transactions with borrowed or leased bonds. In a buyout repo transaction, both parties shall not change the underlying bonds or execute early redemption during the repo, and they shall complete the bi-directional delivery of bonds and funds in the initial term. Therefore, the credit risk of bond repo transactions depends on the credit risk of the pledged bonds. As high credit-rating bonds dominate China's bond repo business, the credit risk restructure in repo business is low.

Association between non-banking institutions and commercial banks through the repo business   In China, the participants in the repo market consist of almost all financial institutions, including commercial banks, credit cooperatives, securities firms, insurance companies, trust companies, fund management companies, asset management plans of various financial institutions, non-financial institutions, and individuals. There are no more duplicated pledges or duplicated buyouts of bonds in the repo market due to the uniformed pledge registration and custody, as well as the strict prohibition of "proportional pledges." The credit risk of trading counterparties was thoroughly reduced, with a full implementation of centralized trading, centralized custody, and payment-against-delivery of bonds or cash. The risk therefore lies completely in the underlying bonds. Moreover, while repo transactions between non-banks and commercial banks are frequent in China, as the high credit-rating bonds dominate the repo market, the possibility of passing risks among institutions is very low.

Money market funds

MMFs are a kind of investment funds that have gradually thrived along with the development of the short-term bond market and the mutual fund system. It is a type of open-ended fund. Compared to other open-ended funds such as stock funds, bond funds, and hybrid funds, it mainly provides investors with a safe alternative for liquidity management. An MMF invests in various high-quality and short-term interest-bearing instruments in money markets. The financial regulatory authorities of every country provide different limitations on the varieties of MMF investment based on the status of their local financial markets. In general, the investment targets of MMF mainly include short-term government bonds, repurchase agreements, negotiable certificate of deposit (NCD) in large amount, bank acceptance bills, commercial paper, bank fixed-term deposit, and other cash items. There are various MMFs internationally, which can be divided into different categories according to classification rules: incorporated MMF and MMF by contract, retail MMF and institutional MMF, and taxable MMF and tax-exempt MMF. According to the *Interim Provisions on Money market Funds Management* in China, MMFs are allowed to invest in the following market instruments: cash, time deposits and large certificates of deposit (CDs) with a fixed term up to and including 1 year, bonds with remaining life up to and including 397 days, bond repo with a term up to and including 1 year, central bank bonds with a term up to and including 1 year, and ABSs with the remaining life up to and including 397 days.

Historical evolution

MMFs originally appeared in the United States in the 1970s, when its economy had stagnated. Two brokers, Rous Bent and Henry Brown, founded the first MMF in 1971. Subsequently, the United States has maintained a leading position in MMF, and MMF became a great success in the global market.

From late 2002 to early 2003, several Chinese fund companies were preparing to launch MMFs in China. On December 9, 2003, the CSRC approved the first issuance of MMF. On December 14 of the same year, the Hua An fund company formally offered "Hua An Xianjin Fuli Investment Fund" to the public, marking MMF's formal entry into China's money market. Due to policy restrictions at the time, the company avoided the internationally accepted term "money market fund" for this first MMF. Instead, it was called a "Xianjin (Advanced) Fund" and was thus regarded as a "Quasi-Money Market Fund." In August 2004, the CSRC and the PBOC jointly issued the *Interim Provisions on Money Market Funds Management* (No. [2004]78 of the CSRC), which regulated the name, the underlying assets, and the MMF's remaining life, and promoted MMF's further development. In the fourth quarter of 2004, the Lion Fund Management Company launched Lion MMF, which was the first product formally named "MMF" after the promulgation of the *Interim Provisions on Money Market Funds Management* (No. [2004]78 of the CSRC). On March 25, 2005, the *Special Provisions on Information Disclosure of Money Market Fund* (No. [2005]42 of the CSRC) and *Notice on Money Market Fund Investment and Other Related Issues* (No. [2005]41 of the CSRC) were released and came into force on April 1, 2005, leading to the legalization and standardization of MMF in China. The implementation of these laws and regulations further regulated the investment operation of MMF and better protected the legitimate rights and interests of fund shareholders.

In August 2005, the CSRC issued the *Notice on Advice Solicitation Regarding Further Expansion of MMF Investment* to solicit advice on broadening the scope of investment, standardization of market operation, and promotion of the MMF development. Subsequently, the CSRC released the *Notice on Investment in Short-term Financing*

Bonds of Money Market Funds on September 22, 2005, and *Notice on Investment in Bank Deposit of Money Market Funds* (No. [2005]121 of the CSRC) on November 21, 2005, which provided standards for and lowered the credit rating of MMFs investing in short-term securities margin trading. The regulation also stipulated in detail the ratio, type, maturity, and interest rate of time deposit investment to reduce liquidity risk.

On October 26, 2011, the CSRC issued new rules on MMF and loosened the limit on MMF's investment in negotiated deposits. MMFs developed alongside the continuous perfection of relevant laws and regulations. At the same time, through continuous innovation, Floor MMF, MMF ETF, +0 Mode MMF, and even MMFs with functions of loan repayment and cash payment all emerged. The market increasingly recognizes and accepts the value investment concept and rich varieties of MMF products, and its influence on the Chinese money market is expanding.

Development incentives

The original goal of establishing MMF is fairly simple, which is to pool the scattered funds of small depositors and invest collectively in the financial market as a "large depositor," to obtain the same interest income as big depositors. It can be found from the characteristics of MMF that the main reasons for MMF's development worldwide are as follows:

LOW INVESTMENT THRESHOLD AND LOW INVESTMENT COST

Before the launch of MMF, the requirement of a minimum trading volume for money market products (e.g., products that only transact in large denominations such as US$10,000) made most individual investors unable to enter the money market and obtain the high yield of certain products. The annual management fee of MMF is generally between 0.2% and 1%, far lower than other types of funds. MMF satisfies investor demands for higher yield with low management fees via collective investment.

LOW RISK AND STABLE INCOME

MMF investment centers on securities with low risk, high liquidity, and stable income, including risk-free treasury bonds and commercial bills issued by banks or financial companies with excellent creditworthiness. These products are unlikely to default, which satisfies risk averse investors' safety requirement and an expectation of stable income. This is the most profound social root of MMF's long-term survival and development.

DUAL-INTERMEDIARIES FOR INVESTMENT AND SAVING

An MMF pools funds together through the issuance of "shares" and then invests the funds in securities and other assets. It thus has the characteristics of an investment intermediary. The investment scope is strictly limited within the liquid money market.

MMF also has the characteristics of an intermediary for savings. Customers may withdraw money at any time or write checks against their accounts to pay off debts. Some funds may also be directly used to make payment for goods. Nevertheless, MMF has significant differences from real saving accounts. It does not fall into the category of commercial banks, there is no strict reserve requirement, and it does not engage in the loan business. It only makes securities investments within a prescribed scope.

In addition to the MMF's characteristics, the special economic development and financial environment in China helped promote the emergence and development of MMF in the country. First of all, although the money market started relatively late in China, it developed quickly in the recent years, breeding the emergence and development of MMF. Second, the development of the Chinese economy lead to surplus social funds from enterprises and individual investors that set a foundation for the emergence and development of MMF. Third, financial institutions that design the MMF products and act as intermediaries of financing also play an important role.

Under the stimulus of certain market factors since 2000, there have been more and more demands for the creation of MMFs in China. China's stock market fell into a serious bear market for nearly 5 years since 2001. This coupled with the subprime crisis caused by the stock market crash in 2008, lead not only to an increase in the risk of stock market investment but also to the sharp decline in the returns of securities funds that mainly invested in stocks. On the other hand, in order to maintain economic growth, stimulate investment and consumption, and raise domestic demand, the Chinese government adopted a low interest rate policy. This lead to low bank deposit rates at a time of high inflation, which meant low or even negative real interest rates. Putting money in banks brought no real returns. In this market environment, investors in China urgently needed a kind of financial instruments with lower risk than stocks and liquidity similar to bank deposits. For fund management companies, they also needed a low-risk financial instrument to diversify their investment risks. MMF was a clear choice to satisfy both demands.

Market size

At the end of March 2013, there were 1,258 funds registered with and regulated by the CSRC, among which there were 40 MMFs,[9] containing 220 products with total assets of RMB 796.2 billion, 88.7 billion more than that at the end of 2012. The total net asset value of MMF reached 796.3 billion, an increase of 12.53%. Although the size of MMF in China was much smaller than that of developed countries, MMF accounted for more than 25% of the fund industry assets, higher than the overall level worldwide and that of developed countries, which indicated that investors preferred MMF in the current Chinese economic climate.

Risk characteristics

According to historical experience, the risks of MMF mainly stem from three aspects: the risks from the investment portfolio; the risks from outside MMF, such as risk of investor redemption when market conditions change; and a change to the layer and structure of money supply that increases the difficulty of measuring M2,[10] which is detailed as follows:

1   The underdevelopment of China's money market leads to a lack of diverse investment tools for MMF. Among the bonds in the money market in China, there are more treasury bonds and less municipal bonds and corporate bonds; among treasury bonds, bonds with medium and long terms are more common than short-term bonds. Moreover, the proportion of central bank bills in the inventory of all short-term bonds and in the trading volume of short-term bonds is too large, which leads to strong reliance on such bills by fund's investment portfolio. The limited investment tools and dependence on certain products limit the diversification of MMF's investment portfolio, which affects the fund's performance and makes it difficult to diversify the risks of fund investment.

2   Investor redemptions in large sums can bring enormous pressure on MMF's liquidity. When the liquidity becomes tight and financing becomes difficult in the market, investors who lack funds will redeem funds deposited in MMF to guarantee the capital adequacy or capital safety of their own, which leads to a sudden rise in the redemption rate. In countries with market-determined interest rates, commercial banks and other depository institutions enjoy protection from national deposit insurance institutions. On the contrary, there is no deposit insurance for MMF. Therefore, redemptions can trigger chain reactions, which in turn will aggravate the pressure on MMFs. In 1994, the United States Federal Reserve Board (FRB) raised interest rates consecutively, which caused losses to the short-term MMF derivatives investing in long-term bonds and reduced MMF net asset value. Fund investors redeemed funds in large sums, leading to chaos in the MMF and financial markets. In the Chinese capital market, on June 20, 2013, news that the short-term funds of several banks defaulted reached the market suddenly and lead to panic. Shibor interest rates soared past 500 basis points overnight. The interest rate exceeded 10% for the first time and reached a record high of 13.4%.

3   MMFs changed the layers and structure of money supply, increasing the difficulty in measuring the M2 index.

MMF has a substantial impact on money supply, but at present MMF has not been included in the statistical coverage of money supply in China. By contrast, it is very clear whether the money deposited in the bank is current deposit or time deposit and how long the fixed term is. However, after the MMF is purchased, the status of investor funds is blurred. If MMF is included in M2, then the proportion of M1 in the money supply structure will decline and that of M2 will increase. Changes in M1 and M2 directly affect the liquidity ratio (M1/M2). A low ratio indicates that the spot purchasing power of currency declines and money's effect on prices becomes weaker. This change to money supply structure will increase the difficulty of central banks to adjust and control money and increase the uncertainty of its implementation effect. Due to the different influences on the three monetary policy tools of central banks, MMFs actually increase the uncertainty of the implementation effect of money market instruments. For deposit reserves, commercial banks will deposit required reserves at the central bank according to the statutory reserve ratio and total amount of deposits. MMFs' role in diversion of deposits pulls part of the bank deposits directly out of the banking system, and MMF does not need to deposit reserves. Consequently, it will be more difficult for the central bank to manage supply in the money market through adjustment of commercial banks' statutory reserve ratio. For the note rediscounting business, commercial banks may choose to sell discounted bills to central banks or to MMFs for liquidity management purposes. Commercial banks' dependence on the rediscounting policy of central bank will decrease along with the development of MMF, and the effects of discount policy will be weakened. MMF's main investment is in money market instruments. With its continuous expansion, MMF has gradually become one of the main participants in the money market, adding a new "counterparty" to the central bank's open market operations. MMFs hold part of the national debt and can be regarded as an important channel for the central bank's adjustment of the monetary base. They can therefore help improve the efficiency of central bank's open market operations.

Determination of shadow banking

MMF is one of the important channels of short-term capital. It is also a key part of shadow banking. In the international financial crisis, due to huge losses to the financial instruments held by certain MMF, investors began massive redemptions, which exposed a potential systemic risk and a spillover effects on the financial system. That's the primary reason why MMF reform is a concern for regulatory authorities. MMF has the following characteristics of shadow banking:

1 Maturity transformation. MMF mainly invests in various short-term (generally, not more than 1 year) instruments in the money market. These include mainly treasury bills, commercial paper, CDs, short-term government bonds, corporate bonds, and other short-term securities. It is important to note that MMFs can transform maturity. Investors may sell their MMF shares on a daily basis, so it is usually used for cash management by investors as a high liquidity tool.

2 High leverage. MMFs may aid credit creation by expanding money supply and the monetary multiplier, namely the combination of multiplier effect and high leverage. With respect to the money supply model, $M = m \times B$, where M represents money supply, m represents the money multiplier, and B represents the monetary base. The monetary base consists of cash held by the public and reserves of commercial banks. As MMF diverts bank deposits and reduces the cash held by the public, it has a certain influence on the measurement of the monetary base. With respect to the money multiplier, $m = (1 + c)/(R_d + R_t \times t + e + c)$, where $c = C/D$. C represents currency in circulation, D represents current deposits, R_d represents the current deposit reserve ratio, R_t represents the time deposit reserve ratio, t represents the time deposit ratio (ratio of

time deposit and current deposit), and e represents the excess reserve ratio of commercial banks. MMFs divert bank deposits, so c increases, but e and t will decrease. Besides, no reserves need to be set aside in the issuance of MMF, so the actual legal deposit reserve ratio decreases and the excess reserves of commercial banks goes down at the same time, both of which raise the money multiplier.

3   The trading model is subscription and redemption. A massive and intensive redemption will give rise to systemic risk. "Subscription" refers to investors applying to buy fund shares after the contract for an open-ended fund becomes effective; "Redemption" refers to fund shareholders' requirement that fund managers repurchase all or part of their share of the open-ended fund. Subscription and redemption of funds can be carried out during the working hours of fund management companies as long as the fund is in existence. Mass redemption by fund holders will trigger chaos in MMFs and financial markets.

4   Association with commercial banks. MMF is a typical shadow banking closely related to commercial banks. Its operational model is similar to that of traditional commercial banks, but there are differences. Most funds do not have sales channels of their own. The bank branches spread all over China bring great convenience for marketing funds through banks. Consequently, most of the fund distributions depend on commercial banks that in turn collect sales commissions. More funds are part of bank's own products or group companies. MMF started late in China, and at present it is issued and managed by (securities investment) fund management companies. The investment scope is narrow, currently limited to short-term debt (including central bank bills), bank deposits, and repo. At present, it mainly operates in the interbank market, and the trading counterparties are banks. As business develops, there may be cooperation with banks and more innovations.

Development trend

Although MMF started late in China, it has been developing at an extraordinary speed together with China's fast economic development. Overall, we believe there are more favorable factors than negative hurdles for MMF's development in China, with a promising perspective.

1   Residents' wealth is growing rapidly, with an increasing demand for low-risk securities investment instruments as an alternative to savings. China's Reform and Opening Up has unleashed a rapid growth of personal wealth. The financial assets in the hands of residents retained after consumption, mainly deposit assets, are huge. Although it is anticipated that China's economy growth will become slower in the future, government policy incentives and measures to increase residents' incomes will raise residents' personal income and savings further, which will give rise to greater financial needs. It has increasingly become an important challenge to increase residents' investment channels, preserve the value of their assets, and ease the pressure of banking management.

As a good substitute to savings, MMF satisfies the current market demand for low-risk products. Therefore, MMF has a great development opportunity in terms of both quantity and scope.

2   In the process of fund industry development, there are constant innovations to products and market segments to meet with investor's different preferences for risk, returns, and liquidity. Equity funds, balanced funds, and bond funds represent certain preferences on risk and reward. The T+0 model, "Huobitong" and "Yu'E Bao" represent different preferences in investor's needs. As part of the fund product spectrum, MMF adds to the diversity of money funds and fills out the spectrum of fund products. To develop and grow, MMF must improve its own supply according to market demand.

3   Continuous improvement of money market conditions will form the basis for MMF's development. At present, as the central bank's open operations in money market become more frequent, commercial banks and other financial institutions increasingly use the money market for liquidity management and short-term investment. The size of the money market has thus made a great leap. The healthy development of the money market in China in the future includes the perfection of market infrastructure, such as clearing structure. Such development should meet MMF's operational demands.

4   The regulation of MMF and the related laws are being perfected, which will greatly standardize and promote MMF's development. The existing *Special Provisions on Information Disclosure of Money Market Fund* (No. [2005]42 of the CSRC) and other laws and regulations have regulated MMF to some extent. The *Money Market Fund Administration Act* should be drafted and enacted as soon as possible to provide legal protection for the issuance, investment scope, income distribution, and risk prevention of MMF. MMF will have even better development opportunities with strict qualifying examination of professionals and senior management in MMF and a strengthening of requirements for information disclosure.

Summary

New businesses in financial markets are one of the main causes of the financial crisis and are often regarded as the main part of shadow banking. As the financial markets in China started late, these businesses are still in a nascent stage and have not reached a large scale. Nevertheless, we must pay close attention to the regulatory experience from other countries and recommendations from the FSB to prevent systemic risk.

Notes

1   According to the quotations from Zopa website.
2   Data from Prosper and Lending Club website.
3   New Finance Research Center of China Business Network. "*White Paper on P2P Lending Service Industry in China (2013)*," China Economic Publishing House, Beijing, 2013.
4   See http://stock.hexun.com/2013-04-24/153499504.html

5 See *A New Round of Securitization of Credit Assets with 300 Billion Pilots to Become Regular within Eight Years*, see www.Treasurer.org.cn/webinfosmains/index/show/92103.html

6 In theory, all assets can be the targets of the repurchase business; however, standardized assets are the most suitable targets for repos. The mortgage and pledge formalities of other assets are cumbersome, which increases transaction costs and thereby frustrates the pursuit of fast and low-cost transactions in the repurchase business. Therefore, bond repurchase is the most common repurchase business. Other target assets mainly refer to the beneficial rights of trusts.

7 There is another kind of repurchase internationally called tri-party repurchase. The tri-party repurchase means delivery of bonds and money to an independent third-party depository such as custodian banks, clearing houses, or securities custody institutions by trading counterparties, which will be responsible to guarantee and maintain the full value of the collateral during the process of the deal. Tri-party repo has developed rapidly in the recent years in the developed bond markets of Europe and the United States.

8 The registration institution is China Central Depository & Clearing Co., Ltd.

9 Galaxy Yinfu money market fund (the following money market funds are referred to "MMF" hereinafter), E Fund MMF, Harvest MMF, Fortune SG Cash Treasury MMF, CIMF MMF, CITIC Cash Advantage MMF, GF MMF, Everbright Pramerica MMF, ABN AMRO TEDA MMF, Changsheng MMF, ICBC MMF, China Universal MMF, CCB Principal MMF, Wanjia MMF, AEGON-INDUSTRIAL MMF, Fullgoal Tianshi MMF, HARFOR MMF, China Nature Tiandeli MMF, SYWG BNP Paribas Earning Treasury MMF, Yimin MMF, Orient Gold Books MMF, Morgan Stanley Huaxin MMF, UBS SDIC MMF, HSBC Jintrust MMF, Harvest Anxin MMF, Tian Hong Cash Housekeeper MMF, Da Cheng MIGD MMF, Hua An Ririxin MMF, Guotai Cash Management MMF, Zhong Ou MMF, Minsheng Royal MIGD MMF, China Universal Earnings Express MMF, Founder Fubon MMF, China AMC Margin MMF, Essence Cash Management MMF, E Fund Daily Finance MMF, HFT Cash Management MMF, Anxili MMF, Dacheng Cash Treasury MMF, E Fund Margin MMF.

10 M0, M1, M2, and M3 are important indices used to reflect money supply. Monetary layers in China are as follows: M0 equals cash in circulation, narrow money (M1) equals M0 plus current deposits (enterprise current deposits plus organization, group, army, rural, and personal credit card deposits), broad money (M2) equals M1 plus deposits of urban and rural residents and those with the nature of fixed term among corporate deposits and trust deposits and other deposits. In addition, M3 equals M2 plus financial bonds and commercial bills and large amount negotiable CDs, and so on. Among them, M2 minus M1 is quasi currency. M3 was set up based on the constant innovation of financial instruments. M1 reflects the real purchasing power of the economy, while M2 reflects the real and potential purchasing power simultaneously. If M1 grows fast, it means the consumption and terminal markets are active. If M2 grows fast, it means the investment and middle markets are active. The central bank and commercial banks are able to determine monetary policy accordingly. If M2 is too high and M1 is too low, it shows that investment is overheating, demand is not strong, and there is a risk of crisis. If M1 is too high and M2 is too low, it shows the demand is strong, investment is inadequate, and there is risk of a rise in price. M2 is a finance concept opposite to narrow money. A form or measure of money supply, represented by M2, the calculation method is the addition of transaction currency, fixed-term deposits, and saving deposits.

6 The impact of shadow banking on the macroeconomy and financial system

The current shadow banking system in China is still in an early stage of development, which is mainly characterized as circumventing lending rate controls, loan volume controls, and other regulatory policies. The overall level of financial innovation associated with shadow banking is relatively low in the current stage, and the asset securitization that brings great risks to a financial crisis has not taken shape yet. The overall risk of shadow banking in this stage is controllable, with both positive and negative impacts on China's macroeconomy. The innovative shadow banking system may to some degree avoid the inefficiency arising from the fluctuation of prices and volume. It may also have an impact on overall social financing and the effectiveness of both fiscal and industrial policies. In this chapter, we mainly analyze the roles that Chinese shadow banking plays in the macroeconomy and financial market system.

Analysis of the scale of shadow banking system in China

To discuss the scale of shadow banking from the perspective of overall financing, it is necessary to expand the definition of total social financing released by the People's Bank of China (PBOC) for the time being. To be specific, first, although the statistical range of total social financing is larger than that of credit, it still excludes the categories, such as financing with trust plans that is not related to the interbank business, deals done jointly by banks and security firms, and direct trust loans, that have significantly impacted financing in the recent years. The cooperation between banks and funds, the cooperation between banks and insurance companies, and loans of small loan companies may also grow fast in the near future. These categories may have the characteristics of shadow banking. Second, with respect to economic growth or domestic production, the capital sources of domestic sectors should include outstanding foreign exchange. Third, the impact of the government or the fiscal system on production sectors is not considered. As a result, in terms of four sectors (banks, manufacturers, government, and overseas sectors), the impact that at least two major sectors (government and overseas) have on domestic manufacturers is not taken into consideration.[1] In the following, we first analyze the capital sources of total social financing. We then provide a supplementary explanation of the statistics for total social financing and analyze the impact of China's shadow banking on total social financing from different aspects. In the end, we estimate China's shadow banking in its narrow sense based on the analysis made earlier.

Capital sources beyond total social financing

To discuss the potential scale of shadow banking, it is necessary to discuss the balance of financing in a comprehensive manner. As estimated, in addition to total social financing, the volume of foreign capital, government budgets, and interbank financing constitute one third of total social financing. The part stated earlier that has not been considered makes up a large proportion and has strong restraint on other financing (in particular on bond purchase and credit supply within the banking system). Figure 6.1 shows the estimation of scale and growth rate of financing from 2002 to 2012, from which it can be seen that all other financings except "RMB loans" had always been in a rapid growth.

In terms of the structure of total social financing (see Figure 6.2), the proportion of credit and outstanding foreign exchange has rapidly declined, while other types of financing that might reflect characteristics of shadow banking were growing quickly.

Take trust loans as an example (Figure 6.3). The scale of new trust loans had grown steadily from 2006 to 2011. New trust loans grew especially rapidly in 2012.

In conclusion, with regard to the structure of overall financing, the proportion of outstanding foreign exchange and loans has decreased rapidly in the financing balance. Since debt financing has expanded, the proportion of net financing via corporate bonds has soared. The proportion of interbank financing fluctuated significantly due to large changes in regulatory policies. Over the years as market demands flourished and the financial business developed, the proportion of financing through

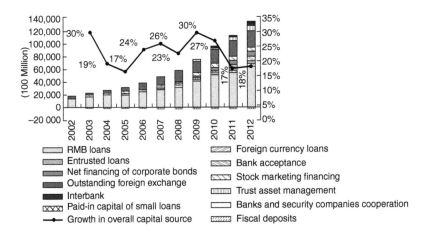

Figure 6.1 2002–2012 financing growth rate statistics.
Source: Quoted from Wind Info (Wind).

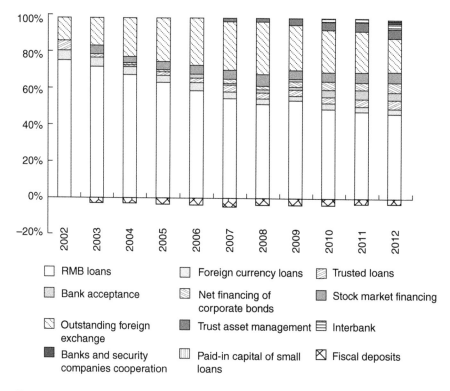

Figure 6.2 2002–2012 changes in financing structure.
Source: Quoted from Wind Info (Wind).

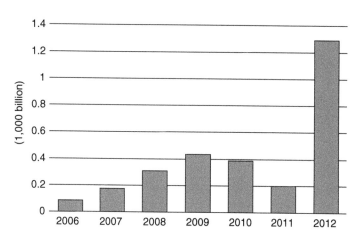

Figure 6.3 2006–2012 new trust loan scale.
Source: Quoted from Wind Info (Wind).

bank-trust cooperation and bank-securities cooperation rose as part of the financing balance. The growth rate over this period reached 646% for bank-securities co-led deals. Meanwhile, the growth rates of net financing balance for both corporate bonds and assets under trust management over the past 5 years stayed above 40%.

Two explanations concerning the statistical results: Calculation method and bank's wealth management products

The statistics of the overall financing scale are already demonstrated earlier, but there are still two issues to explain:

The first issue is the calculation method. We had accurate data for the balance of debt, bond, and stock financing in total social financing, but the remainder was drawn from the sum of the yearly increment based on the total social financing released by the PBOC.[2] The outstanding foreign exchange and fiscal deposits of non-social financing were drawn from data released by PBOC. The interbank business was estimated and calculated through the differences between banks in the balance sheet category of "other deposit types." For cooperative deals between banks and security firms, it was estimated through the balance of targeted asset management products. For cooperation deals between banks and trust companies, it was estimated by deducting trust loans from trust asset growth. To avoid double-counting of financing from the banking system by small loan companies, financing by small loan companies was estimated according to their paid-in capital.

Second, wealth management product (WMP) is not counted in the financing, as WMP is similar to savings deposits. It is an investment target for manufacturing sectors and a capital source for financial institutions, while loans and bonds are capital sources for manufacturing sectors and investment targets of financial institutions. Most of the non-principal guaranteed WMPs are related to trust products. Trust and bank-securities cooperation deals are already taken into account in the statistics of manufacturing sector's capital sources. Most of the principal-guaranteed WMPs are invested in the interbank market and reflected in social capital sources through loans and bond purchases from financial institutions and other channels.

Total social financing and possible scale of shadow banking in a multi-dimensional perspective

The scale of shadow banking essentially depends on our definition of its scope. We have made preliminary estimation and calculation regarding six perspectives of total social financing:

Perspective 1: In terms of domestic sectors, if the non-loan portion in the financing balance is all regarded as "shadow banking," then the scale of "shadow banking" is around RMB 67 trillion.

Perspective 2: If impact of foreign sectors and government is eliminated from the statistics of Perspective 1, then the scale of "shadow banking" is around RMB 44 trillion.

Perspective 3: If foreign currency loans, other credit financing, and equity financing are not taken into account, then the scale of "shadow banking" is around RMB 32 trillion.

Perspective 4: If direct financing of corporate bonds and trust asset management (except trust loans in its narrow definition) are not taken into account, then the scale of "shadow banking" is around RMB 20 trillion.

Perspective 5: If we assume there are no currency derivatives generated or no risks concentrated in banks, "shadow banking" could include entrusted loans, bills, equity financing, paid-in capital of small loans, and so on, with the amount around RMB 28 trillion.

Perspective 6: In terms of effective regulation, "shadow banking" is unlikely to be defined as direct financing such as bond financing and stock financing, nor to be considered as credit assets such as loans in both domestic and foreign currencies. There is no direct connection among outstanding foreign exchange, fiscal deposits, and financial business, so it cannot be regulated. Entrusted loans and trust asset management are normal financing and, if operated in compliance with laws and regulations, are also well regulated. Those that need to be regulated may concentrate in the so-called interbank, trust-securities, and bank-trust cooperation deals that appear as inter-financial-institutional assets but are credit in substance. The real risks of such deals may still concentrate in the financial system. The scale of capital of this kind is estimated to be around RMB 10 trillion.

Based on the statistics of overall financing, the scope and scale of "shadow banking" referred to in the aforementioned six perspectives are shown in Table 6.1.

Estimation of shadow banking in the narrow sense

There is no pure shadow banking institution in China for the time being, but many institutions are involved in the shadow banking business and become one of the links in the capital chain. According to the narrow definition of shadow banking, non-bank credit institutions or businesses may result in systemic risk and regulatory arbitrage with one or more of the four characteristics—maturity and liquidity transformation, high leverage, and credit transfer—and are unregulated or barely regulated; there is no accurate statistic of shadow banking scale due to different calculation methods. Recently, the scale of shadow banking in China is estimated by a variety of institutions to range from RMB 5.8 trillion to RMB 30 trillion.

Based on the definition of shadow banking in both the broad sense and the narrow sense in this book, and according to the judgment of various shadow banking businesses in Chapters 3–5, we roughly estimate the scale of shadow banking in China in a narrow sense as follows:

By the end of 2012, the overall scale of assets under management of quasi-financial institutions and business that were regulated by various ministries and local governments totaled up to RMB 4.5 trillion. Among them, the total assets of the pawn industry in China were RMB 122.9 billion. As of the end of 2012, the balance of guaranteed financing loans was RMB 1.5 trillion, and the balance of financial leasing contracts reached RMB 1.6 trillion. During 2012, over 680 deals were closed

Table 6.1 Scale estimation of shadow banking of various types (unit: RMB 1 billion)

	CNY loan	Foreign currency loan	Entrusted loan	Bank acceptance	Net financing of corporate bonds	Stock market financing	Outstanding foreign exchange	Trust asset management	Trade among banks	Cooperation between banks and securities companies	Paid-in capital of small-loan companies	Entrusted loans	Fiscal deposits	Scale of shadow banking
2012	62,998	5,026	5,654	5,925	7,306	6,824	25,819	7,100	4,208	1,700	510	2,709	−2,426	
Type 1	√	√	√	√	√	√	√	√	√	√			√	67,626
Type 2	√	√	√	√	√			√	√	√	√			44,233
Type 3			√	√	√			√	√	√	√			32,383
Type 4			√	√					√	√	√		√	20,686
Type 5			√	√	√ᵃ	√					√		√	28,908
Type 6								√ᵇ	√	√				10,299

Notes

ᵃCorporate bond financing, if owned by banks, still has its risks concentrated in the banking system.

ᵇEntrusted loans are excluded.

in the private equity market in China, and a total of US$197.9 billion was raised in 606 cases that disclosed such information. By the end of December 2012, there were 6,080 small loan companies nationwide with a loan balance of RMB 592.1 billion. In 2012, there were a total of 2,896 listed assets on the Beijing Financial Assets Exchange, with a total listed amount of RMB 876.6 billion and a turnover of RMB 637.9 billion.

At present, the overall scale of unregulated institutional shadow banking is around RMB 4.5 trillion. In 2010, the overall turnover of the online lending industry in China was around RMB 1 billion; in 2011, RMB 5 billion; in 2012, RMB 20 billion; and in 2013, RMB 105.8 billion. Private lending includes a wide variety of businesses. It includes not only investment companies and wealth management companies (the scale of which is predicted at RMB 3 trillion or so) but also institutions such as chambers of commerce and entrepreneur clubs (the scale of which is predicted to be RMB 500 billion or so). The scale of the traditional underground financial industry such as private unincorporated banks, loan brokers, and trade associations is hard to count, but it is predicted to be approximately RMB 1 trillion.

The total net asset value of market monetary funds in the innovative financial business reached RMB 796.32 billion. By the end of June 2013, asset-backed securities of RMB 89.6 billion were issued. When we add in margin financing, stock lending, and repos, the overall scale of innovative financing is about RMB 1.5 trillion.

In conclusion, at the end of 2012, the overall scale of shadow banking in the narrow sense in China is around RMB 10.5 trillion, ranging from RMB 10 trillion to RMB 12 trillion.

Impact of shadow banking on fiscal and industrial policies

It is fair to say that the shadow banking business is an indispensable part of overall financing. The statistics for capital sources for the outstanding financing of the manufacturing sector provides a way to understand the dynamic relationship between overall social financing and the scale of shadow banking. The following section analyzes the role of shadow banking from a macro perspective and discusses the impact of shadow banking on monetary and industrial policies in more detail.

Impact on fiscal policies

As a supplement to the credit system, shadow banking alleviates pressure on local governments and provides a support to fiscal policies. However, it also creates certain hidden problems.

After the introduction of the dual tax system, local governments in China have faced huge expenditure pressures mainly arising from structural and cyclical aspects. The structural aspect is the long-term trend for an increase of expenditure in normal day-to-day economic activities. Under the current fiscal decentralization system, the central government wields over 50% of national fiscal income. However, unlike other large countries, fiscal expenditure of local governments in China makes up the majority of such expenditure, but the central government only bears around 10%. This results in huge fiscal pressure on local governments. The cyclical aspect is primarily because China's fiscal policies mainly rely on discretionary actions in stabilizing economic cycles, whereas taxation and automatic stabilizers play relatively little role, leading to huge expenditure pressure on local governments. Therefore, one of the primary methods for local governments to solve these issues and achieve fiscal freedom is to establish their own financing vehicles.[3]

In this context, the shadow banking system plays a positive role in alleviating fiscal pressure of local governments and facilitating the development of local economies by providing financing to local governments. First, as responses to the Asian and global financial crisis in 1997 and 2008, respectively, the central government issued national debt and government bonds on behalf of local governments, and local governments raised funds through financing vehicles to provide funds for the economic development. Second, the shadow banking system has been a significant support to welfare improvement and environmental protection. For example, local government debt equivalent to more than RMB 1 trillion had been invested in welfare-improving projects such as education and health care, and RMB 401.6 billion had been invested in energy conservation, emission reduction, ecological construction, and other areas by the end of 2010. Last, the local government debt lays a foundation for safeguarding the sustainable development of the economic system. For example, RMB 6.97 trillion of debt had been used in infrastructure such as transportation and municipal administration, land purchase and storage, and energy construction by the end of 2010.

Still, there are some problems in the issuance and management of local governmental debts, resulting in the accumulation of local and systemic financial risks. First, there are no standards to which the local government can abide by when issuing debt, and most of the debt incomes and expenses are not incorporated into budget management. There are no prevailing laws and regulations that give local governments the legal authority to directly issue debt, nor are there standards for the management of existing governmental debt. Most local governments borrow in disguised form from financing vehicles or financing companies, and some of them even offer illegal guarantees or borrow money directly. Second, some local governments are not capable of repaying their debt, which creates hidden problems. Third, financing vehicles and companies controlled by local governments are large in number and have low management standards.

Therefore, new channels are needed in the future. With improved management, local governments' fiscal freedom should be expanded. With an increase in the transparency of local budgets, structural factors such as the local industrial structures should be closely linked to the extent of local fiscal autonomy. This should encourage structural economic adjustment and may fundamentally eliminate shadow banking's negative impact on fiscal policies.

Impact on industrial policies

According to the European Union (EU) and US standards, any policies that have an impact on specific industries rather than the overall economy are defined as industrial policies. In this regard, industrial policies in China include standards for industrial licensing, systematic management for industrial investment and financing, preferential tax treatment, and many other policies. The impact of shadow banking system on China's industrial policies is mainly reflected in financing.

First, some policy-restricted industries achieved growth by financing themselves through shadow banking. As a result, the impact of industrial policies is compromised. For example, trust loans that financed the real estate sector are shadow banking system in the broad sense. Since it is increasingly difficult for real estate developers to borrow from traditional banks due to unfavorable regulation of the real estate industry over the years, they are forced to choose the shadow banking system. Support from this type of shadow banking compromised the credit-tightening policies on China's real estate sector. Such issues arise from the fact that government's industrial regulations are more policy based than market driven and therefore violate market rules. The market takes advantage of gray channels to circumvent the government's administrative intervention and essentially renders the industrial policies ineffective. Therefore, shadow banking is not the only reason to blame; unreasonable industrial policies should take responsibility as well.

Second, since differences in industrial policies result in different financing costs, some enterprises directly became part of the shadow banking system. Currently, China's banking industry is operating within an environment of price controls, and the number of banks is strictly restrained. Regulation on loan scale makes commercial banks "focus on big state-owned enterprises and neglect the small private ones" in the capital distribution of on-balance sheet loans, which enables state-owned enterprises to obtain funds with lower costs than private enterprises would pay. In this context, state-owned enterprises with the advantage of low financing cost will arbitrage by relending their bank financing, which is manifest in the explosive growth in entrusted and trust loans in recent years.

Impact of shadow banking on monetary policy

Impact on the objectives of monetary policy

Generally speaking, the central bank has three types of policies available for endogenous money. First, quantitative policies such as regulation of loan scale can be replaced with interest rate policy. To further facilitate interest rate liberalization, the interest rate becomes an intermediate target of monetary policy, based on which we can promote structural economic adjustment. Based on the current policies, the following points need to be taken into serious consideration:

1 *Weaken the use of the reserve ratio.* In the context of endogenous money, the bank reserve is "adaptable," in other words, the central bank will increase reserve supply when loans in the banking system are issued. Generally, the central bank may reject certain commercial banks' demand for increasing reserves but not for all banks. If all commercial banks fail to make provisions, financial panic will rise, and interbank interest rate will fluctuate severely, and the whole financial system would fall apart in the end. The central bank, however, needs to maintain the stability in the financial system. Therefore, to prevent the collapse of the financial system, the central bank supplies reserves passively. In this case, the passive supply of reserves depends on conditions in the whole financial system. The central bank will add to supply when the market badly needs capital.

2 *Abolish limits on bank's total loan scale.* The limit on loan scale makes little difference in the context of endogenous money. When the scale of loans is controlled, banks will exchange assets to transfer the loans into off-balance sheet assets to circumvent supervision without being noticed and continue to meet financing demands. Higher risks then arise in the financial system. Due to limits on loan scale, credit rationing will be an increasingly serious problem. In China, credit rationing mainly affects private enterprises and is harmful to both employment and economic development. We therefore predict that other private financing methods will replace bank loans, and trade credit will be deployed more frequently in the future.[4]

3 *Increase the transparency of the central bank.* In the context of endogenous money, increase of investment makes inflation more serious, so central bank transparency should be increased to contain inflation expectations. Currently, the

PBOC is heavily in favor of discretionary approaches, and its conventional behavior has been inadequate, which jeopardizes the control of inflation expectations.

First, the central bank prefers to communicate its policies via announcements and post-explanations. Such a simple communication method is harmful to the control of expectations. The communication patterns of the PBOC at present include monetary policy reports, policy change announcements, news conferences, central bank officials' speeches, other formal speeches in public, and so on. The communication primarily expresses the economic trend analyses by the PBOC, monetary policy positioning, the background and condition in which policies are made, operating methods, and other information. To control inflation expectations, it is necessary to make a judgment on the future economic trends, communicate the central bank's policymaking standards, and formulate China's monetary policies and rules based on such future predictions and policy-making standards.

Second, control the loan-to-value ratio (LTV). Generally, interest rate policies impact loan and deposit rates of traditional banks. In a shadow banking system, financing mainly relies on collateralized intermediary loans or repos, so financing costs should be determined independently. One of the key variables in collateralized intermediary loans and repos is the LTV. When determining the LTV, we should avoid pro-cyclicality and take the risk characteristics under adverse conditions into consideration and prevent systemic risks due to the declining value of collateral after adverse events.

Lastly, macroprudential regulation is an important monetary policy tool in the context of endogenous money. Currently, there is no standard for uniform macroprudential regulation. Each country, follows the transfer of systemic risks and manages risks step-by-step based on its own conditions. For macroprudential regulation, China needs to pay the most careful attention to prevent liquidity fluctuations in the financial markets that would result in man-made systemic risks. Since liquidity is extremely sensitive to central bank actions, it needs to provide clearer statements of its objectives and transparency of its actions to appropriately guide the market rather than make the market speculate about its action. This will help us develop a good balance between liquidity and macroprudential regulation. Otherwise, panic will arise in financial institutions, the market will fluctuate wildly, and regional systemic financial risks will emerge.

Impact on the monetary transmission mechanism

Since the reform of banking system in 1984, the PBOC exclusively functions as the central bank. The objectives and control methods of Chinese monetary policies have been changed significantly. At the beginning of 1998, China cancelled the overall loan limits and quota and expanded open market operations. Monetary policies went through a transformation from direct to indirect control. This evolution and progress are summarized in Table 6.2.

Table 6.2 Evolution of Chinese monetary policies and strategies

		30 Years before opening up and reform (1948–1978)	*20 Years after opening up and reform (1979–1997)*	*Initial stage of indirect control (1998–2000)*	*Deepening stage of indirect control (2001–2007)*	*Mixed stage of indirect control (2007–2011)*
Policy Tool	Major tools	Credit cash plans	Credit cash plans Central bank loans	Central bank loans Interest rate policies Open market operation	Open market operation Deposit reserve Interest rate policy	Open market operation Deposit reserve Interest rate policy Window guidance
	Auxiliary tools	Credit policies Interest rate policies Administrative methods	Interest rate policies Credit policies Rediscount Open market operation Special deposit	Deposit reserve Rediscount Guidance credit plans Credit policies Window guidance	Loans issued by the central bank Rediscount Credit policy Window guidance	Loans issued by the central bank Rediscount Credit policy
Operation target			From loan scale to monetary base	Monetary base (to monitor the liquidity)	Monetary base Short-term interest rate	Monetary base Short-term interest rate
Intermediate target		Major four balances	From loan scale to money supply	Money supply (to monitor interest rates and currency rates)	Money supply Long-term interest rate	Loan scale Money supply Total financing
Ultimate target		Economic growth Price stabilization	From economic development, price stabilization to currency stabilization to facilitate economic growth	Stabilize currency to facilitate economic growth	Stabilize currency to facilitate economic growth	Stabilize currency to facilitate economic growth

Source: Systemized according to *Research on the Transmission Mechanism of Chinese Monetary Policies* (Beijing, Economic Science Press, 2001) mainly compiled by Dai Genyou and data on the central bank website.

From the perspective of intermediate targets, Chinese monetary policies have gone through a development process from a focus on the loan scale to a focus on the money supply and then a focus on both. Overall loan limits were eliminated in 1998 and then reintroduced in 2006 to control inflation. Since then, they have remained in force. However, in any event, the central bank now primarily focuses on the quantitative target among medium-term objectives. Since the interest rate is controlled in China, the PBOC adopts quantitative tools like deposit reserves and central bank loans as control tools. The open markets business focuses more on the quantitative intermediate target.

Such quantitative intermediate targets and operational tool selection have played an important role in China's financial system and provided important financial support during the initial stage of China's Reform and Opening Up. However, Chinese monetary policies have had weak transmission effects over the years, which indicates the current monetary policies and strategies have failed to adapt to the current economic environment. For example, to make loan limits effective, loan scales should be closely linked to GDP. But as more financing channels have emerged in the recent years, loans play a less significant role in total financing.

The primary cause of the weak transmission mechanism of monetary policy in China is the fact that currency is taken as an exogenous variable controlled by the central bank. However, in essence, money is endogenous in the economy and uncontrollable by the central bank. Generally speaking, money stock depends on exogenous variables. The central bank controls the injected amount of monetary base, while the monetary base and money multipliers decide the money stock. Under this framework, fluctuation of money supply in real economy comes from two factors: monetary base and money multipliers. Therefore, the central bank controls money stock by controlling the monetary base and money multipliers.

However, the causal relationship could be that the monetary base depends on money supply. The causal relationship starts from financial tools such as bank loans borrowed by non-bank financial institutions or bonds of financial institutions purchased by banks. According to double-entry bookkeeping, it creates money stock with the debtor, and the central bank supplies reserves needed for the money stock. The logic is that "loans create deposits, and deposits necessitate reserves." In this process, the central bank duly supplies reserves because the reserves actually depend on the "collective" action of all banks. The central bank may refuse other banks' borrowing demand for legal reserves. However, if raising the legal reserve results in financial strain for all banks, the liquidity risk increases. The central bank may then need to supply reserves to maintain financial stability. Therefore, money stock is an endogenous economic variable and is determined by the financing willingness of enterprises and credit standards of banks. In this sense, the central bank is passive in the modern monetary system. In this vein, Paul Volcker, former Federal Reserve chairman, mentioned in a speech that he repeatedly considered what other ways the Fed could use to regulate the financial system during his term.

Endogeneity of the money supply has different mechanisms in different financial systems. In the modern market economy's manufacturing process, financing demand arises because production and sales take time, and enterprises need to pay employees in advance. A typical process goes as follows. If banks consider an enterprise to be reliable, they will supply enterprise credit or accept purchase notes issued by the enterprise, based on which the enterprise pays and purchases. After the enterprises obtain loans, bonds, or income from stock issuance, the enterprise may pay employees. The employees then gain incomes that are reflected as bank deposits. They use bank deposits to consume and allocate the remaining in the form of bank deposits or other financial assets (stocks, funds, etc.). Money (deposits) then turns into a stock (as opposed to a flow), which corresponds to part of the financial assets owned by employees. As long as bank debts are accepted as a payment method, banks are able to create money.

The modern banking system is shown in Figure 6.4. According to money supply endogeneity, the logic of this figure flows from bottom to top.[5] At the bottom of the figure is the participant of the economy: clients (enterprises and individuals). Enterprises and individuals are connected to the financial market through the product and factor markets, which constitutes a cycle in the economy. This circulation is complete due to commercial banks on the second layer. Commercial banks issue loans to enterprises that purchase equipment for production in the factor market to obtain products. Factor suppliers purchase products with incomes acquired in the factor market. Enterprises repay the loans after obtaining the money and the production cycle comes to an end. At this point, the remainder of factor suppliers' bank deposits and cash becomes societal money stock. If there are legal reserves, then commercial banks have to borrow from the central bank. Since such borrowing arises from the whole banking system, the central bank is obliged to supply or face systemic financial risks. Meanwhile, due to diversification, some banks are better at issuing loans while others may be better at attracting deposits. In this case, money exchange occurs among banks. After Bank A issues loans, part of the loans are transferred to Bank B as deposits, so Bank A needs to borrow from Bank B. Borrowing in this manner is actually a settlement among banks. In the modern banking system, such settlement must be completed with the commercial banks'

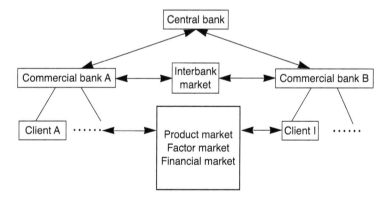

Figure 6.4 Modern banking system.

deposits at the central bank, which makes commercial banks borrow from and deposit in the central bank. Reserves and settlement needs are commercial banks' demand for an account balance at the central bank. In the meantime, commercial banks can adjust their central bank account balance in the interbank market. In the modern banking system, endogenous money supply channels should come from the independent lending and investments by banks. The central bank accepts loans for legal reserves and settlement funds.

To apply the aforementioned situation in China's investment system, there is another financing channel in addition to the financing demands from enterprises. After the National Development and Reform Commission (NDRC) approves a project and allocates the fiscal capital, along with bank loans, the money supply increases. Namely, investment demands lead to money supply. For example, according to historical data, broad money in 2009 increased by around RMB 9 trillion compared to 2008, and it increased by about RMB 11 trillion in 2010 compared to 2009. The Chinese government initiated a RMB 4 trillion investment plan (stimulus) as a response to the financial crisis. Pushed by such investment, the exogenous RMB 4 trillion investment plan was like a loan of the same amount. People have a stronger preference for liquidity in a financial crisis, so the RMB 4 trillion investments were equivalent to savings rather than other financial assets. Therefore, M2 increased by about RMB 13 trillion in 2009 according to the aforementioned analysis. Based on actual data, broad money increased by RMB 13.51 trillion in 2009, while the broad money increased by RMB 11.56 trillion in 2010, a return to normal. The data almost coincide with predictions based on endogenous money. Therefore, in 2009, the increased endogenous investments in China exactly indicated that the causal chain for money supply and growth is from credit and loans to deposits and then to reserves, not the other way around.

One of the reasons that shadow banking exists is the pursuit for high-income private money. The economy creates private money through the shadow banking system, which manifests in the endogeneity of money. Thanks to money supply endogeneity, control of the money supply is an invalid intermediate target, and quantitative tools are ineffective. Therefore, monetary policy should be subject to the price and the market.

Impact of shadow banking in China on the financial system

The shadow banking in China is a double-edged sword for the financial system. It both promotes efficiency and accumulates systemic risks that weaken the financial system.

Impact on the safety of the financial system

Shadow banking may accumulate some systemic risks and endanger the financial system due to three different aspects of its business. First, there was a massive influx of funds channeled through shadow banking either into the real estate market, other industries with excess capacity, or into repayment for government debts. In the long run, shadow banking is likely to bring risks to local government financing vehicles (LGFVs), the real estate market, and industries with high energy consumption, high pollution, as well as sectors with excess capacity. These systemic and regional financial risks pose a hazard to economic restructuring. Second, the shadow banking business poses higher systemic risks due to its maturity transformation, liquidity transformation, credit risk transfer, and high leverage. Meanwhile, shadow banking in China is very closely connected to commercial banks through factors such as liquidity support and implicit guarantees supplied by commercial banks. They are inextricably intertwined. Such close contact is extremely likely to bring risks of shadow banking to the traditional banking industry.

Third, the shadow banking system weakens the effectiveness of microprudential regulation prescribed in the *Basel Accords* through regulatory arbitrage. As analyzed earlier, regulatory arbitrage arising from shadow banking is inevitable in the course of market self-correction, which is a typical prisoner's dilemma.[6] In this context, numerous financial institutions clamor to enter the shadow banking system, which may result in malfunction of original regulatory framework and accumulate systemic risks.

Impact on the traditional banking system

First, the shadow banking business in China is largely seen as a banking system response to regulations and supervisions. The current regulations on deposit interest rates, lending limits, and supervision under the *Basel Accords* increase the cost of on-balance sheet assets and liabilities. Chinese commercial banks therefore moved into innovative financial products and various off-balance sheet assets/liabilities. Such products circulate among various financial intermediaries and become shadow banking in a broad sense.

Second, shadow banking challenges the traditional operating model of commercial banks. The large-scale development of shadow banking products challenges the traditional business model that makes money from the interest rate spread between deposits and loans at commercial banks. The high profits of such new products compensate banks' shrinking interest incomes caused by a narrowing net interest margin (NIM) over the years. In fact, this process lays a foundation for further market reform of banks by changing banking's business model. If commercial banks place a high emphasis on interest income, market reforms of Chinese deposit rates will be further delayed.

Third, the business between shadow banking and traditional banking is closely connected and inseparable, resulting in high risks. To obtain more advantageous credit in the market, shadow banking products rely too much on the liquidity support and credit enhancement provided by commercial banks. This interconnection clearly increases risks for banks. However, these risks are hidden under the prevailing accounting and legal frameworks and only came out during the financial crisis in 2008. Therefore, development in the shadow banking system does not relieve risks in commercial banks. Rather, it creates and even magnifies such risks.

Impact on the development of capital markets

Shadow banking faces both challenges and opportunities in capital markets. First, shadow banking stimulates capital market development. Shadow banking is an intersection of financial intermediaries and financial markets. Traditionally, financial intermediaries are the strongest largest pieces of the financial system, while the capital market is the smallest and weakest. Shadow banking needs to link with various financial intermediaries to perform its functions, which then creates a stimulus for capital market development. The rapid growth in MMFs and the repo market in the recent years are evidence of this exact phenomenon.

Second, shadow banking magnifies risks in the capital market. Shadow banking is a business chain that links financial intermediaries in all types of financial markets: bonds, short-term commercial paper, and repos and many others. Financial market participants are traditionally connected through interest arbitrage, which in fact effectively disperses risk in multiple markets. However, shadow banking provides another connection which better synchronizes each market and magnifies risks. In the recent financial crisis, the "run" on the repurchase market of the United States via the shadow banking system caused the whole financial market to shut down.

Impact on financial regulation

Shadow banking has posed a huge challenge to financial regulation. First, regulation should be comprehensive and evolve with the times. Shadow banking is a complex financial network composed of financial intermediaries. A unified regulatory framework is therefore necessary to cover all relevant financial institutions and markets. Any regulatory difference between those for various intermediaries and markets will result in regulatory arbitrage, which in turn brings out new forms of shadow banking. Meanwhile, it requires regulators to develop and maintain a forward-looking view in designing the regulatory system to adapt to the new shadow banking business.

Second, there have been new regulatory requirements on shadow banking institutions. Regulators should be more specific and focused in their supervision and pay attention to new sources of contagion and systemic risks arising from the shadow banking system. Shadow banking system creates new channels for financial risk contagion that have not been supervised efficiently by current regulatory policies. Meanwhile, the shadow banking system has become a new risk source. In the shadow banking system, money market funds are an important financing channel, and its liquidity problem is equivalent in spirit to that of a bank run. These new risk sources need to be further addressed in regulation. In conclusion, regulators should maintain creativity and concern themselves with new trends and characteristics of financial intermediaries within shadow banking. There should be an unprecedented exchange of ideas and continuous attention to regulation of the financial intermediaries involved in shadow banking.

Third, systemic risks that were easily neglected in the past should be addressed in the supervision of shadow banking's financial products. Various products including wealth management, trusts, asset securitization, collateralized intermediary loans, or repo are increasingly prevalent. They have created excessive risks due to shadow banking. At present, the supervision of these products is mainly centered on the standardization of issuance and trading, rather than systematic consideration of these products' role in the financial system. It is the key issue that regulators need to tackle in the future.

Fourth, macroprudential regulation is increasingly important and needs work together with microprudential regulation. The original assets of shadow banking are loans, regardless of form. The nature of regulation is thus control over the speed of lending. One of macroprudential regulation's goals is to control aggregate loan growth. When the shadow banking system is growing, macroprudential regulation plays an extremely important role. For the time being, there is no universal macroprudential regulation toolbox. Chinese regulators need to apply such tools with local considerations. During this process, the coordination between macroprudential regulation and microprudential management is key to avoid unnecessary fluctuations in liquidity.

Fifth, data collection needs to be further improved. Complete statistical data of shadow banking is a basic prerequisite for effective regulation. There are multiple sources of statistical data regarding shadow banking, which causes problems such as differences in standards, definitions, and presentation, as well as inappropriate application of statistical methods. This book regards data collection as the most urgent issue at present. Lack of data is already the number one issue for regulators.

Quantitative analysis on shadow banking in the broad sense

Shadow banking's economic impact requires measurement according to financial function. We employ measurement according to financial function to measure the impact of China's shadow banking scale in a broad sense on the macroeconomy, for which we use the scale of trust loans as a proxy variable. Admittedly, trust loans do not all fall in the shadow banking category. When the capital for trust loans is collected directly from the issued trust plans, there is no liquidity requirement or term transfer, and it is no longer technically shadow banking. New trust loans in 2012 in China were RMB 1.3 trillion. Up to March 2013, the balance of trust loans was about RMB 3.8 trillion. Overall, compared with Chinese economic aggregates, the loans make up a small proportion.

To further analyze the shadow banking impact in broad sense on the macroeconomy, we adopt monthly data from January 2007 to April 2013 to analyze the impact of new trust loans on industrial added value, fixed-asset investment, and consumer price index (CPI). Trust loan data come from Wind Info (Wind), and other data come from the CEInet database.

For a robust result, we use a unit root test. Using an augmented Dickey–Fuller (ADF) test, the month-on-month (mom) growth rate of trust loans does not have a unit root, but the year-on-year (yoy) growth rate of trust loans has a unit root. The first difference is stationary. The yoy CPI and mom CPI do not have unit roots. The accumulative growth rate of fixed-asset investment yoy has a unit root, but its first difference has no unit root. The growth rate of industrial added value on yoy basis has a unit root, but its first difference has no unit root.

We use stationary time series to create a vector autoregression (VAR) model to analyze the relationship between new trust loans and all economic variables. First we analyze the impact of new trust loans on the CPI. The impulse response function (IRF) in Figures 6.5 and 6.6 shows that the relationship between new trust loans and CPI is not significant with yoy ormom. Therefore, there is no evidence showing that shadow banking will intensify inflation in China.

The horizontal axis suggests the tracking period of impacts (to better observe the dynamic impact among all variables, we have a 10-period track for all variables), and the vertical axis suggests the changes in variables. The solid line is the path of the IRF change in time, and the dashed lines on both sides are the confidence interval of the response function value plus or minus 2 standard deviations. Figures 6.6–6.8 show the repeated analysis for yoy versions of the trust lending variables.

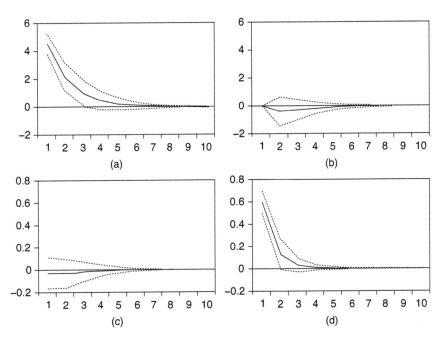

Figure 6.5 Impact of the mom growth rate of new trust loans on that of CPI. (a) Response function diagram of mom growth rate of subsequent new trust loans arising from the impacts of the mom growth rate of new trust loans. (b) Response function diagram of mom growth rate of subsequent new trust loans arising from the impacts of the mom growth rate of CPI. (c) Response function diagram of mom growth rate of subsequent CPI arising from the impacts of the mom growth rate of new trust loans. (d) Response function diagram of mom growth rate of subsequent CPI arising from the impacts of the mom growth rate of CPI.

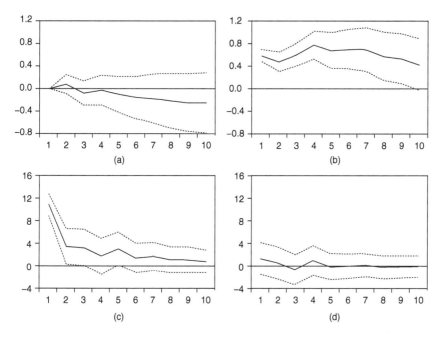

Figure 6.6 Impact of the yoy growth rate of new trust loans on that of CPI. (a) Response
function diagram of yoy growth rate of later new trust loans arising from
the impacts of the yoy growth rate of new trust loans. (b) Response function
diagram of yoy growth rate of later new trust loans arising from the impacts of
the yoy growth rate of CPI. (c) Response function diagram of yoy growth rate
of later CPI arising from the impacts of the yoy growth rate of new trust loans.
(d) Response function diagram of yoy growth rate of later CPI arising from the
impacts of the yoy growth rate of CPI.

Following is the impact of new trust loans on investment. Figure 6.7 shows the
relationship between new trust loans and fixed-asset investment, and Figure 6.8
shows the relationship between new trust loans and industrial added value.

In the IRF shown in Figure 6.7, it is obvious that the yoy growth rate of new trust
loans does not increase the yoy accumulative growth rate of fixed-asset investment.
There are mainly two reasons. First, the trust loans for the LGFVs and those for real
estate enterprises are not presented as loans but in other forms such as equity investment. As a result, they are not standard shadow banking. Second, as analyzed earlier, the
generation of shadow banking in China is, to some extent, due to the regulatory limits
on deposit interest rates. Therefore, these shadow banking products mainly function as
high-interest investments and make little difference to the economy.

Last, the IRF shown in Figure 6.8 suggests that new trust loans have a slightly
positive impact on industrial added value. In this way, the existing shadow banking system has a slightly positive impact on China's economy, with high interest
investment.

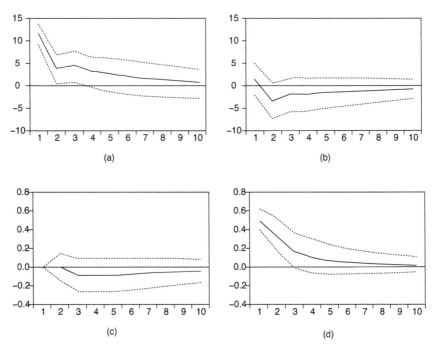

Figure 6.7 Impact of yoy growth rate of new trust loans on accumulative growth rate
of fixed-asset investment. (a) Response function diagram of yoy growth
rate of subsequent new trust loans arising from the impact of the yoy growth
rate of new trust loans. (b) Response function diagram of yoy growth rate of
subsequent new trust loans arising from the impact of the accumulative growth
rate of fixed-asset investment. (c) Response function diagram of yoy growth rate
of subsequent CPI arising from the impact of the accumulative growth rate of
fixed-asset investment. (d) Response function diagram of accumulative growth
rate of fixed-asset investment arising from the impact of the accumulative
growth rate of fixed-asset investment.

Generally speaking, shadow banking currently has little impact on China's
economy, if anything, the impact is somewhat positive. On the one hand, shadow
banking amplifies "financial idling," resulting in a disconnect from real economy.
On the other hand, shadow banking bypasses regulations on interest rates and
lending volume, prevents financial distortions to some extent, and improves the
efficiency of economy. Therefore, shadow banking serves as a complement to current macroeconomic regulatory tools and therefore stimulates economic growth.
However, shadow banking also made some regulatory tools ineffective, which forces
the government to adjust macroeconomic regulation. In addition, shadow banking
risk should be managed with tools designed correspondingly to reduce the leverage
ratio and mismatches in maturity and liquidity.

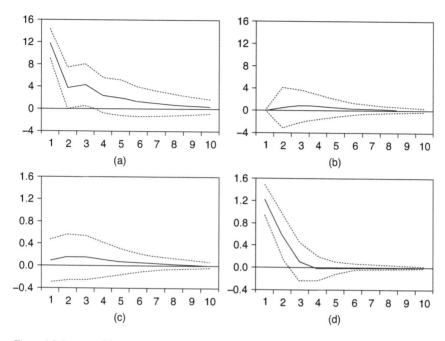

Figure 6.8 Impact of the yoy growth rate of new trust loans on that of industrial added value.
(a) Response function diagram of yoy growth rate of subsequent new trust loans arising from the impacts of the yoy growth rate of new trust loans. (b) Response function diagram of yoy growth rate of subsequent new trust loans arising from the impact of the yoy growth rate of industrial added value. (c) Response function diagram of yoy growth rate of subsequent CPI arising from the impact of the yoy growth rate of industrial added value. (d) Response function diagram of yoy growth rate of industrial added value arising from the impact of the yoy growth rate of industrial added value.

Notes

1   Financing of foreign sectors and government behaviors may play a great role in the capital source of domestic producers.
2   Total social financing in the data may be underestimated, but it has grown rapidly over the past decade. The accumulative increment is estimated to make up over 95% of the accumulative balance. Therefore, the sum of new flows over the past decade is almost on par with historical stock.
3   According to data by the audit office, until the end of 2010, the ratio of debt ratio of local governments at provincial level, municipal level, and county level with repayment obligation (i.e., the balance of debts) to comprehensive fiscal power is 52.25%. When we add in contingent debt in connection with guarantee liabilities, the ratio is 70.45%.
4   Many businessmen "ran away" (disappeared) to get rid of huge debts over the years, which suggests that private lending was more sensitive to economic conditions.
5   The logic in endogenous money theory is from the bottom-up. The top two layers shown in Figure 6.4 determine the nominal value only, while actual value completely

and independently depends on the third layer, the economic cycle among enterprises and individuals.

6   For example, if a bank does not strip assets through the shadow banking system, it will use more core capital and increase costs. Thus, shadow banking becomes a dominant strategy, that is, no matter what other financial institutions do, shadow banking is the best way. Therefore, shadow banking results in market malfunction and fails to reach the Pareto optimal state.

7 Recommendations for the regulation of Chinese shadow banking

Whether it is the United States' Dodd Frank financial reform bill or the Financial Stability Board's (FSB) regulatory framework, there are clear international principles for shadow banking regulation. They involve simultaneous encouragement of its development, increased regulation, and reduction in the systemic risks it implies. Although China's level of financial development is different from nations like the United States, we still need to balance the same fundamental considerations for regulatory policy: reasonable apportionment of regulatory responsibility, manageable levels of financial innovation, and stable financial development. This chapter first systematically covers the FSBs regulatory framework for shadow banking and then uses the framework to provide specific recommendations for its regulation in China.

International regulation of shadow banking

The most systematic international research on shadow banking comes from the FSB. The regulations they propose are in three parts: general principles, basic policies, and concrete policy toolkits. They also outline five economic functions and the policies to deal with each, and how to implement them.

FSB's general principles and basic policies[1]

The FSB proposes five general principles for shadow banking regulation in any country: focus, proportionality, forward-looking and adaptable, effectiveness, and assessment and review.

1 Focus implies regulation that is targeted specifically to the risks of the shadow banking system and any externalities it causes.
2 Proportionality means that measures should be tailored to match the magnitude of shadow banking risks.
3 Forward-looking and adaptable means looking out for risks that may emerge in the future.

4   Effectiveness means taking into account differences in financial systems and a balance between these considerations and the reduction of cross-border regulatory arbitrage.
5   Assessment and review means policies should continually be reviewed to improve them based on experience.

In addition, there are four overarching principles to follow:

1   Authorities should define, and keep up to date, the regulatory perimeter.
2   Authorities should collect information needed to assess the extent of risks posed by shadow banking.
3   Authorities should enhance disclosure by other shadow banking entities as necessary so as to help market participants understand the extent of shadow banking risks posed by such entities.
4   Authorities should assess their non–bank financial entities based on the economic functions and take necessary actions drawing on tools from the policy toolkit.

Policy toolkits[2]

The FSB refined policy toolkits that are tailored to specific economic functions. We briefly cover these in this section.

Economic function 1: Management of collective investment vehicles with features that make them susceptible to runs

TOOL 1: TOOLS FOR MANAGING REDEMPTION PRESSURES IN STRESSED MARKET CONDITIONS

Tool 1a: Redemption gates   Redemption gates put limitations on the amount investors can redeem in a given day. With redemption gates, the redemption pressure is spread out and prevents a run. However, utilizing this tool itself could lead to panic that forces other collective investment vehicles (CIVs) to use redemption gates in the fear of an imminent run.

Tool 1b: Suspension of redemptions   Suspension of redemption is essentially a stronger version of redemption gates. With the investors unable to redeem, the managers could utilize this prolonged period to analyze the situation and make necessary responses before they remove the suspension. There are drawbacks to this tool: it robs the investors of a timely redemption in full amount; it could send a bad signal into the market, triggering runs in other CIVs; it may also arouse fear among the investors and cause a run to take place after the suspension is removed. Nevertheless, in practice, this tool has proven its value in preventing runs in many incidents.

Tool 1c: Imposition of redemption fees or other redemption restrictions   We can mitigate the risks posed by maturity transformation through certain tools to impose extra costs on investors who want to redeem their funds. They retain the option to redeem, but it becomes more costly to do so. It is important to design these well and understand that their imposition can send a negative signal to investors, which may then intensify the redemption wave.

Tool 1d: Side pockets   Side pockets provide a way to separate problem assets from funds and potentially avoid runs. They can be used when a specific type of asset becomes difficult to value due to financial market conditions. For example, there may be a market in which liquidity disappears and the only sales left to provide reference prices are fire sales that do not necessarily reflect the underlying value of the assets. In this case, this type of asset would be separated from the fund for the purposes of fulfilling redemptions and measuring returns until the markets return to normal and the assets can be properly valued. However, these should be applied carefully and sparingly. Managers should not be able to decide when to use them to avoid conflicts of interest and loss concealment.

TOOL 2: TOOLS TO MANAGE LIQUIDITY RISK

Tool 2a: Limits on investment in illiquid assets   These involve certain limits on the proportion of portfolios that may be invested in illiquid assets. Assets that have a nonexistent or spotty secondary market will be difficult and potentially costly to unwind in the case of heavy withdrawals. Since portfolio managers want to avoid such "fire sales," they will likely liquidate the most liquid assets first. If this occurs in large amounts, "herding" will depress prices for these liquid assets as well and potentially cause broader problems in the financial system as this becomes a self-reinforcing cycle. The costs of such measures include possible lower returns, an altered risk-return profile, and more restricted investment opportunities.

Tool 2b: Liquidity buffers   Liquidity buffers can ensure that the CIV has enough liquid assets to handle sudden spikes in redemptions. These can be enforced as a portion of CIV assets based on the risk-return profile, redemption policies, and potential stress. However, these may be insufficient to prevent fire sales during extraordinarily high redemption demand, and there may not be enough safe assets available in some areas.

Tool 2c: Limits on asset concentration   Sometimes, it may make sense to limit the proportion of CIV assets exposed to a particular issuer or sector of the economy. If problems arise, and the existing position is too large, it may be costly or impossible to liquidate it to satisfy redemptions. These should be used carefully, however, as this may be incompatible with certain investment strategies, such as those designed to gain exposure to a specific sector.

TOOL 3: LIMITS ON LEVERAGE

Leverage can be a positive factor that magnifies returns, but it can also be difficult to unwind in periods of market distress. Authorities can reduce this risk, and that of implicit government guarantees for highly levered funds, by limiting overall leverage or imposing minimum liquidity limits to avoid a disorderly unwinding of positions. Difficulties include determination of specific limits for different investment strategies.

Tool 4: Restrictions on maturity of portfolio assets   These are applicable for funds that are generally presented as "low risk." They may take the form of limits on duration of fund assets, weighted average maturity of assets, and stepped maturity profiles to ensure that CIV maturity transformation does not prove too risky.

Economic function 2: Loan provision that is dependent on short-term funding

TOOL 1: IMPOSE BANK PRUDENTIAL REGULATORY REGIMES ON DEPOSIT-TAKING
NON-BANK LOAN PROVIDERS

Non-bank financial entities that have bank characteristics possess the same risks as banks, but without regulation. As a result, these entities must be regulated the same way as banks. Otherwise, they may harm the interest of investors and threaten financial stability.

TOOL 2: CAPITAL REQUIREMENTS

Financial entities may be required to maintain a certain level of capital so when they incur losses, their own capital can cover them. This tool will also be essential in deleveraging since they will motivate the entities to pay more attention to credit risks. With the existence of these financial entities, businesses can have an easier access to loans. As a consequence, they are more likely to expand in a sound economy and shrink in rough times. Therefore, the capital requirement should be set to counter such behavior. Setting the appropriate level of requirement is both crucial and difficult, as financial entities generally possess a much greater level of variety than banks.

TOOL 3: LIQUIDITY BUFFERS

Setting appropriate liquidity buffers can be very crucial in preventing runs, mitigating stress, and managing risks. Moreover, when an entity that is closely tied to its parent group suffers, the damage to reputation may be on the entire group. Liquidity buffers can provide protection in these situations. In practice, choosing buffer size and selecting eligible assets must be done with care, as many entity types are very different from banks.

TOOL 4: LEVERAGE LIMITS

Leverage limits are useful in stopping certain entities from creating excessive leverage, which could harm the economy. It can decelerate procyclical behavior that prudential regulation may not be able to deal with. It is important to tailor the specific limits to fit each type of financial entity, as the normal level of leverage differs by market. Certain types of regulatory arbitrage with banks may be under the Basel III leverage ratio regime, which is important for the authorities to consider.

TOOL 5: LIMITS ON LARGE EXPOSURES

Claims on the obligated entity may be limited when a certain entity possess a large asset concentration to a small number of entities. In practice, before placing the limits, the nature of the industry must be reviewed to prevent excessive intervention to an industry where asset concentration is regarded as normal.

TOOL 6: RESTRICTIONS ON TYPES OF LIABILITIES

The likelihood of runs may be lowered or erased by placing a restriction on certain types of liabilities. Moreover, if certain restrictions are placed on lenders, sectors, or instruments, risks from maturity transformation or liquidity transformation can also be lowered or eliminated.

Economic function 3: Intermediation of market activities that is dependent on short-term funding or on secured funding of client assets

TOOL 1: IMPOSE PRUDENTIAL REGULATORY REGIMES EQUIVALENT TO THOSE FOR BANKS

Non-bank financial entities that use similar leverage and maturity/liquidity transformation could be equally risky as banks. Even with long-term assets as collateral, they may still face certain risks such as runs. As a result, authorities may choose to place these entities under prudential regulation like banks to prevent financial instability and regulatory arbitrage. However, authorities must be aware that such measures may not be appropriate, especially for entities that take no deposits and make no long-term loans.

TOOL 2: LIQUIDITY REQUIREMENTS

Liquidity requirements can be placed on certain entities provided that they perform liquidity transformation. In doing so, these entities may be less susceptible to runs, which will help prevent systemic crises from happening. Authorities may consider learning from the spirit of the Basel III liquidity requirements. The specific requirements should differ depending on the entity.

TOOL 3: CAPITAL REQUIREMENTS

Capital requirements such as minimum capital ratio or minimum levels of liquid net capital can be useful tools to prevent overleverage and reduce procyclicality. The level of risk is an indication on whether to set the minimum requirements or not. Like other tools, authorities need to weigh the pros and cons before imposing capital requirements.

TOOL 4: RESTRICTIONS ON USE OF CLIENT ASSETS

If non-bank entities decide to fund their own long-term assets with the assets of their clients, then they are essentially performing maturity/liquidity transformation. Such actions create risks similar to that of the banks. Therefore, these entities may be restricted from funding with clients' assets unless in re-hypothecation, which only entities with proper regulation should be able to perform. Client disclosure should be in place to keep them informed. When re-hypothecation is permitted, either by regulatory regimes or clients, the authorities may choose to limit re-hypothecation in order to mitigate risks of runs. Like other tools, the pros and cons must be weighed before any decision is final.

Economic function 4: Facilitation of credit creation

TOOL 1: CAPITAL REQUIREMENTS

Imposing this tool will help deleverage the financial system, as they will motivate the entities to pay extra attention to credit risks. With the existence of these financial entities, businesses can have an easier access to loans. As a consequence, their activities are likely to be highly procyclical. Therefore, the capital requirement should be designed to be countercyclical. Authorities need to pay attention to international stakeholders to prevent cross-border arbitrage and mitigate common risks.

TOOL 2: RESTRICTIONS ON SCALE AND SCOPE OF BUSINESS

Entities that provide credit insurance or financial guarantees must be designed to manage risks associated with credit creation. Restrictions on the scale and scope of business are tools for authorities when internal risk management is not so well developed. After authorities set up adequate risk profiles, the entities will be put under appropriate regulation. This will give the authorities the chance to decide on the exposure limits for these entities and prevent the entities from suffering too many losses due to unfamiliar activities.

TOOL 3: LIQUIDITY BUFFERS

Liquidity buffers can reduce run risks for entities that unintentionally perform maturity/liquidity transformation. Without them, entities may fail due to creditor runs and trigger chain reactions in the market. Authorities can use this tool to safeguard entities in turbulent times by requiring them to constantly maintain an appropriate level of liquidity.

TOOL 4: ENHANCED RISK MANAGEMENT PRACTICES TO CAPTURE TAIL EVENTS

Entities that provide financial guarantees and credit insurances must be aware of their potential loss levels in the event of recession. This can be done through enhanced risk management practices such as loss modeling with stress testing. Stress testing will help the entities understand their exposure to risks. With this understanding, entities are more likely to better position themselves, which will contribute to financial stability.

TOOL 5: MANDATORY RISK-SHARING BETWEEN THE INSURER/GUARANTOR AND INSURED/GUARANTEED

An effective method to mitigate imperfect credit risk transfer is to have the insured financial entities bear some credit risk themselves. There are two ways of doing this: a deductible and a co-payment. In both the cases, the entity bears a portion of the clients' losses. Risk sharing also provides the entities an incentive to better qualify their borrowers, which will help keep leverage at appropriate levels. However, risk sharing also has drawbacks: the entities are forced to absorb additional risks, and it may incentivize some lenders not to lend. Therefore, information sharing is crucial for the effectiveness of this tool.

Economic function 5: Securitization-based credit intermediation and funding of financial entities

TOOL 1: RESTRICTIONS ON MATURITY/LIQUIDITY TRANSFORMATION

An effective tool to mitigate risks from maturity/liquidity transformation through securitization is to limit differences in maturity between underlying assets and the securities issued from them. Limits on securitization vehicles will both reduce liquidity transformation risks and increase the flexibility of the entities. Additional benefits include reducing asset-backed securities' rollover risk and decreasing entities' dependency on sponsors. However, other than those that should be restricted, making accurate assessments of maturity mismatches can prove challenging. Moreover, in order to be effective, this tool must be adjusted to fit different entities.

TOOL 2: RESTRICTIONS ON ELIGIBLE COLLATERAL

When funds cannot be obtained from the wholesale market, banks sometimes utilize non-bank entities to inject capital into some of their illiquid portfolios. This increases the level of leverage in the financial system and may cause chain reactions in the market if the quality of portfolios starts to decline. Placing restrictions on collateral can help reduce the risks. If collateral is liquid, it can be sold quickly to compensate losses, such as in the event of a default. On the other hand, restrictions on eligible collateral could reduce funding, not to mention that collateral often loses its value quickly during recession.

As exemplified in the subprime crisis, when banks and entities explore other funding channels such as securitization, they tend to create too much credit and excessive leverage. In doing so, they also create spaces for regulatory arbitrage, increasing risks in financial markets. Restrictions on exposures to banks and other financial entities may help mitigate risks and cut their dependency on channels such as securitization by limiting the funds from banks and single counterparties. Authorities should ponder the negative effects of this tool before imposing restrictions in order to minimize damage on market efficiency or pressures on funding.

Establishment of a monitoring and regulatory system

The establishment of a monitoring and regulatory system should include following aspects:

First, authorities should refer to the experience of developed countries to build a dynamic monitoring system based on the flow of funds among markets and participants. This will allow them to make accurate estimations of quarterly flows and stocks to improve regulation and avoid hindering innovation, distorting market prices, and weakening market allocation of economic resources due to a lack of information.

Second, authorities should strengthen consolidated supervision. It is extremely important that shadow banking entities that banks sponsor are consolidated in the group and are thus included on their balance sheet positions for the purpose of risk-based capital and liquidity buffers as well as leverage ratio calculations. Such prudential measures will then take the risk posed by sponsored shadow banking entities into account. According to accounting principles, both structured and traditional institutions need to conduct consolidated supervision. As for structured institutions, even if those without voting rights, consolidated supervision is still complicated because each has a unique structure and operational model. Yet for traditional institutions, such management is simple as long as they have voting and control rights. Under the risk-based principle, all non-bank financial institutions should be involved in consolidated supervision and disclose both qualitative and quantitative information, especially for securities that require capital reserves commensurate to their risks. However, different accounting standards will result in risk-based differences in management. Therefore, consolidated management is only a way of covering banks' risk exposure and needs an appropriate risk-weight.

Third, authorities should restrict traditional banks' risk exposure to shadow banking institutions. Currently, no countries have specialized large risk exposure principles for shadow banking. In addition, current large risk exposure principles more or less conceal some risks. Therefore, it is necessary to build a globally consistent standard to avoid cross-border arbitrage and monitor deals between traditional and shadow banks. Two possible methods would be to implement stricter restrictions on traditional banks' risk exposure to single shadow bank or to improve large risk exposure restrictions. At the same time, authorities should take four factors into consideration: rules inside groups, relevance and transparency, short-term risk exposure, and implicit support. Rules inside groups are key because shadow banks inside groups are usually outside similar risk evaluation, control, and information disclosure when dealing with their parent firm or other subsidiary companies. Relevance and transparency come into play because shadow banking risks are often connected with potential capital pools, and important information is often hidden from the view of market participants. The mechanism should cover risks produced by short-term trades, high-quality guarantees, implicit support and sovereign backing.

Fourth, traditional banks should implement risk-based capital requirements for risk exposures to shadow banking. The Basel Committee is studying the implementations of capital requirements for funds (e.g., hedge funds) and whether to expand capital requirements that provide short-term liquidity facilities for securities tools to all non-bank institutions including shadow banking.

Basel II does not provide detailed guidance on how to calculate the risk weighting and has not reflected the leverage ratio when counting investment capital requirements. Therefore, it is necessary to establish a new framework that is more structured, more risk-sensitive, and more applicable to all types of funds and banks. The new framework should take decision trees with three steps depending on available information. First, if the bank has adequate, frequently audited information, it can apply a look-through approach. If a bank cannot use the first approach, then it uses the "middle ground" option, which assumes that the fund invests in assets with the highest capital requirements. Finally, if the previous options cannot apply, fallback treatment can apply a uniformly high risk weight. For all funds or shadow banks, the risk weight of investments is 1,250%, 625% for other funds. Also, funds' leverage ratios should be considered.

For short-term liquidity facilities, the Basel 2.5 enhancement of July 2009 increased the credit conversion factor (CCF)[3] for short-term liquidity facilities (less than 1 year original maturity) provided to entities that fall under the Standardized Approach Securitization Framework (i.e., securitization vehicles) from 20% to 50%. The same CCF remains at 20% for liquidity facilities (off-balance sheet exposures) provided to other type of entities. There are four possible policy solutions that allow us to deal with relevance, systemic risk, and possible factors that cause counterparties' creditworthiness to deteriorate. First, retain a 20% CCF for short-term liquidity facilities; second, increase the CCF of banks' total short-term facilities from 20% to 50% for backing of financial institutions (e.g., hedge fund, mutual funds in the money market, and conduits) that are unregulated and consolidate management; third, increase the CCF of banks' total short-term facilities from 20% to 50% for unregulated financial institutions; fourth, increase the CCF of banks' all short-term facilities from 20% to 50% for all financial institutions. For the moment, the second solution is theoretically more reasonable. However, there are subjective differences in defining "support," so the third solution is more practical.

Fifth, authorities should strengthen regulations on reputational risk and implicit support. According to the Basel Committee's survey, most countries have partly implemented Basel's 2009 guidance. However, there are still problems on prudential measurement, stress testing, and policy for reputational risk and implicit support. Only one-third of members have adopted regulations on implicit support. Implicit support recognition remains the biggest challenge. Some jurisdictions depend on consistent surveillance for commercial behavior, market information, and spot inspection to identify implicit support. They ask banks to establish frameworks and policies dealing with corporate governance, management, and monitoring by moral suasion or force banks to disclose information. Implicit support regulation mainly focuses on asset-backed commercial paper (ABCP) conduits and securities. Some jurisdictions forbid traditional banks to provide implicit support for shadow banks and ask for improved deal structure to minimize implicit support risk and consolidated supervision in accordance with accounting and prudent regulatory principles. We recommend supervision of banks' reputational risks or implicit support risk with case studies or information sharing, strengthening of 2009 guidance, improvement in risk management, and formulation of clear rules to estimate implicit support and related capital adequacy.

All in all, increasing transparency by strengthening data reporting and information disclosure is essential to reduce market participants' motivation to take advantage of arbitrage opportunities resulting from banks' regulatory boundaries. FSB published Shadow Banking: Strengthening Oversight and Regulation on October 27, 2011, in which it advised authorities to adopt high-level principles, including authorities' right to collect necessary data as well as information to identify regulatory boundaries and monitor the shadow banking system.

Ideas, boundaries, and principles for shadow banking regulation

The Chinese shadow banking system mainly comprises financial innovations, which attempt to circumvent regulations. While their existence is driven by the market and should be viewed as positive, they must be properly regulated.

Ideas guiding Chinese shadow banking regulation

The unique problems the Chinese financial industry faces are insufficient innovation and a lack of diversified business models. At the same time, intermediary businesses and off-balance sheet businesses still have a large potential for growth. The way to think about the Chinese shadow banking regulation includes a few important considerations. First, the regulators need to bear in mind that finance serves the needs of real economy. Regulation should be at levels that match what the market can accept, the tolerance of investors, and regulatory capacity. Regulators should continue to encourage financial innovation in banks and other institutions, further the development of financial infrastructure, and increase market efficiency to provide a better environment for the development of new businesses.

Second, regulators must pay close attention to risks associated with financial innovation, both on a macro level and on a micro level. Regulators must prevent the risks from spreading before damage is inflicted. To achieve this, they need to strengthen routine monitoring activities and track the chain of risk transmission associated with shadow banking businesses and products.

Target of Chinese shadow banking regulation

The focus of regulation differs during different stages of financial development. Since the global financial crisis in 2008, financial regulations have been targeted at the prevention of systemic risks and the preservation of financial stability. At the same time, more emphasis has been placed on protecting consumers. The target of Chinese shadow banking regulation includes the following four aspects: preventing systemic risks that shadow banking may cause to maintain stability in the Chinese financial market, safeguarding individual financial markets by preventing risk that may be associated with shadow banking organizations and their products, encouraging financial innovation to increase the competiveness of the financial system, and improving the efficiency of resource allocation, and strengthening regulation of shadow banking activities and procedures in order to protect consumers.

The boundaries of Chinese shadow banking regulation

Since Chinese shadow banking covers a wide range, the boundary of its regulation must also be broadened. All non-bank credit intermediaries related to shadow banking and any industry that could threaten the financial system must be regulated. At the same time, the process of information collection must be secure.

Regulators must be aware of credit intermediary activities outside the traditional banking system, especially those that operate similar businesses as traditional banks with inadequate or nonexistent regulatory standards. By doing so, regulators can better monitor all or at least a portion of the credit intermediary activities that occur outside the traditional banking system. As a result, they can identify potential shadow banking systems and associated risks.

Principles of Chinese shadow banking regulation

The principles of financial regulation are its basis. They are crucial throughout the procedures of financial regulation. Since shadow banking is an important, constantly changing part of the financial system, the following principles must be followed in addition to the core principles of banking regulation.

1   Regulation according to law. Laws and regulations suitable for the current characteristics of shadow banking should be enacted in order to preserve authority, seriousness, forcefulness, and consistency in supervision.

2   Moderation and effectiveness. The regulatory department must select measures that match the risk level of the shadow banking system.
3   Foresight. Assessments of the risk level of shadow banking need to be adjustable according to the changes in the market. Overall, the measures must be chosen with flexibility and foresight.
4   Combination of microprudential and macroprudential supervision. Regulators need to strengthen the regulation of shadow banking institutions with systemic importance, as well as markets and risk positions, to establish a counter-cyclical macroprudential supervisory framework. Such a framework can help reduce systemic risk and safeguard the stability of the financial system. At the same time, individual shadow banking institutions, markets, and stability cannot be compromised.
5   Combination of external supervision and self-discipline. With a system of external supervision in place, shadow banks should be allowed to perform self-regulation and internal control. This can be an active measure to manage and prevent risk.

Regulatory guidance and frameworks

Institutions, markets, tools, and products of the shadow banking system span many industries, such as banks, trusts, securities, insurance, and funds. Together, they help increase the efficiency of the financial system, but they add linkage and potential contagion to financial risks. Therefore, regulation of shadow banking should have various tools focused on financial security, stability, efficiency, and innovation to protect the rights of consumers of financial products. Since China's current principle distributes regulatory responsibilities among different regulatory bodies by operating function, this chapter introduces overall guidance at first and then analyses supervisory frameworks of financial and other regulators separately.

Overall guidance for institutions and specific business-oriented regulation

China's non-bank financial institutions are subject to more stringent regulation than their counterparts in most other countries. They do not have some obvious features of shadow banking, but we still need to pay close attention to avoid a blowup of risk. More attention should be paid to types of financial institutions and businesses outside the current regulatory system to prevent systemic risks. Overall guidance for the stable development of the Chinese financial system should be as follows:

–   First, standardize regulatory standards for non-bank financial institutions. Authorities should recognize institutions that are already regulated and have shadow banking features. Then, they should clarify regulators' responsibilities and strengthen appropriate measures.
–   Second, authorities should strengthen supervision of non-financial institutions. Authorities should intensify research on non-regulated institutions and businesses, including small loan companies, pawn companies, and non-financial

guarantee companies to further identify their impact on the system and whether they have shadow banking features. Once they have such results in hand, authorities should use the information to take proper measures to ensure their prudent regulation.

– Third, authorities should strengthen research on private financing. Authorities should know its methods, institutions, size, and risks, especially the effects of illegal financing and financial pyramid schemes on banks. Regulatory authority and policies should be more clearly delineated.

– Fourth, tighten management and regulation on systemic risks. Authorities should urge banks to improve their ability to undertake consolidated supervision and control counterparty risk. The key is to keep banks from taking on large shadow banking risk exposure, liability transfer, and implicit support to prevent contagion.

Chinese regulatory framework for the shadow banking system

Shadow banking system generally crosses various industries and markets, which does not fit the current Chinese supervisory framework. To avoid the need for a fundamental change in supervisory model, financial authorities should optimize sectoral regulation, information sharing, and coordination. In the short term, regulators can adopt some quick countermeasures to aim at major problems to standardize shadow banks' development. At the same time, they should consider a medium- and long-term financial regulatory frameworks.

Regulatory issues for Chinese financial authorities

First, we need to standardize the information disclosure mechanism of the shadow banking system and reduce information asymmetry. From the American experience, we know that all financial institutions are exposed to financial crises due to high leverage, high systemic importance, high information asymmetry, and unregulated over-the-counter (OTC) trading. Thus, future shadow banking regulation should focus on designing a proper information disclosure mechanism. Exploring new information disclosure mechanisms, increasing financial product and transparency, improving information disclosure of OTC trading, and clearly informing investors are important measures to prevent these market risks. A reasonable information disclosure mechanism should include at least two aspects: a comprehensive platform and inclusion of the OTC market. This could unify regulatory standards among different departments and institutions and collect, analyze, and publish market data regularly to make sure that all participants in both shadow banking and traditional financial systems can obtain sufficient information. For OTC trading, authorities should accelerate the building of information disclosure and regulatory regime to lower information asymmetry, which also helps match debtors and creditors, reduces transaction costs, restricts high leverage, and prevents some trading risks.

Second, we must build a firewall between commercial and shadow banks to cut off direct channel for risk contagion. Off-balance sheet activities (e.g., trust-bank financial products, financial products issued by banks or financing guarantees for other institutions) add potential risks to commercial banks. There is no deposit insurance system in China, nor a thorough legal system for bankruptcy of financial institutions. In this context, risk contagion would be inevitable if a crisis breaks out in the shadow banking system, leaving government and central bank to bear the final costs. Therefore, it is necessary to insulate commercial banks from shadow banking and build a firewall to protect the banking system. We recommend the following three steps to establish this firewall: Strictly prevent commercial banks fund flows to the shadow banking system (e.g., PE funds or microfinance companies). Cooperative business between banks and trusts should be pure asset transfers without implicit/explicit support.

Strengthen risk management of the asset securitization business. This should pay attention to debtor capacity and willingness to pay. Banks should not lower standards for securitization. Overly complex securitization and re-securitization should simply be banned. Banks should also strictly control product leverage.

Strengthen management of operational risks. Financial institutions' employees should not be allowed to participate in private financing activities. Otherwise we leave an open risk conduction channel from private financing to banks.

Third, we should strengthen the early warning and monitoring mechanisms to build effective ways to prevent risks and deal with crises. Based on the mutability and conductivity of systemic risks in shadow banking system, authorities should build dynamic and prudent mechanisms for risk warning and conflict resolution. The central bank should keep an eye on the shadow banking system, with special attention for size and pace of credit creation. There should be a special department to regulate the shadow banking system. This will strengthen studies on its development and use econometric methods in assessment of each business, innovative derivative risks, and risk management capacity. A real-time monitoring system should be built to supervise shadow banking leverage and absorb both leverage ratios and asset prices into the macroprudential regulatory framework. We can then update regulatory standards in real time. This will strengthen dynamic monitoring of systemic risks as well as a risk warning mechanism to avoid excessive leverage and asset price bubbles. In order to improve capacity, there should be an emergency linkage mechanism that is coordinated, orderly, and efficient. All regions and departments should also have integrated processing networks to deal with shadow banking emergencies.

Fourth, we must strengthen the means of liquidity regulation. Specifically, authorities could require richer information, including detailed maturity structure as well as liquidity analysis of trading assets and off-balance sheet positions under various scenarios. Authorities could then publish timely, systematic reports on liquidity trends and reduce risk with a variety of tools (such as liquidity buffer requirements and core funding ratios). In addition, we should urge financial institutions to increase investments in their risk management departments, develop rigorous risk management processes, and strengthen information disclosure to ensure that investors understand basic product features (e.g., risks, trading structure, and relevance); strengthen leverage limits and establish management mechanisms for total leverage, on-balance sheet leverage, and off-balance sheet leverage.

Fifth, it is key to enhance investor education and improve general risk awareness. Investors must objectively know the potential risks of the products they purchase and perform self-assessments of risk tolerance. In the absence of a lender of last resort (LOLR) inside the shadow banking system, investors will play the role by themselves and bear their own investment risk in the absence of foul play by financial institutions.

Building a long-term framework for information sharing

Currently, separate supervision based on separate operations in the shadow banking system is likely to produce holes in regulation, especially when some institutions may make use of regulatory competition ("turf wars") or blind spots. For this reason, regulatory bodies should build efficient cooperation and information sharing mechanisms to deal with potential risks in the shadow banking system and cope with the shortcomings of the current regulatory framework.

First, the central bank should coordinate with statistics departments to provide a monitoring framework for flows in the shadow banking system. The Chinese shadow banking system is still immature. Without complex financial derivatives and credit intermediation chains, the shadow banking system basically consists of single, mostly isolated entity or quasi entity. This makes monitoring more straightforward. If authorities monitor and manage the shadow banking system efficiently at the very beginning, then risks will be controlled and the development is promising. However, under separate supervision, most financial institutions are divided into different regulation sectors, so they face inconsistent standards set by various regulators. There is no unified standard for statistical information among different departments, let alone collection and analysis. It is necessary to build a comprehensive, unified, and standardized statistical system for improved coordination between regulatory bodies.

Second, we must build information collecting and sharing mechanisms based on a unified statistical framework that provides quantitative foundations for macroprudential and microprudential regulation. Various regulatory departments would then be able to estimate the risks of shadow banking institutions or businesses from an overall perspective, which helps them distinguish possible risks transferred from shadow banking to traditional banks. In addition to quantitative information, regulators can also use information obtained from conversations with market participants and investigations to be aware of the latest trends and risk diversification. This information can make regulation more forward-looking and adapt to rapid changes. All these quantitative and qualitative information requires information sharing among various regulatory authorities and establishment of a coordinated and comprehensive risk assessment.

Third, regulators must work together to strive for a rational division of regulatory responsibilities and push key points for regulation at appropriate stages. Regulators need to pay more attention to information sharing and coordination mechanisms among supervision departments to optimize China's current framework. Good coordination mechanisms can make up for dispersed regulatory responsibilities and arbitrage in shadow banking. Such mechanisms can take the form of joint conferences or committee of representatives from various regulatory agencies. Four factors should be taken into consideration: information sharing, coordinated decisions, mutual compliance rulemaking, and conflict resolution. First, regulators should share information and refer to each other's experience. Second, related departments should work together to make decisions based on consensus. Third, regulators should respect and obey other departments' legal responsibility to secure effective adjudication and prevent potential conflicts between regulators and regulation arbitrage. Finally, there should be a conflict resolution mechanism to provide proper solutions.

Fourth, we must clarify the mode and scope of the LOLR. As an innovative business model, shadow banking system faces inevitable risks. When all market risks can be traced back to those responsible for them, then shadow banking will have specific and diversified risks and a more healthy development. Under the condition that the market risk diversification mechanism is not well developed, the LOLR for the shadow banking system (including local government, commercial banks, and private enterprises) will surely shoulder the liabilities. This solution only passes risks to the next counterparty instead of resolving risks by market, which in the end is not in the interest of taxpayers. In the long run, it is necessary to clarify the methods and scope of LOLR assistance, let financial institutions have clear expectations, and then clarify market risks. If the shadow banking system is not allowed to access the LOLR, then there should be other market ways to reduce and diversify its risks.

Regulatory framework for other Chinese government departments

Regulatory focus for lending by legal non-bank financial institutions

China's shadow banking system includes many non-bank institutions that have legal credit activities. Their regulation should focus on issues much broader than initial authorization to establish a business.

MICRO-LOAN COMPANIES

Micro-loan companies operate mainly with their own funds in the lending business, but they do not belong to formal financial system. Therefore, the regulation of micro-loan companies is less strict than that of the formal banking system despite strict regulation at the time of establishment. Formal banks usually treat them as ordinary businesses and can grant them loans.

Unlike their foreign counterparts, Chinese micro-loan companies are neither nongovernmental organizations (NGOs) nor banks. Thus, their regulation must be different. According to their "lending only" feature, we can classify them as "quasi-financial institutions." Regulators must control micro-loan company leverage ratios to ensure that owners of capital in this business bear the risks they undertake. Even though micro-loan companies can obtain credit from banks, the amount is generally small. This in turn limits potential losses and the scale of contagion.

The other key for their regulation is to inspect compliance. Since micro-loan companies lend their own money, there is no need for normal protection of depositors' interests. Risks are mainly concentrated in internal and external losses brought by illegal business or possible group events caused by illegal sequestration, fund-raising, and intermediation. The main task for regulators is thus to prevent illegal operations, not to adapt prudential regulatory rules used for banks.

PAWNSHOPS

Pawnshops play a unique role in social financing, especially in promoting financing diversification and the development of small and micro enterprises. The current problem is that some consignment shops undertake the pawn business or other illegal activities in disguise. Thus, regulation should focus on firm crackdowns on these pawn businesses in disguise, maintenance of normal management order, and further clarity for the administrative regulatory relations between regulators and pawnshops. The People's Bank of China (PBOC), Public Security Bureaus (PSBs), industrial departments, and the commerce departments should separately supervise pawnshop establishment, management, and exit. We advise related departments to build cooperative relationships and clarify their respective competencies.

GUARANTEE COMPANIES

Regulators have been concerned about recent chaos in the guarantee industry. Some companies engage in high-risk investments, high-interest loans, and illegal public financing under the guise of guarantee companies. Once a crisis occurs, the guarantee company itself will face serious problems that could then also drag down banks and even whole financing environment in a chain reaction due to guarantee companies' high leverage. In March 2010, seven ministries jointly issued the "Interim Regulation on the Administration of Financing Guarantee Companies" which completely reorganized the guarantee industry, reconstructed the regulatory system, and clarified transition security from a filing to business licensing system. This document also made clear rules about registered capital, business license, regulation standards, business domain, and limits of financing guarantees as well as equity funds. The regulatory focus is to continue standardizing operations, strictly restrict business through laws and regulations, and further improve relevant regulatory policies for guarantee companies.

Regulatory focus for private lending and network loans

PRIVATE LENDING

For private lending practices, the main regulatory task is to promote its transparency by blocking some channels while opening others. Private lending, which reflects the allocation of financial resources by the "invisible hand," objectively promotes the formation and development of multi-level credit markets. What we need is to improve the current legislative norms for private lending that define its legal boundary. In sum, we should promote legalization, standardization, and transparency in the private lending business.

First, we should give regulatory authority and supervisory power to local governments of all levels. Local government regulators are responsible for compiling information, dealing with problems and possible crises, developing regulatory measures based on local circumstances, cooperating with the central government, participating in local legislation, and issuing legitimate licenses. Meanwhile, they should resolutely combat and eliminate illegal fund-raising, relending at usurious interest rates, financial pyramid sales, and money laundering to prevent as well as reduce potential risks private lending poses.

Second, we should cultivate industry self-regulation and encourage the public to take a supervisory role. In this vein, self-regulatory organizations for the private lending industry will require training to ensure that they can understand and take the guidance of government regulatory authorities into account. They can then self-regulate according to law and are responsible for the implementation of inspection rules, publishing information related to private lending and resolving disputes to gradually form a virtuous interaction between government supervision and industry self-regulation. We can also publish information about registered lending institutions through mass media and set up a reporting network (e.g., telephone hotlines and websites) to further allow the public to play a regulatory role.

Third, we must establish an effective monitoring system for private financing information. Local governments can establish a sound registration system for private lending and clearly define registration by sector. To register and file private lending information, make inspections more effective, and to track private funds, authorities should build a dedicated information management system for private lending. Provinces, cities, and counties should set up monitoring sites on private lending information that are exclusively responsible for the collection of private lending information within their jurisdictions. They would then submit this to the information system to provide information support to relevant departments' work to strengthen private lending management and formulate macroeconomic policies.

NETWORK LOANS

Private lending, P2P, and other forms of new Internet finance businesses are currently in a regulatory gray area. Once they register in business administration departments, companies can open online financing businesses. Existing laws and regulations have no clear rules about P2P companies' entry qualifications, information disclosure, internal management, and industry regulator. Therefore, we should improve the regulatory system and laws as soon as possible to make clear rules for the nature, organization form, business scope, and disclosure Internet loans.

It is necessary to include Internet loans like P2P in the regulatory system and clearly define relevant regulatory authorities, responsibilities, and monitoring tools.

At the same time, these should be looped into a nationwide information monitoring mechanism for network loans that includes frequent surveys, statistics, and reports. A mandatory information disclosure mechanism will require relevant companies and business sponsors to fully disclose their personal financial status and operating conditions, names of companies' legal representatives, contact information, and other relevant information. All of these information newly collected by authorities and combined in the nationwide system will improve the ability of authorities at all levels to effectively manage the development of this sector.

Specific recommendations for institutions and business lines

Regulatory proposal for financial institutions under the supervision of the CSRC, CBRC, and CIRC

Recommended regulatory tools for bank wealth management

To promote the sustainable and healthy development of bank wealth management (WM), here are some regulatory policy recommendations:

1 Since the "Interim Measures for the administration of the personal WM business of commercial banks" promulgated and carried out in 2005, bank WM started from scratch. Since then, the market has undergone significant changes. Authorities should strengthen top-level design, gradually form a forward-looking regulatory system, improve the formation of regulation (including financial services management practices, investment management approaches, etc.), and clarify financial services' legal status to highlight the WM business's bankruptcy isolation mechanism.

2 Strengthen statistical monitoring, improve information sharing, and build a platform to exchange statistics and information. In the recent years, the media has often used incorrect, exaggerated data and false reports on bank WM in their stories. Since information about banks' financial services was not public, it was difficult to ensure that the public understands the true scale of these activities. These stories misled market participants and forced regulators into a reactive position with respect to both the development and regulation of bank WM.

3 Emphasize regulatory compliance and improve enforcement. Since 2005, regulators have issued a number of regulations and risk warnings on bank WM and constantly reiterated compliance requirements in WM research, design, investment operations, and marketing. However, some banks failed to properly carry out regulatory policies. To reflect the seriousness as well as regulatory authority and highlight regulation's consistency, authorities need to improve enforcement of laws and regulations and to enhance supervision for market access in banking WM, including on- and off-site inspections.

Regulatory proposal for trust WM

1   Bank and trust cooperation that is currently subject to strict regulations is not narrow shadow banking. However, they do undertake credit transformation that could have shadow banking characteristics. It is necessary to further strengthen regulations for these products and eliminate credit transformation to take away shadow banking factors. Commercial banks and trust institutions may refuse to implement rules or conceal facts to protect their interests, so authorities need to take appropriate measures and strengthen supervision.

2   Lead trust companies shift from bank-and-credit cooperation to trust industry through bonus mechanism. For trust companies, their cooperation with banks has many advantages. It is simple, has lower management cost, can expand asset scale, and help company become both more profitable and higher positioned within the industry. However, in the long run, these cooperations cannot reflect the true advantages of the trust industry. Trust companies should gradually focus more on the asset and WM businesses, reverting their original purpose.

Regulatory recommendations for securities company WM

There are two main recommendations for this sector: improvement of statistics gathering and strengthened regulation of the specialized asset management business.

1   Strengthen statistics and regulations on bank and securities company cooperation. Many targeted asset management businesses in securities companies are so-called channel businesses that result in double counting because they are included in securities companies' asset management [assets under management (AUM)] and banks' WM at the same time. Authorities should independently measure the scale and nature of bank purchases of finance bought from securities companies in a careful and timely manner. Strengthening statistics and regulations on bank-securities cooperation can help authorities know how bank funds flow from off-balance sheet to on-balance sheet, standardize sales of cooperative products, and enhance consumer protection.

2   Strengthen regulations on specialized asset management businesses. Compared with that of aggregated and targeted asset management businesses, relevant implementation rules for the specialized asset management business have failed to emerge. Today, the specialized asset management business is small and almost negligible compared with the total size of the asset management business. Authorities have not uniformly defined and standardized its definition, scope, implementation details, and other issues. With the development of the securities financing business, regulation on specialized asset management services needs further improvement.

Regulatory recommendations for funds' WM business

First, we must improve regulation of the managed accounts business and prevent the operation of channel businesses. Fund companies' managed accounts business could very well become another way for banks to operate channel businesses, which could lead to double counting between banks' WM businesses and fund AUM. Therefore, we recommend that authorities implement an independent measurement system for these products and work with the banks to plan their specific characteristics and scale.

Second, authorities should step up monitoring of fund companies' net capital and improve their ability to withstand risk. At present, these managed account businesses must only register RMB 20 million in capital, which is much weaker than the net capital requirements securities companies and trusts must fulfill. Our concrete recommendation is to implement net capital and operating capital requirements for managed accounts as well as regular statistical monitoring of this business. To avoid stunting the growth of managed accounts, the wide gap between these two types should be closely monitored. At the same time, it will allow authorities to quickly and effectively react to areas of potential high risk.

Third, PE funds require more robust regulation. PE funds receive far lighter regulation than public and non-public equity funds. They have the most flexible investment scope, the most diverse forms of investment, and most clearly exhibit shadow banking characteristics when compared with other funds' asset management products.

Regulatory recommendations for insurance companies' WM business

INSURANCE COMPANIES' WM BUSINESS

First, authorities should implement a filing and dynamic reporting system for universal and dividend insurance. These funds' investment transparency is much lower than investment-linked insurance products, and investor understanding of their operation is relatively low. Therefore, authorities should ensure that universal and dividend insurances are subject to increased disclosure requirements. Investors can then better understand their investing principles and scope.

Second, we must release laws and regulations to keep insurance companies from hidden dealings in the short-term WM business. Insurance companies' main competency is risk management; WM is only a derivative side function. Recent insurance innovations have leaned more toward investment products at the expense of risk management, but they should keep their focus on the latter. Although this shift may lead to higher short-term profits, their maturity and liquidity mismatches are accompanied by accumulating risk that poses a threat to the entire shadow banking system. Therefore, authorities should release rules to restrict insurance companies' involvement in short-term WM and bring them back to their original purpose.

FOR INSURANCE ASSET MANAGEMENT COMPANIES' WM

Detailed rules and regulations are necessary to set up systems for the establishment and operation of insurance asset management companies. Authorities should also limit the scope of their products' operations. At present, they are restricted only by the China Insurance Regulatory Commission (CIRC) relatively strong framework: Circular on Issues Relevant to the Pilot Project Business by Insurance Asset Management Companies (No. [2013]124 of the CIRC). This is incomparable to both the China Banking Regulatory Commission's (CBRC's) refined standards for trust companies and the CSRC's refined process for the regulation of securities companies and fund companies. Differences in regulation are a key factor that gives insurance asset management companies much room to grow. Authorities should thus use regulations that apply to trusts, securities companies, and funds as a reference to create detailed regulatory standards for this sector. They will then be able to get to the bottom of and cutoff potential risks these institutions pose.

These companies need comprehensive rules and stronger regulation. The Circular on Issues Relevant to the Pilot Project Business by Insurance Asset Management Companies (No. [2013]124 of the CIRC) instituted a shift from a CIRC-led product approval mechanism to one of post-issuance registration. In reality, this initial approval and reporting process constitutes very loose regulation. The industry is in an early stage, and its scale is not yet clear, so such loose regulation makes it difficult to effectively control its shadow banking risk.

These companies also need a disclosure system to increase transparency. A look through the information reported by the CIRC, industry groups, and individual companies reveals the insufficiency of publicly available information. Their transparency is the lowest of all formal financial institutions and does not suffice for external regulators. To fix this, we can use external help in regulation to reduce risk as much as possible and ensure that these institutions remain healthy.

Regulatory recommendations for financial leasing companies

Regulation needs to keep these companies focused on their core business of leasing and increase and improve professionalism, competitiveness, differentiation, specialization, development strategies, and market position. They should develop internal control mechanisms to create the foundation necessary for better governance, information management, evaluation/rating, and especially risk management. For better risk management, specific attention should be paid to changes in the structure of the economy, overcapacity, downturn risks, debt ratios, asset management risks, and liquidity risk.

Regulation must also improve the external environment for financial leasing companies. The legal status of leasing companies deserves further research, which should include cooperation with and feedback from the highest levels of the court system for explanation of the Company Law's application in this case. This should help alleviate current issues in the establishment and legal registration of leasing companies. Improved communication between taxation authorities is also necessary to resolve the issues raised by the changeover from business taxation to value-added taxation. There must also be more equity in terms of tax advantages.

Regulatory recommendations for auto and consumer finance companies

We must complete the existing framework and tools used to regulate and rate these companies by type. The next step will be to further refine these tools. Authorities should set up coordination to support and encourage the expansion of medium- and long-term financing channels through debt issuance and securitization. Liquidity management is a key aspect of these processes and their proper regulation.

Regulatory recommendations for regulatory bodies: Commissions and local government offices

Recommendations for pawnshop regulation

The main regulation for pawnshops is the Measures for the Administration of Pawning, Ministry of Commerce (No. [2005]8), jointly issued by the Ministry of Commerce (MOFCOM) and the PSB. It lays out a framework for the establishment, operation, scope, regulation, and supervision of pawnshops in China. Most provincial commerce departments then built their own specific regulations according to the general framework laid out in the Measures. Together, this regulatory framework is sufficient to cover the daily operation of pawnshops and prevent them from posing systemic risks. Therefore, the focus for regulation of this sector should be to ensure that local rules are properly implemented in line with the regulations that already exist.

Regulatory recommendations for guarantee companies

Due to an incomplete regulatory framework, guarantee companies have been demonized in the past few years. They are seen as the main representatives of illegal fund gathering. In order to properly regulate them, we should focus on three main tasks. The first is to create a task force to halt illegal fund-raising by institutions that only nominally act as guarantee companies and shut down unlicensed operators. The second is to restrict guarantee company operations according to the CBRC and six other departments' Interim Measures for the Administration of Financing Guarantee Companies (No. [2010]3). This includes a ban on taking in funds resembling deposits, taking on debt, receiving entrusted loans, and other activities. The third is to promote more understanding and awareness of guarantee companies among the general populace.

Regulatory recommendations for small loan companies

According to *Guiding Opinions of China Banking Regulatory Commission and the People's Bank of China on the Pilot Operation of Small-Sum Loan Companies* (No. [2008]2 of the CBRC), province-level finance offices or related departments have the duty to supervise small loan companies. It does not expressly designate a certain department for regulation of micro-loan companies. This function is delegated to the local governments, so the level of regulation in different jurisdictions varies greatly.

Current provisional efforts have seen all sorts of departments in this role, from finance and commerce departments to public securities bureaus and many others.

These local governments have almost all implemented the previously mentioned Guiding Opinions in a prudential supervisory framework similar to those used for financial institutions. They carefully monitor and control market entry, qualifications of high-level management, interest rates, accounting processes, information disclosure, risk mitigation, and disposal measures.

The aforementioned regulatory system and supervisory standards have positively influenced the stable development of the small loan business. However, fund integration limits have been too strict. These have stopped small loan businesses from reaching their full potential. Regulators should relax these restrictions and allow them to both issue debt and securitize assets in the near future.

Regulatory recommendations for financial asset exchanges

China currently lacks clear legal and regulatory statuses for financial asset exchanges. In addition, it remains unclear which supervisory body should be/is responsible for their regulation. Since these organizations play an increasingly important role in China's financial system, we recommend the following regulatory measures:

- clarify their legal status and create legal, supervisory, and departmental norms for their regulation;
- empower local governments to regulate them;
- put transparent regulation at the core of all efforts;
- comprehensively regulate their operation, including establishment, trading, corporate governance, investor protection, and delisting procedures.

These measures will help protect investor interests and contribute to financial stability.

Regulatory recommendations for currently unregulated organizations

New forms of Internet finance

The rapid development of Internet finance's territory has brought with it both unhealthy competition and problems with risk management and operating models. These are manifest in issues such as the "Ha Ha Dai" website, which recently stopped service due to a sudden break in its capital funds. Regulation and laws specifically for this sector are urgently needed, as those currently in existence are insufficient to meet the needs of practitioners. Therefore, we recommend the following steps:

- establish a strategy for the parallel development of Internet finance with traditional finance;
- create a management advisory body specifically for Internet finance;
- accelerate the creation of rules and regulations for Internet finance;

- develop professionals qualified to develop and manage this complex form of finance;
- reform the sub-sectoral management mechanism.

Recommendations for P2P financing

Unregulated P2P financing poses numerous hidden risks. For example, unreasonable interest rates, over indebtedness, debt disputes, threats to social and financial stability, treats to macro and monetary policy, disruptions to market and macro regulation, encouragement of gray market transactions, and illegal fund-raising. We have four main recommendations to deal with these issues: complete the legal and regulatory system, create a center for their regulation, establish a credit reporting system, and perfect the P2P service system.

First, we must complete the legal and regulatory system. Regulations currently in force have neither clearly defined P2P capital nor empowered/charged a regulatory body to implement relevant regulation or establish norms. *Several Opinions of the State Council on Encouraging, Supporting and Guiding the Development of Individual and Private Economy and Other Non-Public Sectors of the Economy* (No. [2005]3 of the State Council), also called "non-public document 36" or "old document 36," uses the phrase "non-public capital," while *Several Opinions of the State Council on Encouraging and Guiding the Healthy Development of Private Investment* (No. [2010]13 of the State Council) (also called "new document 36") jettisons the previous phrase in favor of "private capital." No official decision has clarified how these phrases are related, so we recommend that authorities clarify this and other aspects of P2P capital through the establishment of a legal basis for P2P capital. This should clearly designate regulatory obligations, rules for market access, operational processes, and legal responsibilities. It will be much easier to take on illegal activities once there is a clearly established legal framework on which we can rely.

Second, we should create a center for P2P lending regulation as soon as possible. This center should have the CBRC as its head and coordinate comprehensive regulatory operations with all relevant stakeholders. It should also focus on data collection related to the scale, interest rate levels, counterparties, and ultimate effects of P2P lending on society. These data will be key in supporting policymakers in their goals to establish effective macroeconomic policies.

Third, we should establish a credit reporting system. This would build on the existing reporting framework to extend it from financial institutions and markets to individuals. P2P lenders will face lower risk because they will be able to quickly grasp the creditworthiness of potential borrowers. The end result will be a more socialized form of credit rating and a new form of public good.

Last, we should perfect the P2P service system. P2P will prove a better partner to the currently capital-starved SMEs once we encourage consultants, lawyers, accountants, and notaries adapt to round out gaps in its service delivery and participate in its further development.

Recommendations for third-party WM

For third-party WM, we have four main areas of focus: development of the legal and economic environment, establishment of a strict regulatory system, use of policy to guide further development, and adaptation to local conditions.

First, we must cultivate a solid economy under the rule of law. In all countries in which third-party WM is well developed, we also see well-developed economies and credit systems. These market economies create the right conditions to encourage the healthy development of the industry, its legal environment, and its regulation. For China, we should attach the most importance to a credit system that ensures those engaged in industrial activities fulfill their obligations. These activities should fall under the orbit of regulators and be part of our efforts to cultivate a market economy solidly rooted in law.

Second, we must emphasize establishment of a strict regulatory system for WM. The flourishing development of WM outside China is rooted in a strong regulatory scheme, clear legal frameworks for trusts and financial planning, and ways to reduce tax liabilities. These factors in turn provide opportunities for wealth preservation and creation through asset allocation. China's situation is the opposite. This WM is foreign to China's tradition, and there is a general lack of honesty in our society. Thus, third-party asset management's underdevelopment in China should come as no surprise.

Third, use policy to guide further development. Over the long term, organizational development is inseparable from good policy. Third-party wealth managers are currently in a weak position compared to banks and securities companies but will find more opportunities as the number of qualified wealth managers grows. Policy should reflect and encourage these developments.

Finally, the government should weigh economic, cultural, and policy-related questions when designing regulation to ensure the choice of suitable, horizontally integrated regulation. Only if this succeeds can China obtain positive legal and regulatory outcomes.

Regulatory recommendations for new forms of shadow banking on financial markets

RECOMMENDATIONS FOR ASSET SECURITIZATION

Securitization regulation should focus on four main areas: improve our understanding of securitization and its effects, include credit rating institutions, improve information disclosure, and establish a regulatory framework.

To better understand the role of securitization in China, we need to understand the contingent risk it poses locally and for the rest of the financial system. Such knowledge will allow authorities to put it in the proper place within the regulatory system. We should also deeply examine the balance between financial stability, innovation, and efficiency. Proper formulation of concrete strategy depends on an effective balance between these goals.

The second focus of securitization regulation is regulation of rating agencies. They must be both better regulated and more transparent to avoid a repeat of previous problems in the sector. We need to establish a single regulator with defined rating standards and regulatory norms. Norms for the rating process within these firms should be more transparent and fall under regulatory standards. Analysts, as the main operating bodies of rating agencies, should be required to enroll in a registration system. To avoid improper ratings, we should start at the analyst level to ensure that they do not violate relevant rules. We can then close loopholes by establishing an industry-wide employee management system to properly punish those who violate the professional ethics.

The third focus is to improve the quality and breadth of disclosure. The current form and focus of information disclosure in the securitization industry are different than those of traditional finance businesses. We can borrow from the United States' experience in financial regulation to learn the following lessons:

- Disclosure standards and forms should fit the issuer and type of securitization.
- Disclosure should make it simple for investors to understand and compare products/information from different issuers.

These principles can help regulators make these markets more transparent. This transparency then aids investors and issuers by facilitating the disclosure process.

The fourth focus area is an adjustment of the Chinese regulatory framework to better fit the challenges posed by securitization. Today's financial products are increasingly integrated, but China's regulatory system remains fragmented. Future development will necessitate integrated regulatory system to fit the integrated financial system. We urgently need a single regulatory body to undertake the coordination of securitization regulation.

Recommendations for regulation of securities lending and repo

Securities lending and repo have growth rapidly in the recent years, which has posed challenges for regulators. First, we should strictly monitor their risk indicators. Securities companies may blindly seek to grow their business scale to maximize profits regardless of risks. Regulatory oversight must ensure they conform to minimum net capital requirements, possess the ability to control risk. They should also determine reasonable levels of credit transaction exposure. In addition, regulators should keep the entire industry's scale within certain limits determined by its risk absorption capacity.

Second, authorities must adjust risk reserve in a timely manner. These reserves are an important indirect regulatory tool that can be adjusted to fit money supply, inflation, or market conditions. Authorities can adjust the required reserves, cash reserves, or haircuts on collateral to put a damper on speculative activity. For example, if equity prices increase too quickly, we can relax securities lending to encourage shorts. If they are falling too quickly, we can loosen financing. Current reserve requirements in China are relatively high. Although this reduces potential risk, it has stunted the development of this industry by weakening the ability of industry participants to use leverage, which makes it a less attractive business.

Third, authorities should strengthen dynamic management of market risk. In this vein, it is key to improve the daily mark-to-market mechanism. The debt ratio for each margin account should be calculated daily based on updated collateral values to avoid excessive buildup of debt and risk. Next, we should focus on the compulsory liquidation system, which with margin accounts and client credit rating systems constitutes the most important risk control measures. Finally, we should establish a forced liquidation system. This is a risk prevention mechanism used in future markets when prices move unilaterally (in only one direction) over two or more days and hit a trading floor or ceiling. Such a situation can make it impossible to find a counterparty to a trade necessary under compulsory liquidation. The exchange or market managers thus use their authority to act as an intermediary and force a transaction between losing parties (obliged under compulsory liquidation to liquidate a certain holding due to losses) and gaining parties (positions gained value during unilateral price movements) according to a matching principle. The concept can be more simply described as "making the loser lose little and the winner win little" or "opening an escape hatch" for the loser. This operation can work to alleviate excessive risk in these special conditions.

Fourth, authorities should improve the investor composition in various markets. From a risk perspective, the price discovery and value creation mechanism is different in each, from the main board, second board, margin, and equity futures markets. Each successive market is riskier and thus fits investors with different risk preferences, so we should regulate each in a way that fits its specific characteristics. For margin trading, we should use fund and experience thresholds to ensure that the right type of investors buy the right type of products. Individual investors should be able to understand and take on this market's risks. In addition, institutional investors like QFII participants, securities investment funds, insurers, social security funds, and securities companies have long only been able to make money through sufficient scale. In a unilaterally declining market, there are few channels for institutional investors to participate. Authorities should allow institutional investors to participate in the margin trading market to encourage its development for more effective risk hedging and price discovery.

Fifth, we should establish a unified regulatory system. Since the PBOC, CBRC, and Ministry of Finance all have a role in overseeing the securities markets, it is easy for each to implement uncoordinated policies according to its institutional preference. The solution is to put the repo market under the regulatory authority of a single government department/commission. The government can then effectively monitor the entire securitization process, including both organizers and transactors and on- and off-market transactions.

Recommendations for money market funds

First, we should focus on the existing Chinese money market and its difference with those of more developed markets. For example, the success and rapid growth of American MMFs is due to a certain constellation of factors in the American money market:

- great variety of money market instruments to trade, especially commercial paper;
- free, market-determined interest rates;

- many types of market participants;
- advantageous structure and configuration, including different levels of creditworthiness and taxation.

Second, we should select a few fund management companies to set up money market funds. They should be under the same operational management system as other securities investors, but managed separately. In addition, we should prohibit transactions between them.

Third, we should strengthen the market infrastructure. To do this, we should increase integration of the interbank and bond markets to form a unified, nationwide bond market. We must also focus on intermediation and brokerage in these markets. Securities companies should be allowed to represent large companies in issuance and trading of commercial paper, including secondary market transactions. These steps will aid the further development of the market for commercial paper.

Fourth, we should accelerate the creation of relevant laws and regulations. To complete the legal system, we need a legal definition of the money market, legislation for their regulation, clear procedures for entry/exit of market bodies, and a reduction in uncertainty for the funds' future development. On this foundation, China's money markets will experience smooth, healthy, and rapid development.

Fifth, we must protect the effective operation of the money market. The Chinese money market has enormous room for growth, especially in the market for corporate debt. However, the operation of such markets inevitably gives birth to risk. Risk prevention is at the very core of ethical operation for any business. Regulators should thus raise the standards of credit rating for all transactors entering the market and establish a comprehensive credit rating system.

The birth and development of shadow banking is inextricably bound to the whole financial system. The relationship between regulation and development has been a cycle of regulation, development, further regulation, and then further development. Our major premise is that shadow banking is a neutral concept, and narrow shadow banking has a limited scale. Regulators must balance the desire to protect and support its financial innovation with that to limit its potential negative influence on the financial system and economy as a whole.

Notes

1   This section follows the structure and wording for the principles in the FSB's "Strengthening Oversight and Regulation of Shadow Banking: An Overview of Policy Recommendations." August 29, 2013.
2   This section refers to the toolkits in the FSB's "Strengthening Oversight and Regulation of Shadow Banking: An Overview of Policy Recommendations." August 29, 2013.
3   Credit conversion factors (CCFs) are used to turn off-balance sheet exposures, which may pose credit risk (such as those arising from securitization) into "credit exposure equivalents" for the purposes of calculating risk weights and capital requirements under the Basel framework. The position is multiplied by the relevant CCF, whose result is then placed in the proper risk-based category as a risk-adjusted, on-balance sheet equivalent.

Conclusion

This book defined the range of shadow banking on broad and narrow foundations. Broad shadow banking is financial intermediation outside the traditional banking system, while narrowly defined shadow banking has our four special characteristics: maturity mismatch, liquidity risk, credit transfer, and high leverage. Broadly defined shadow banking has no inevitable negative effect on macroeconomic stability. Rather, it is the narrowly defined type that can spark a systemic crisis. These require stronger safeguards for their risk and closer regulation.

Shadow banking is thus a neutral concept with a sort of objective necessity. From the supply side, its drivers are the search for return on capital, financial innovation, and regulatory arbitrage. Ample global liquidity and high domestic savings provided the necessary capital. From the demand side, the formal financial system was put under regulations that limited their scale of lending, loan-to-deposit ratios, and capital adequacy. These made it impossible to fully satisfy credit demand from local governments, property developers, and small- and medium-sized enterprises (SMEs). Shadow banking objectively widened financing channels, made the financial system more effective, pushed the innovative transformation of commercial banks, and aided the development of the real economy. They exposed the financial system's shortcomings and future development path.

Chinese shadow banks have a background and special characteristics that make them distinct from their foreign counterparts. European and American shadow banks concentrate on securitization and repos, while Chinese shadow banks focus on credit and lending businesses. The strict regulation they receive disqualifies them as narrow shadow banks. Financial market innovations were the main cause of the American and European crises in addition to the main component of shadow banking, but this type of business is still in a nascent stage in China. They are still small, but must be closely watched. In an attempt to lay out a basic definition for shadow banking, this book attempts to quantify its scale in China. We define objectively and avoid unnecessary exaggeration through differentiation by risk and regulatory requirements. In our estimation, we use our standards of judgment to analyze non-bank and even non-financial institutions and industries to see if they fit our characteristics of shadow banks.

From a risk perspective, shadow banking has continuously expanded in the past years. Securities companies, trusts, and insurance companies mingle together and cause systemic risk to accumulate. These lurking risks come from their maturity and liquidity transformation, risk transfer, and high leverage. The risk of contagion has also risen with the intimate relations between banks and their shadow counterparts. Current legal and accounting frameworks underestimate risk because they are unable to effectively differentiate and monitor this part of it. Shadow banks' massive hidden creation of related loans, self-serving loans, and collaborative loans raised risk and spurred a proliferation of illegal activity in the financial industry. Regulatory arbitrage by shadow banks weakened the effectiveness of microprudential regulation such as the Basel Accords. Additionally, the unending expansion of shadow banking has created entrenched interests that resist financial regulation and reform.

We can improve financial stability by strengthening regulation of shadow banking. It also helps reforms establish a more stable economic and financial environment. Shadow banking's establishment and expansion is a conscious market behavior. Objectively, if we have banks, then we have shadow banks too. They cannot be eliminated. To effectively govern shadow banking, we must go beyond stopping up their negative effects and intervene at the source, whether organization or mechanism.

To improve regulation, we must also regulate different types of shadow banks with the most effective methods for that type. This will require a combination of macroprudential and microprudential regulations to make it more effective. For broad shadow banks, we can wrap them into the management of the normal credit system and increase microprudential regulatory tools. We thus reduce the ease with which its credit creation can engender systemic risk. For narrow shadow banks, we can use macroprudential measures to avoid welfare losses and economic damage due to price or quantity controls. For newly emerging forms of debt outside our current management system, such as Internet finance and peer-to-peer(P2P) lending, we must pay careful attention to contagion and put them under the microscope of regulators. At the same time, we should do more to coordinate laws and regulations to increase their effectiveness.

China must horizontally integrate the central bank and its three regulatory commissions to constitute a high-level network. This is the only way to ensure proper regulatory coverage and avoid coddling of specific industries. The other key structural reform will be to clearly delineate the regulatory competency of local governments versus those of the central government, which will ensure that fewer organizations escape proper supervision.

Finally, these reforms must go hand in hand with broader financial reform to improve China's financial system. These reforms, taken together, will help China take the key next steps in its development and effectively manage the risks posed by shadow banking.

Appendix

CF40 Organizational Structure and Club Members (2015)

CF40 Advisors (names are in alphabetical order)

1	**CHEN Yulu**	President, Renmin University of China
2	**HU Huaibang**	Chairman, China Development Bank
3	**HU Xiaolian**	Chairman, The Export-Import Bank of China
4	**HUANG Qifan**	Mayor, Chongqing
5	**JIANG Chaoliang**	Governor, Jilin Province
6	**JIANG Jianqing**	Chairman of the Board of Directors, Industrial and Commercial Bank of China
7	**LI Jian'ge**	Chairman of the Board, Sun Yefang Fiscal Science Foundation
8	**LIN Yifu**	Professor, National School of Development, Peking University
9	**LIU Wei**	Executive Vice President, Peking University
10	**PEI Changhong**	Director, Institute of Economics, Chinese Academy of Social Sciences
11	**QIAN Yingyi**	Dean, School of Economics and Management, Tsinghua University
12	**QIN Xiao**	Director, Boyuan Foundation
13	**SHEN Liantao**	Former Chairman, Securities and Futures Commission, Hong Kong
14	**TANG Shuangning**	Chairman of the Board, China Everbright Ltd.
15	**WANG Jiang**	Professor of Finance, MIT Sloan School of Management
16	**WU Jinglian**	Senior Research Fellow, Development and Research Center the State Council
17	**WU Xiaoling**	Vice-Chairwoman, the Financial and Economic Affairs Committee, the National People's Congress of the People's Republic of China (Former Deputy Governor of the People's Bank of China)
18	**XIE Ping**	Vice President, China Investment Corporation

19	**YI Gang**	Deputy Governor, the People's Bank of China; and Chief Administrator, State Administration of Foreign Exchange
20	**YU Yongding**	Senior Research Fellow, Institute of World Economics and Politics, Chinese Academy of Social Sciences
21	**ZHU Guangyao**	Vice Minister, Ministry of Finance
22	**ZHU Min**	Vice President, International Monetary Fund

CF40 Executive Council

The CF40 Executive Council is the supreme authority of the Forum, which is led by the Chairman of CF40 Executive Council.

Chairman of CF40 Executive Council

| **CHEN Yuan** | Vice-Chairman, the National Committee of the Chinese People's Political Consultative Conference |

Vice-Chairman of CF40 Executive Council

| **XIE Ping** | Vice President, China Investment Corporation |

Members of CF40 Executive Council

1	**CAI Mingxing**	Vice-Chairman, Fubon Financial Holding Company
2	**CHEN Dongsheng**	Chairman and CEO, Tai Kang Life Insurance Co. Ltd.
3	**CHEN Wenhui**	Vice-Chairman, China Insurance Regulatory Commission
4	**CHEN Yuan**	Vice-Chairman of the National Committee of the Chinese People's Political Consultative Conference
5	**DING Xuedong**	Chairman, China International Capital Corporation Limited
6	**JI Xiaohui**	Chairman, Shanghai Pudong Development Bank
7	**LI Renjie**	President, Industrial Bank Co. Ltd.
8	**LI Ruogu**	Former Chairman and President, The Export-Import Bank of China
9	**LI Zhenjiang**	Vice President, Agricultural Bank of China
10	**LIU Yong**	Chief Economist, China Development Bank
11	**LV Jiajin**	President, Postal Savings Bank of China
12	**MIAO Jianmin**	President, China Life Insurance (Group) Company

13	**QIAN Yingyi**	Dean, School of Economics and Management, Tsinghua University
14	**QIU Guogen**	Chairman, Chong Yang Investment Co. Ltd.
15	**REN Huichuan**	Executive Manager, Ping An Insurance (Group) Company of China
16	**SHEN Rujun**	Vice President, Bank of Communications
17	**SONG Liping**	President and CEO, Shenzhen Stock Exchange
18	**TU Guangshao**	Executive Vice Mayor of Shanghai
19	**WANG Dongming**	Chairman, CITIC Securities Co. Ltd.
20	**WANG Haiming**	Secretary-General, China Finance 40 Forum
21	**WANG Zhe**	Secretary of the Party committee, China Foreign Exchange Trade System & National Interbank Funding Center
22	**XIE Ping**	Vice President, China Investment Corporation
23	**YAN Qingmin**	Vice Mayor, Tianjin
24	**YANG Dehong**	Chairman, Guotai Junan Securities Co. Ltd.
25	**YANG Jiacai**	Assistant Chairman, China Banking Regulatory Commission
26	**ZHANG Jialin**	Chairman, Aiyixinrong Capital Management Co. Ltd.

Members of CF40 Council

1	**CAI Mingxing**	Vice-Chairman, Fubon Financial Holding Company
2	**CHEN Dongsheng**	Chairman and CEO, Tai Kang Life Insurance Co. Ltd.
3	**CHEN Yisong**	Chairman, Citic Trust Co. Ltd.
4	**CONG Lin**	CEO, ICBC Financial Leasing Co. Ltd.
5	**DING Xuedong**	Chairman, China International Capital Co. Ltd.
6	**FU Gang**	President, China Bohai Bank
7	**GAN Weimin**	President, Bank of Chongqing
8	**GAO Feng**	President, Deutsche Bank (China) Co. Ltd.
9	**GAO Shanwen**	Chief Economist, Essence Securities
10	**JI Xiaohui**	Chairman, Shanghai Pudong Development Bank
11	**LI Renjie**	President, Industrial Bank Co. Ltd.
12	**LI Ruogu**	Chairman and President, The Export-Import Bank of China
13	**LI Zhenjiang**	Vice President, Agricultural Bank of China
14	**LIAN Ping**	Chief Economist, Bank of Communications
15	**LIU Mingjun**	Vice Mayor, Qingdao

16	**LIU Yong**	Director-General, Business Development Department, China Development Bank
17	**LV Jiajin**	President, Postal Savings Bank of China
18	**MIAO Jianmin**	President, China Life Insurance (Group) Company
19	**NORMAN Ni**	Vice President, Point72 Asset Management
20	**QIU Guogen**	Chairman, Chong Yang Investment Co. Ltd.
21	**RACHAEL Hoey**	Head of CLS Aisa
22	**REN Huichuan**	Executive Manager, Ping An Insurance (Group) Company of China
23	**WAN Fang**	Chairman, Ping An Asset Management Co. Ltd.
24	**WANG Dongming**	Chairman, CITIC Securities Co. Ltd.
25	**WANG Jinshan**	Chairman, Beijing Rural Commercial Bank
26	**WANG Jun**	Chairman, Zhejiang Tailong Commercial Bank
27	**WANG Zhe**	Secretary of the Party Committee, China Foreign Exchange Trade System & National Interbank Funding Center
28	**XIA Shu**	Chairman, Fu Dian Bank Co. Ltd.
29	**YANG Dehong**	Chairman, Guotai Junan Securities Co. Ltd.
30	**YU Yeming**	Managing Director, China Pacific Asset Management Co. Ltd.
31	**ZHANG Jialin**	Chairman, Aiyixinrong Capital Management Co. Ltd.
32	**ZHANG Xiaolei**	Chief Executive Officer, Standard Chartered Bank in China
33	**ZHAO Min**	Chairman, Beijing ADFAITH Consulting Firm Co. Ltd.
34	**ZHAO Wei**	Deputy Chairman and General Manager, China Re Asset Management Co. Ltd.
35	**ZHENG Yang**	Director, Shanghai Financial Services Office

Member Unit of CF40

BOC International (China) Limited

CF40 Academic Committee

The CF40 Executive Council authorizes the Academic Committee to be responsible for the academic management work of the Forum. The Academic Committee is the supreme academic authority.

Chairman of CF40 Academic Committee

QIAN Yingyi   Dean, School of Economics and Management, Tsinghua University

Members of CF40 Academic Committee

1	GUAN Tao	Senior Fellow, China Finance 40 Forum
2	HUANG Yiping	Vice Dean, National School of Development, Peking University
3	PAN Gongsheng	Vice President, People's Bank of China
4	YAN Qingmin	Vice Mayor, Tianjin
5	YUAN Li	Vice President, China Development Bank
6	ZHONG Wei	Director, Finance Research Center, Beijing Normal University

CF40 Supervisory Committee

CF40's Supervisory Committee is responsible for assessing and auditing the Forum's financial affairs. It is also entitled to supervise the performance of duties of the Academic Committee Chairman and Secretary-General when they are in office.

Chief Supervisor

YU Yali   Executive Director and Vice President, Bank of Communications

Supervisors

1	GUAN Tao	Senior Fellow, China Finance 40 Forum
2	LU Lei	Director, Research Bureau, the People's Bank of China
3	WU Hemao	Professor, China Europe International Business School
4	ZHONG Wei	Director, Finance Research Center, Beijing Normal University

CF40 Secretariat

The Forum, which is led by the Executive Council, follows secretary-general responsibility system. The Secretariat, led by the secretary-general, is a permanent operative and executive body of CF40.

Secretary-General: WANG Haiming

40 × 40 Club Members

Government Officials

1	**BA Shusong**	Chief Economist, China Banking Association
2	**CHEN Wenhui**	Vice-Chairman, China Insurance Regulatory Commission
3	**FAN Wenzhong**	Director, International Department, China Banking Regulatory Commission
4	**FANG Xinghai**	Director, International Economic Bureau, Office of the Central Leading Group for Financial and Economic Affairs
5	**JI Zhihong**	Director, Financial Market Department, the People's Bank of China
6	**Li Bo**	Director, Monetary Policy Department, the People's Bank of China
7	**LIU Chunhang**	Director-General, Department of Research, China Banking Regulatory Commission
8	**LIU Jian**	Director, International Division, Ministry of Finance
9	**LIAO Min**	Director, Shanghai Office, China Banking Regulatory Commission
10	**LONG Guoqiang**	Vice Minister, Development Research Center of the State Council
11	**LU Lei**	Director, Research Bureau, the People's Bank of China
12	**MA Jun**	Chief Economist, Research Bureau, the People's Bank of China
13	**PAN Gongsheng**	Vice President, the People's Bank of China
14	**QI Bin**	Director, International Department, China Securities Regulatory Commission
15	**SHEN Xiaohui**	Director, International Department, Research Office of the State Council
16	**WEI Jianing**	Vice Director, Department of Macro-Economics, Development Research Center of the State Council
17	**WEI Shangjin**	Chief Economist, Asian Development Bank
18	**YAN Qingmin**	Vice Mayor, Tianjin
19	**ZHANG Tao**	Director, Legal Affairs Department, the People's Bank of China
20	**ZHANG Xiaopu**	Vice Director-General, Department of Research, China Banking Regulatory Commission

Academics

22	**BAI Chong'en**	Vice Dean, School of Economics and Management, Tsinghua University
23	**DING Zhijie**	Assistant Principal, University of International Business and Economics
24	**GUAN Tao**	Senior Fellow, China Finance 40 Forum
25	**HUANG Jinlao**	Senior Fellow, Chongyang Institute for Financial Studies, Renmin University of China
26	**HUANG Yiping**	Vice Dean, National School of Development, Peking University
27	**LI Daokui**	Director, Schwarzman Scholars at Tsinghua University
28	**QU Qiang**	Director, China Financial Policy Research Center
39	**YAO Yang**	Dean, National School of Development, Peking University
30	**ZHONG Wei**	Director, Finance Research Center, Beijing Normal University

Business

31	**GAO Shanwen**	Chief Economist, Essence Securities
32	**HA Jiming**	Vice-Chairman of China, and Chief Investment Strategist, Department of Investment Management, Goldman Sachs
33	**HUANG Haizhou**	Managing Director, China International Capital Co., Ltd
34	**LI Fu'an**	Chairman, China Bohai Bank
35	**LIAN Ping**	Chief Economist, Bank of Communications
36	**SUN Mingchun**	Chairman and CIO, Deepwater Capital Co., Ltd
37	**WANG Qing**	President, Shanghai Chongyang Investment Management Co., Ltd
38	**YUAN Li**	Vice President, China Development Bank
39	**ZHANG Jianhua**	President, Beijing Rural Commercial Bank

CF40 Invited Members

1	**CHEN Long**	Chief Strategic Officer, Ant Financial Services Group
2	**CHEN Weidong**	Deputy Director, BOC Institute of International Finance

3	**GAO Zhanjun**	Managing Director, CITIC Securities Co., Ltd
4	**GUO Lian**	Director-General, Financial Research Centre, China Development Bank
5	**HUANG Zhiqiang**	Vice President, China Export & Credit Insurance Corporation
6	**HE Dong**	Deputy Director, Monetary and Capital Markets Department, International Monetary Fund
7	**Jin Zhongxia**	Executive Director for China, International Monetary Fund
8	**LI Lin**	Director, Strategic Development Department, Shanghai Pudong Development Bank
9	**LI Xunlei**	Chief Economist, Haitong Securities
10	**LIANG Hong**	Chief Economist, China International Capital Corporation Limited
11	**LIN Caiyi**	Chief Economist, Guotai Junan Securities Co. Ltd.
12	**LIU Shangxi**	Director-General, Research Institute for Fiscal Science, Ministry of Finance
13	**LU Zhengwei**	Chief Economist, Industrial Bank Co. Ltd.
14	**PENG Wensheng**	Global Chief Economist, CITIC Securities
15	**SHENG Songcheng**	Director, Statistics and Analysis Department, the People's Bank of China
16	**SUN Guofeng**	Vice Director, Monetary Policy Department, the People's Bank of China
17	**STEPHEN Green**	Economist, Capital Group
18	**WU Jian**	Full-time Director of the Board, China Everbright Bank
19	**XIE Duo**	Party Secretary, National Association of Financial Market Institutional Investors
20	**XIONG Zhiguo**	Director, Policy Research Office, China Insurance Regulatory Commission
21	**XU Xianchun**	Deputy Director, National Bureau of Statistics
22	**XU Zhong**	Vice Director, Financial Market Department, the People's Bank of China
23	**XUAN Changneng**	Director-General, Financial Stability Bureau, People's Bank of China
24	**YIN Jianfeng**	Vice Director, Research Institute of Finance, Chinese Academy of Social Science
25	**ZHANG Bin**	Senior Fellow, China Finance 40 Forum
26	**ZHANG Chenghui**	Director, Research Institute of Finance, Development Research Center of the State Council
27	**ZHENG Jingping**	Deputy Director, National Bureau of Statistics
28	**ZHU Jianfang**	Chief Economist, CITIC Securities

29	**ZHU Ning**	Vice President, Shanghai Advanced Institute of Finance, Shanghai Jiaotong University
30	**ZHOU Chengjun**	Vice Director, Monetary Policy Department II, the People's Bank of China
31	**ZHOU Daoxu**	Deputy Secretary-General of the People's Government Guizhou Province, Director of the Financial Service Office, the People's Government Guizhou Province
32	**ZOU Jiayi**	Assistant Minister, Ministry of Finance

CF40 Senior Fellows

1	**JIA Kang**	Former Director-General, Research Institute for Fiscal Science, Ministry of Finance
2	**WU Hemao**	Professor, China Europe International Business School

CF40 Invited Researchers

1	**CHENG Manjiang**	Director, Research Department, and Managing Director, BOC International Holdings Limited
2	**MIAO Yanliang**	Senior Advisor to the Administrator, China's State Administration of Foreign Exchange
3	**REN Zeping**	Managing Director and Chief Macroeconomic Analyst, Guotai Junan Securities Research and Consulting Company
4	**WANG Xin**	Manager, Nanchang Sub-Branch, the People's Bank of China
5	**XIANG Songzuo**	Chief Economist, Agricultural Bank of China
6	**ZHU Dantao**	Section Chief, Associate Researcher, Central Financial Work Leading Group Office